A HISTORY OF
THE SOUTHERN SUDAN
1839–1889

A HISTORY OF
THE SOUTHERN SUDAN
1839–1889

BY

RICHARD GRAY

OXFORD UNIVERSITY PRESS

Oxford University Press, Amen House, London E.C.4

GLASGOW NEW YORK TORONTO MELBOURNE WELLINGTON
BOMBAY CALCUTTA MADRAS KARACHI LAHORE DACCA
CAPE TOWN SALISBURY NAIROBI IBADAN ACCRA
KUALA LUMPUR HONG KONG

FIRST EDITION SET BY SANTYPE LIMITED, SALISBURY
AND PRINTED BY W. & J. MACKAY & CO., LTD., CHATHAM
PUBLISHED IN 1961
REPRINTED LITHOGRAPHICALLY AT THE UNIVERSITY PRESS, OXFORD
FROM SHEETS OF THE FIRST EDITION
1964

PRINTED IN GREAT BRITAIN

ONULP

TO
MY PARENTS

PREFACE

PREVIOUS historians have dealt with aspects of the history of the southern Sudan in the nineteenth century. Professor M. Shukry's *The Khedive Ismail and slavery in the Sudan* throws much light on Ismāʿīl's policy in the Sudan, and the three parts of G. Douin's *Histoire du règne du Khédive Ismail* which deal with Ismāʿīl's African empire are authoritative and valuable. Developments in the southern Sudan, however, are seen by these writers mainly as an important incident in Ismāʿīl's reign, and historians have shown but little interest in the conflicts which decisively influenced developments within the area itself. There has been no previous attempt to study as a whole the contact between the outside world and the pagan hinterland of Khartoum in the nineteenth century, or to see it as a significant chapter in the history of tropical Africa.

The materials for this study—the impressions of observers recorded in the letters, diaries and writings of consuls, missionaries, explorers, traders and administrators—are abundant. The interest in the quest for the sources of the Nile made the southern Sudan, for two or three decades, perhaps the best documented area in the interior of tropical Africa, and it is almost the only region for which records are available from the first moment of contact. The area is fortunate also in the quality of the observations; few explorers in Africa have equalled the accuracy and detail of Schweinfurth, Junker and Emin. By themselves these materials do not of course constitute anything like a complete record of tribal histories. They do, however, reveal a great deal about conditions over a wide area, and they make it possible to provide a documented, though incomplete, account of the southerners' relationship with the alien intruders. I hope that this outline will soon be given greater depth by accounts based on the oral traditions of the peoples themselves, for there is an urgent need to record these sources before they are finally forgotten.

In the spelling of tribal names I have generally followed those used by the Survey Department of the Sudan Government, and in that of place names I have in most cases adhered to the original. Having no scholarly knowledge of Arabic, my spelling of Arabic terms has no claim to consistency: for personal names I have attempted to follow the guidance of R. L. Hill's *Biographical Dictionary of the Anglo-Egyptian Sudan*, and for other words I have adopted that most commonly in use. A guide to the abbreviations used in the footnotes will be found in the list of manuscript sources.

The research on which this book is based was undertaken as a post-graduate student at the School of Oriental and African Studies, London, and the thesis was approved for the Ph.D. degree. Many of the source-materials are in France, Italy, Austria and Germany; I gratefully acknowledge a grant from the Central Research Fund of London University which enabled me to travel and to study these documents—and, incidentally though most fortunately, to meet Gabriella who has become my wife. I would also like to acknowledge the assistance of owners and custodians of these papers both in England and on the Continent who most generously gave me access to them. Many other people have helped me in this work and I am deeply grateful for all the kindness and help that I have received. It is impossible to mention them all, but I must specifically thank the Master and Fellows of Downing College, Cambridge, for making it possible for me to embark on historical research, and Dr. Roland Oliver, whose supervision of my thesis and continued advice and encouragement have been my main guide and stimulus in the study of African history.

RICHARD GRAY

Valverde, Bergamo
  April 1960

CONTENTS

LIST OF MAPS

GLOSSARY

Abid	slave
Baqqara	cattlemen; tribes living south of the 12th parallel where camels do not flourish
Bashi-buzuk	irregular Turkish troops, also loosely used in the Sudan of other irregulars
Bazinger	armed negro employees, watchmen, porters, messengers and soldiers; often freed slaves
Dahabiah	Nile sailing-boat
Dongolawi, *pl.* Danaqla	Inhabitant of Dongola riverain-area
Durra	millet, sorghum
Effendia	intelligentsia
Fakir	professional holy man, religious teacher
Hotteria	possibly corrupted from *awturiya*, a militiaman, it was applied in the Bahr el Ghazal to irregular soldiers and Danaqla tax-gatherers
Jebel	hill, mountain
Jellab, *pl.* Jellaba	pedlar, petty (itinerant) trader
Kantar	100 rotl = 99·05 lb. = 44·93 kilogrammes
Khedive	title used informally by the Viceroy of Egypt since *c.* 1850, but officially recognized by the Porte in 1867
Mudir	Governor, loosely used also of a commander of a large district
Mudirieh	province
Nugger	large broad-beamed boat used on the upper Nile
Qadi	Islamic religious judge
Quintal	100 lb.
Rakuba	grass shelter
Razzia	raid, or plundering expedition
Reth	divine King of the Shilluk
Rotl	0·99 lb.
Sagia	water-wheel
Shaikh	tribal chief or notable; religious leader
Sudd	papyrus swamps of the White Nile
Vakil	agent, deputy
Vali	Viceroy; the Governor-General of a province of the Ottoman Empire
Zeriba	thorn enclosure

One Egyptian pound = 100 Piastre Tariff = £1.0.6. = 25.9 fr. = 5 Maria Theresa Thalers.

Map 1. THE NORTHERN SUDAN 1839

I

THE DISCOVERY

1. The northern Sudan before 1839

ON 16 November 1839 an expedition of ten boats commanded by Salīm, a Turkish frigate captain, left Khartoum with orders from Muḥammad 'Alī, ruler of Egypt, to explore the White Nile. South of the junction with the River Sobat the boats entered the sudd, a vast extent of permanent, fifteen-foot high papyrus swamp, which obscured and obstructed the channel of the main river. Eighteen centuries previously this obstacle had defeated Nero's centurions in the only other official expedition ever to have attempted to discover the sources of the White Nile, but Salīm succeeded in breaking through the sudd and reached Gondokoro a thousand miles south of Khartoum. Thus, at a time when Livingstone had yet to embark for the Cape, when Sultan Sa'īd had only just established his dynasty at Zanzibar, and when direct European influence in west Africa was practically restricted to coastal contact, the outside world suddenly discovered a navigable waterway stretching far into the unknown interior. During the following decades the southern Sudan by virtue of this discovery occupied a position of primary importance in the exploration and colonization of tropical Africa.

This lunge deep into central Africa was but a spectacular part of the process by which Egypt, stimulated by the growing influence of European technology, concepts, and commerce, had recently started to explore and to develop the economic and strategic possibilities of the Sudan. Parts of the northern Sudan had been closely connected with the civilization of ancient Egypt, but with the decline of Egyptian power the contact had withered. The Nile, with its cataracts and the enormous circling detours of its course, did not provide a practicable link between the two countries, and the Sudan was left to evolve by itself, relatively isolated behind the expanse of the Nubian desert. The degree of isolation was indeed illustrated by the fact that kingdoms with a Christian tradition survived in the Sudan for several centuries after Islam had become dominant in Egypt. The final overthrow of these kingdoms was as much due to their internal weakness as to the gradual infiltration of Arab traders and tribes, and Egyptian influence remained on the whole peripheral until the nineteenth century.[1]

The Arabs, however, brought an underlying unity to the northern Sudan and linked it tenuously to a wider community. Racially they were mainly assimilated by the indigenous peoples, but their language, religion, and to a large extent their tribal structure were superimposed throughout the area, distinguishing it sharply from the Kingdom of Abyssinia or the medley of pagan tribes which were its southern neighbours. Despite this degree of cultural homogeneity, however, ecological diversity and the poverty and vastness of the area thwarted the development of a close-knit social unity: the outlook and way of life of the Nubian and Danaqla cultivators in the narrow riverain strip were greatly different to those of the camel-owning nomads of the desert or the Baqqara tribes of the Kordofan savannah grasslands with their large herds of cattle and their many Negroid slaves.

From the sixteenth to the nineteenth centuries a semblance of political unity was given to this northern area by the supremacy of the Fung Kingdom of Sennar. In the seventeenth century this kingdom extended from the third cataract to the Abyssinian mountains and from the Red Sea to Darfur; but direct rule was only exercised over the vast promontory or 'island' (Gezira) between the Blue and White Niles, and in the rest of the kingdom the influence of Sennar was virtually restricted to the occasional collection of tribute. The principal contacts with the outside world were not with Ottoman Egypt: religious links were with Arabia and were maintained by the pilgrimage, while commercially the country derived its chief importance from its position on the route between the Red Sea and the Islamic kingdoms of Darfur, Wadai and Bornu.[2] By the end of the eighteenth century even this loose political confederation was in decline, as Dongola and Kordofan had broken away. In 1820 therefore the kingdom of Sennar and the rest of the northern Sudan were easily captured by the invading armies of Muḥammad ʿAlī, whose personal dynastic ambitions and adoption of European technology were converting Egypt once again into an expansionist power.

The country was conquered by men of varied ethnic origins:

[1] J. S. Trimingham, *Islam in the Sudan*, 1949, pp. 39–105.
[2] H. C. Jackson, *Tooth of Fire*, Oxford, 1912.

Ottoman Turks, Circassians, Kurds, Greeks and Albanians. They were all called 'Turks' by the Sudanese and the period 1820–1884 is still known as the 'Turkīya'. Egypt was technically a province of the Ottoman Empire, and Muḥammad ʿAlī was recognized as Vali, or viceroy, by the Sultan in 1805. The areas conquered in 1820 became a dependency of the Vilayet, or province, of Egypt, and the firmans of 1841, which regulated the relations between the Porte and the Vilayet, recognized Muḥammad ʿAlī's rule, for his life only, over 'Nubia, Darfur, Kordofan, and Sennar with all their dependencies situated beyond the borders of Egypt'.[1] The administration of the Sudan was therefore independent of the Porte and was closely controlled by Muḥammad ʿAlī himself. The Governors and other officers of the administration were bound to him by a personal allegiance and their tenure of office was largely dependent on his personal will. There was no regular audit but officers were sporadically sent from Egypt to inquire into suspected irregularities. The country was expected to be self-supporting and to render tribute to Egypt in cattle, timber, grain, gold, ivory, and slaves. Sudanese participated in local government from the beginning of Egyptian rule, since this proved to be an economical way of keeping order and collecting taxes. Village sheikhs and tribal authorities retained their offices, and Sudanese were gradually encouraged to take posts as legal, military, and administrative officials.[2]

Military power remained however the basis of Egyptian rule. The new Egyptian army was modelled on the latest European examples. In 1821 a training camp at Aswan was started for Negro soldiers. Here they were vaccinated, instructed in Islam, and trained by French military officers who had served under Napoleon, and who brought with them French military discipline, promotion on merit, and desert drill. Many of these troops saw service in Syria and the Hejaz, while others formed the permanent garrison in the Sudan. In addition to these regular troops, locally recruited irregular bands, armed and paid by their officers, were extensively used for tax-collecting and the raiding of recalcitrant tribes.[3]

The immediate result of the Egyptian conquest was to intensify commercial activities in the Sudan, and the rapid growth of

[1] M. F. Shukry, *The Khedive Ismail and slavery in the Sudan*, Cairo, 1937, p. 8.
[2] Richard Hill, *Egypt in the Sudan 1820–1881*, 1959, pp. 35–64.
[3] Shukry, pp. 51–6; Hill, pp. 24–29.

Khartoum was a symbol of the new régime. Before the conquest
it had been a small fishing hamlet, but as the Egyptian military
and administrative headquarters it had become by 1837 the leading
city of the Sudan with an estimated population of about twenty
thousand.[1] Yet although its growth was the result of Egyptian
influence it was still for the most part primitive in character. Only
the Mosque and a part of the Governor's palace were of kiln-burnt
brickwork; all the houses were built of mud, even the best of them
needing extensive repairs after every rainy season. Some Greek
traders and a few Italian doctors and chemists were the principal
European residents, and European wares were sold only in private
houses. Khartoum had yet to become one of the most important
river ports in Africa; it was still merely a 'junction of caravan
routes'.[2] Its vast, southern, riverain hinterland abutting the White
Nile still remained unexploited.

These caravan routes, leading west and east to Kordofan,
Sennar and the Red Sea, and northwards to Egypt across either the
Bayuda steppe or the Nubian desert, were but the eastern extension
of the ancient network of trade-routes linking the coast lands of the
Mediterranean with Africa south of the Sahara. Islam had given
this network both unity and exclusiveness, so that it was possible,
though sometimes dangerous, for a Muslim to travel throughout
its length and breadth for trade and the pilgrimage. It was the
character of this trade, however, rather than religion by itself,
which excluded European merchants. Burckhardt, who visited the
Sudan before the Egyptian conquest, had seen that 'commerce is
the very life of society in these countries'.[3] In the towns every
family was in some way connected with trade and as late as 1863
an intelligent French observer perceived that credit was here
supplied not by commercial and legal institutions but by 'the
spirit of association'.[4]

The conquest centralized this activity and Khartoum rapidly

[1] J. Russegger, *Reisen in Europa, Asien, und Afrika*, Stuttgart, 1843, Bd. II,
Th. ii, pp. 17–38.
[2] Ibid.
[3] J. L. Burckhardt, *Travels in Nubia*, 1822, p. 289.
[4] A. E. Corr. Comm. Masaouah, Vol. 12. Lejean-M. le Min., 1/VIII/1863
enclosing 'Aperçu général sur le commerce de l'Est Afrique'. Lejean continues:
je suis convaincu qu'une maison européenne arrivant avec un capital de 100,000 fr.
sur les places del Gallabat et Messalamie, s'y fera battre par ces ·Hadarba et
Danagla dont le plus riche n'a jamais 1,500 en caisse'.

became the focus of the activities of several thousand Danaqla and
Ja'liyin, whose tribes inhabited the cultivated riverain areas south
of Wadi Halfa, and who excelled in the adventurous, quarrelsome
life of mercenary fighters and itinerant traders. With a minute
capital investment in cloth or beads they penetrated through
Kordofan and Sennar to the borders of the pagan lands and returned
to sell their purchases of slaves and ivory to Egyptian traders at
Khartoum and Dongola.[1] In this closely interwoven activity, which
was dependent on kinship contact, a simple standard of living, and
a small margin of profits, there was no scope for European capital
and enterprise. The opportunity for Europeans to break through
this closed network of Muslim trade only arrived with the possibility
of penetrating by river into the pagan lands of central Africa; for
this penetration required capital and equipment on a scale which
only Europeans could provide.

A small amount of gold and ivory from the Abyssinian borders
and an increasing quantity of gum from Kordofan were exported
by the caravans, but slaves were the country's most important
export. Before the Egyptian conquest Sennar exported about one
thousand five hundred slaves a year to Egypt, and at the end of the
eighteenth century it was estimated that the annual caravan from
Darfur brought five to six thousand, the majority of whom were
girls destined for the harems and domestic service.[2] The caravan
from Darfur was, however, subject to interruptions; between 1810
and 1817 no caravan arrived, and the resolve to secure a regular
supply of 'recruits' for his army was one of the reasons for
Muḥammad 'Alī's decision to invade the Sudan.[3] After the
conquest periodic raids were undertaken by the Egyptians into
the mountains south of Sennar and Kordofan and eye-witness
accounts state that as many as five thousand captives were taken
in one campaign; the government retained half, and the rest were
paid to the soldiers, many of whom sold them to the Danaqla
traders, who also occasionally purchased slaves from independent
pagan chiefs.[4] By 1838 it was estimated that about ten to twelve

[1] Russegger, pp. 18–20.
[2] G. Douin, *Histoire du Soudan Egyptien*, Vol. I 'La Pénétration, 1820–22',
Cairo 1944, p. 64; P. S. Girard, 'Mémoire sur ... le commerce de l'Egypte',
in *Description de l'Egypte*, II. i, pp. 630–6.
[3] Douin, pp. 56, 66–68.
[4] F.O. 141/10. Beke-Stokes 10/X/1843, enclosed in Stokes-Aberdeen,
17/XI/43; also Douin, p. 314.

thousand slaves were annually imported into Egypt; a Frenchman was reported to be shipping whole boatloads down the Nile; and although the desert crossing here was reputed to be much less disastrous than the Atlantic middle passage, many died on the route and many were retained in the Sudan.[1]

In 1838 Muḥammad 'Alī obtained a first-hand impression of this situation during a visit to the Sudan. The decision to undertake this journey was characteristic of the septuagenarian's energy and courage; his principal motive was also typical. Conflicting accounts of the gold fields in the mountains south of Sennar had been reported to Cairo and he resolved to inspect them personally, hoping to initiate an intensive exploitation which would solve his continual and increasing financial difficulties.[2] The eldorado was found to be non-existent, but Muḥammad 'Alī was an eye-witness of the ravages caused by the recruiting raids. Influenced by the firm anti-slavery sentiments of both the French Saint-Simonians who accompanied him and the British diplomatic agents in Cairo, he took the opportunity to forbid his troops to hunt for slaves in the future and he released five hundred taken in a recent raid.[3] His action received favourable publicity in Europe,[4] but after his return the raids recommenced, for the capture of slaves continued to maintain the social and commercial life of the northern Sudan.

Many of the male captives were retained in the Sudan as cultivators of the riverain areas; others were exported as labourers to Egypt. Many of the women were absorbed into domestic service and the lighter-coloured Galla from the Abyssinian borders fetched a high price as concubines. Some of the youths were mutilated, chiefly by Coptic monks near Asyut, and the few who survived were sold as eunuchs.[5] Above all recruits were continually needed by the army, and in reply to the remonstrances of the British Consul-General in Cairo it was pointed out by the Egyptian authorities that recruitment could not be entirely voluntary, that the raids were undertaken in response to the appeals from friendly

[1] F.O. 78/381. The MS. draft of a report on Egypt by Dr. John Bowring, March 1839, p. 347; Russegger, p. 21.

[2] A. Sammarco, Il viaggio di Mohammed Ali al Sudan, Cairo, 1929.

[3] E. Driault, 'Mohammed Aly au Soudan', Bull. Inst. Egypte., 1927; Shukry, p. 77.

[4] e.g. T. F. Buxton, The African slave-trade and its remedy, 1840, pp. 428–35.

[5] Burckhardt, pp. 329–30.

tribes, and that since 'the people of these countries are savages, humanity cannot approve leaving them in that state'.[1] The reasoning of the authorities revealed their attitude not only towards slavery but also to the whole pagan world. Islam rigidly divided the world into two categories, Dar al-Islam and Dar al-Ḥarb (the domain of war). Beyond the boundaries of Dar al-Islam the taking of slaves in war was therefore permitted, and a hostile contemptuous attitude towards the pagan peripheries was natural to Islam. But after the horrors of capture and the degradation of the slave-market were passed, Islam attached no social stigma to slavery. Burckhardt could even state that 'slavery in the East has little dreadful in it but the name',[2] and it must be remembered that at this period in South Africa the Boers were invoking a religious sanction for somewhat similar raids against their pagan neighbours.

Yet although Muḥammad 'Alī's visit had little permanent influence on this problem of slavery in the Sudan it did achieve one major result. Gold-mining could not solve his economic difficulties, but there remained the unexplored potentialities of central Africa. Abyssinia guarded the sources of the Blue Nile, but the course of the White Nile was still completely unknown, and here Muḥammad 'Alī made a decisive contribution.

Interest in the ancient geographical mystery of the sources of the Nile began to revive in Europe during the eighteenth century. Bruce's famous journey to Abyssinia and the Blue Nile was supported by Lord Halifax, President of the Board of Trade, and his report published in 1790 led to an English translation of the travels undertaken by the Portuguese Jesuits who had preceded him in the early seventeenth century. Attention was then also turned to the problem of the White Nile. Bruce was followed by Browne who successfully entered Darfur in 1793 but was unable to fulfil his plan of reaching the White Nile. Finally at the end of the century the Napoleonic invasion of Egypt began to unite the geographical quest with the strategic importance of guarding the route to India.[3] The African Association, founded in 1788 by

---

[1] F.O. 84/486 Barnett-Aberdeen, 6/XI/1843, enclosing Borghos Bey 2/XI/1843, and F.O. 84/540 B. to A., 19/III/1844, encl. Private Sec. of Viceroy, 20/II/44.

[2] Burckhardt, p. 305; Ahmed Chafiq Bey, *L'Esclavage au point de vue musulman*, Cairo, 1938.

[3] Sir H. Johnston, *The Nile Quest*, 1903, pp. 75–95.

British scientific, industrial, humanitarian, and political interests, was chiefly concerned with the exploration of the Niger,[1] but it also sponsored several attempts to explore the course of the Nile. The Swiss, John Lewis Burckhardt, travelled under their auspices in the Sudan before the Egyptian conquest but was unable to penetrate to the south.

Muḥammad 'Alī's conquest however opened up new prospects of navigation. In 1827 the African Association financed an expedition by Linant de Bellefonds, a French engineer who later played a distinguished part in the development of Egyptian irrigation. He sailed up the White Nile and reached El Eis, one hundred and fifty miles south of Khartoum. Beyond this point, however, bands of Shilluk warriors were reported, and, since it was impossible to persuade his crew to venture further among the vanguard of these hostile and numerous pagans, he returned bringing with him the report that the Nile was supposed to lose itself in a series of vast lakes stretching away to the west.[2] This report reinforced a common belief that the source of the White Nile lay in the neighbourhood of Lake Chad and it seemed possible that the river might give access to the vast areas south of Darfur, Wadai, and Bornu. Fully alive to the commercial and strategic possibilities Muḥammad 'Alī prepared plans for an expedition up the White Nile, and during his visit to Khartoum active preparations were begun.[3] Supplies were brought up from Alexandria and eventually Salīm's expedition was sent forth to explore the nature of the southern Sudan.

2. The situation in the southern Sudan

The peoples of the southern Sudan were ill-prepared to encounter this sudden intrusion. Their manner of life was in many respects extremely well adapted to their harsh peculiar environment, but in no way had they shared in the life and thought of the north from which they were separated by centuries of development. Their scanty technological equipment, their complete illiteracy, their ignorance of commerce, their minute social horizons, and their lack of any broad political allegiance were

---

[1] C. Howard and J. H. Plumb, *West African Explorers*, 1951, pp. 4–23.
[2] J. Mazuel, *L'Oeuvre géographique de Linant de Bellefonds*, Cairo, 1937.
[3] Sammarco, p. xxxvii; Hill, pp. 31–33.

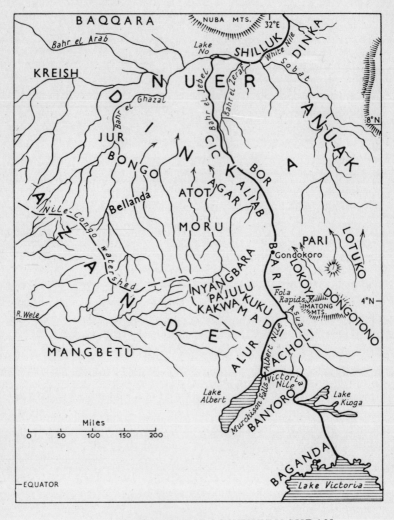

Map 2. TRIBES OF THE SOUTHERN SUDAN
AND ITS HINTERLAND

decisive disadvantages which help to explain the difficulties, conflicts, and tragedy which subsequently developed.

The southerners were previously sheltered and isolated from their powerful neighbours in the northern Sudan and Abyssinia by a series of formidable geographical barriers. The Nuba mountains, to the south of Kordofan, and the foothills of Abyssinia provided strongholds for small groups of agricultural pagan people. Beyond these bulwarks large swamp lands and vast stretches of inhospitable, arid clay plains sheltered the south. The scrub lands of the fierce yet scattered Baqqara tribes were bounded to the south of the Bahr el Arab by the swamps of the western tributaries of the Bahr el Ghazal. Rising on the Nile-Congo watershed, these tributaries spill their waters across a vast clay plain, so that their course in most cases becomes completely lost in a maze of high swampy vegetation until the residue that does not evaporate finds its way into the sluggish channel of the Bahr el Ghazal. On a far larger scale this process is repeated with the waters of the White Nile. Flowing from the immense reservoir of the Equatorial Lakes, the river, after cutting a relatively narrow channel through the Fola Rapids and the hilly country in Lat. 3′ 50°–5°, encounters the plain and for four hundred miles it winds its way slowly northwards with many side channels leaving behind a deep border of permanent swamp, while over the whole plain vast areas of grassland are seasonally under water. In the eastern part of this plain the waters from the Abyssinian escarpment are gathered into the tangled skein of the river Sobat and its tributaries, or disappear into an extension of swamp and grasslands which merges gradually into the scrub lands of the Baqqara. Thus across the width of the southern Sudan a vast area of swamp and 'cracking-clay' plain, buttressed by the Nuba mountains and Abyssinian foothills, protected its grazing lands and enabled its inhabitants to live virtually undisturbed.

Yet this was merely a protection of isolation, and the peoples of the southern Sudan had gained no benefit from their proximity to centres of great cultural importance. The knowledge of iron-working probably passed into Negro and central Africa from Meroe, a kingdom which for six hundred years from the third century B.C. flourished in the northern Sudan. It is possible that a concept of divine kingship also spread from this same centre. But both these achievements seem to have by-passed the swamps and they were assimilated and developed elsewhere.[1] These barriers had also completely prevented any gradual penetration of Islam, and even more important was the fact that the area had merely the slenderest link with the northern network of caravan trade. On its fringes—the steppes south of Darfur, the Nuba mountains, the Abyssinian foothills, and the southern plains of the Gezira—the raids for slaves were increasing in intensity after Muḥammad 'Ali's occupation and it seems possible that a few Jellaba (itinerant traders) were simultaneously establishing contacts with independent pagan chiefs,[2] but beyond this fringe the geographical obstacles baulked these activities. A minute quantity of trade-goods reached the interior,[3] but even the most rudimentary commercial practices had not developed, and there were here no tribes like the Yoruba and other peoples of western Africa, prepared to act as independent middlemen. Yet when Salīm's expedition finally pierced the sudd, the peoples of the southern Sudan were rapidly exposed on a relatively large scale to the rigorous demands of commerce and it was in this realm that the crucial adaptation was demanded.

In this contact, so suddenly brought upon them, internal instability was an even greater disadvantage than the previous isolation. Just as the Nile spilt its waters across the plains, so waves of migrations spread their ripples throughout the area, setting up continual eddies, and leaving behind small stagnant remnants. This unsettled history, together with material conditions unfavourable to the formation of large-scale political systems, resulted in large numbers of small tribal or kinship groups within the broad divisions of Nilotes, Nilo-Hamites, and Western Sudanic peoples. Conditions varied considerably, but nowhere were the tribes united and prepared to confront on equal terms the forces of the outside world.

The Nilotes, descended from peoples of Negro stock who at a period of probably 'high antiquity' received an infusion of Hamitic blood,[4] were separated in three broad divisions: Dinka, Nuer and Luo. The way of life of the pastoral nomadic Dinka and Nuer was

[1] *History and Archaeology in Africa*, S.O.A.S., London 1955, pp. 16–19, 38–39.
[2] Russegger, p. 19; Werne, passim.
[3] see below, pp. 38, 65–66.
[4] C. G. and Brenda Z. Seligman, *Pagan Tribes of the Nilotic Sudan*, 1932, pp. 12–18.

well adapted to the vast clay plain with its magnificent dry season grazing grounds. Other peoples might well have found it a harsh, inhospitable environment, but the Dinka, as they still say, 'hate the hoe' and despised their neighbours who cultivated the richer ironstone lands to the south. Observers have pointed out that 'it is not easy for anybody unacquainted with the Nilotics to realize the overwhelmingly important part that cattle play in their lives'; almost their only possession, cattle have a predominant role in economic, social, religious and aesthetical life, 'and to their acquisition almost everything is sacrificed'.[1] Local kinship groups were centred round the activities of a cattle camp, and society was organized in a series of small, mutually opposed segments, which occasionally combined for a cattle raid but whose tribal life was normally 'a kind of ordered anarchy in which every section plays the game of feud according to the rules'.[2] The economic self sufficiency—albeit at a meagre subsistence level—and independence arising from this pervasive pastoral emphasis did not predispose them to co-operate easily with the outside world, and when tension developed their social divisions were only too easily exploited. Fortunately for the majority, however, the inaccessibility of their territory, their nomadic mobility, and their very independence gave them a remarkable resilience.

The other broad Nilotic division, the Luo, consisted of a number of widely separated tribes stretching from the Kavirondo Luo on the shores of Lake Victoria to the Shilluk who inhabited the west banks of the White Nile. Luo traditions[3] ran back to an original division into two major groups probably somewhere near the area later occupied by the Bari. One group seems to have turned south and later divided into the Acholi, Alur and other tribes in Uganda. The other group turned north and, leaving small segments behind on the fringe of Dinka territory in the Bahr el Ghazal, it crossed the Nile and founded the Shilluk nation, while yet another section, the Anuak, penetrated up the Sobat and settled round its tributaries.

---

[1] *Report of the Jonglei Investigation Team*, Khartoum, 1949, p. 1.
[2] E. E. Evans-Pritchard, 'The Nuer, Tribe and Clan', S.N.R. 1933,–34,–35. p. 87.
[3] My account is based on a re-assessment of the published traditional evidence, which is contained in articles by several authors and in two major works: W. Hofmayr, *Die Schilluk*, Vienna, 1925, and J. P. Crazzolara, *The Lwoo*, Part I Lwoo Migrations; Part II Lwoo Traditions, Verona, 1950 and 1951.

Of all the peoples in the southern Sudan, the Shilluk were perhaps best equipped to meet the impact of the outside world. Adequate dry season grazing by the banks of the Nile favoured a settled pastoral, fishing, and agricultural economy. Contiguous village settlements occupied a long narrow strip of about a hundred miles, and those Europeans who accompanied the first expeditions from the north were astounded at the apparent density of population.[1] Their traditions of the long migration, of a line of rulers stretching back probably into the sixteenth century, and of successful resistance to the sporadic attacks of their northern neighbours, were unusually strong; and they possessed in their ruling institution a form of divine kingship rich in ritual significance. They believed that the spirit of their first leader was reincarnated in successive 'reths' (kings) upon whose well-being rested the fertility and success of men, cattle and crops. Through the widely distributed shrines the whole nation participated in the cult, and amidst great emotional tension the whole tradition was reborn at the reth's investiture.[2] Anthropologists however have emphasized that the reth's function in Shilluk society was religious and ritual rather than political and administrative, and that the Shilluk shared with the other Nilotic peoples a tendency to divide into mutually opposed segmentary sections.[3] The evidence of the earliest travellers suggests that there was a rudimentary administrative machinery with the reth at its central point,[4] but the Shilluk never possessed a political organization comparable for example to the kingdoms of Bunyoro or Buganda, and although under favourable conditions this machinery might have developed,

---

[1] D'Arnaud to Jomard, 10/V/43, in *Bull. Soc. Géog. de Paris*, 1843, p. 445, estimated it at over a million. Knoblecher thought that one to three million was not impossible. (Knobl. MS. 28/XI/1849).

[2] P. P. Howell, and W. P. G. Thompson, 'The Death of a Reth of the Shilluk and the installation of his Successor', *S.N.R.*, 1946.

[3] E. E. Evans-Pritchard, *The Divine Kingship of the Shilluk of the Nilotic Sudan*, 1948; P. P. Howell, 'Observations on the Shilluk of the Upper Nile', *Africa*, 1952.

[4] Knoblecher, a careful observer, noted in his diary, after contact with numerous Shilluk: 'Die Einigkeit und politische Verbindung unter einem König, der sie durch Ortschaftsvorsteher, deren Deputierte sich alle drei Wochen bei ihm versammeln, regiert, macht sie stark und ihren Feinden fürchterlich' (Knobl. MS. 4/XII/1849). Early traders also found that the reth exercised an effective control over trade, (e.g. J. Petherick, *Egypt, the Soudan and Central Africa*, Edinburgh, 1861, p. 352. See also G. Beltrame, *Il fiume bianco e i Denka*, Verona, 1881, p. 74.)

it was by no means powerful enough to withstand the disruptive forces which were later brought to bear on Shilluk society.

To the south-east of the Dinka and Nuer were the northern Nilo-Hamites, a group of peoples whose strong Hamitic element was possibly that of a Sidama type driven south-west from Ethiopia as a result of Galla pressure.[1] The Bari, numerically the most important tribe, stretched along the east bank of the Bahr el Jebel. On the west bank the Nilo-Hamitic speaking Kuku, Kakwa, Pajulu, and Nyangbara were probably of basic Bari stock with which were mixed strong Sudanic elements. To the east of the river the land gradually rises to form the Imatong mountains and near the Bahr el Jebel it has a wooded parkland aspect, which, unlike the vast grassy plains with their seasonal inundations, favoured a more settled form of pastoral and agricultural communities. The village and not the cattle camp was therefore the focal point of their social organization; its horizons however were just as restricted. Loosely divided into mutually hostile sections and clans, the Bari had no conceptions of a tribal administrative chief. Instead the affairs of the village were settled by the clan and council of elders, with, in some cases, the guidance of a ritual expert. The most important of these experts were the hereditary rain-making chiefs, the leading line of which had a genealogy which stretched back possibly into the sixteenth century. An off-shoot of this line had settled on Belinian, a hill a few miles south of Gondokoro, and was destined to play a prominent part in the history of the Bari's contact with the outside world, but its political influence was entirely indirect, being dependent on the fluctuating prestige of the rain-makers as ritual experts.[2] The Bari therefore possessed no recognized leader capable of adapting their society to the changes which suddenly arrived; while their eastern neighbours, the Lokoya, Lotuko, and Dongotono lived as relatively small, jealous communities in mountainous country which enabled them to preserve a fierce independence and to undertake periodic raids into Bari country.[3]

Thus although the Nilotes and Nilo-Hamites were proud, independent peoples, they completely lacked any broad internal

---

[1] G. W. B. Huntingford, *The Northern Nilo-Hamites*, 1953, pp. 10–11.

[2] A. C. Beaton, 'A Chapter in Bari History', *S.N.R.*, 1934, and 'Clan and Age-Class Systems', *S.N.R.*, 1936.

[3] Huntingford, pp. 11–19.

cohesion or focal points of authority. They inhabited a good pastoral area but large parts of it were quite unsuitable for intensive agriculture, and consequently the invading pastoralists had encountered no thriving agricultural populations, which might have provided the basis of powerful states as in Bunyoro and the other Lacustrine Kingdoms. Instead, in 1839, the outside world encountered a series of mutually hostile, economically independent, small 'democratic' units divided both by their way of life and their diverse historical experiences.

To the west of the Bahr el Jebel, across the Nile-Congo watershed, the situation was even more complicated and fluid. Waves of Sudanic speaking people, driven from the area south of Lake Chad and the Chari river, had entered the Wele basin. There, finding that the dense belt of equatorial forest presented an impenetrable barrier to the south, they had been deflected north-eastwards and forced into the south-western area of the southern Sudan by the continual pressure of fresh invading waves. Linguistic considerations suggest an ancient common origin of the Bongo-Baka and Moru-Madi groups who were the first Sudanic speaking people to infiltrate into the area of the river Wele long before the sixteenth century. In the succeeding centuries they were forced north-eastwards until they stretched in a broken line from the Madi in northern Uganda, through the Moru, Bongo, and many smaller groups on the ironstone slopes of the south-western Sudan, to the Kreish in the Dar Fertit area south of Darfur.[1] The Bongo, typical of these groups, were established at an early date in the neighbourhood of the Tonj river. By the nineteenth century they were divided into a large number of clans pursuing a settled agricultural existence, separated by miles of uninhabited bush, and often harassed by fierce local feuds, the whole hemmed in between the Dinka on the plains and the later waves of Sudanic invaders to their south and west.[2]

By far the most important of these later waves were the Azande. According to traditional evidence it must have been about the end of the sixteenth century that the earliest of these waves reached the M'Bomu river. It consisted of people belonging to the same linguistic group as the Azande, and amongst the second wave were the Abele, the first Zande group to invade the area. Con-

---

[1] A. N. Tucker, *The Eastern Sudanic Languages*, Vol. i, 1940, pp. 40–54.
[2] E. E. Evans-Pritchard, 'The Bongo', *S.N.R.*, 1929.

currently with these two waves there occurred invasions of Bantu speaking people coming from the south-west into the Wele basin. None of these people acted under a strong or united leadership and they pressed into the area as a series of confused and conflicting groups; but in the middle of the eighteenth century the Avongura crossed the M'Bomu coming from the valley of the river Chinko.

Amidst the welter of particular local loyalties the Avongura were a unique phenomenon. A proud, military, aristocratic clan they created and controlled the Zandé empire. Under a chief called Gura they established control on the M'Bomu and started to subject and assimilate the Abele and other Zande speaking groups. During the first half of the nineteenth century Gura's descendants, each jealous of the others, sought to conquer fresh subjects with the aid of a small following of Avongura and assimilated people. Since the Abandia prevented an expansion to the west, they moved into the Wele basin and up across the Nile-Congo watershed to the tributaries of the Bahr el Ghazal, assimilating the hitherto-divided groups.[1]

Their organization was the secret of their success. Warriors and adaptable agriculturalists, the Azande lived in isolated family homesteads often set in dense vegetation. They were however intimately linked with their Avongura chiefs both through officials (Bakumba) appointed to exercise authority over a small group of homesteads, and also through a system in which all boys on approaching puberty were enrolled as a body-guard for the chief. These boys received a uniform education which created an intellectual and moral homogeneity and ensured the swift assimilation of conquered peoples. The Avongura dynasties owned the soil, collected taxes, decided legal disputes, and declared war. Instead of small, exclusive, turbulent democracies, 'une compréhension impériale' was established over great regions, representing a form of political organization which was the antithesis of those which for the most part prevailed in the Nilotic and other societies of the southern Sudan.[2] Their achievement contained however a serious flaw. It has been noted above that their expansion sprang from

[1] The main source for Zande traditions is A. de Calonne-Beaufaict, *Azande*, Brussels, 1921. My condensed account owes much to an unpublished seminar paper by D. H. Jones, 'Tribal movements in the Wele basin and the Bahr el Ghazal', 1952.

[2] de Calonne-Beaufaict; E. E. Evans-Pritchard, 'The Nuer, Tribe and Clan', *S.N.R.*, 1935.

dynastic rivalries. Although a chief often established control over a vast area, the latent rivalries of his sons or relatives remained, bursting forth as his powers declined, and these rivalries eventually prevented even the Azande from presenting anything approaching a united front to the forces of the outside world.

3. The expeditions, 1839–1841

Although Salīm and the first Egyptian expeditions penetrated far to the south, they only encountered the fringe of this unknown world. On 30 November 1839, at Lat. 13° 57′ they left their last link with civilization: a small, struggling outpost of water-wheels established some years previously by an Egyptian who survived the annual raids of the Shilluk only by periodically removing the machines to safety inland.[1] For the next ten days they sailed through a suspicious and hostile country. The long, wooded islands, scattered on the broad expanse of the river, sheltered small groups of piratical Shilluk, who continually harassed the nomadic Baqqara Arabs,[2] while further south other Shilluk groups were seen on the west bank and Dinka on the east. On the approach of the expedition these groups hastened into the inaccessible interior.[3] Eventually, on 8 December 1839, the expedition established its first contact with the main body of Shilluk at Kaka, where at a distance of about a mile from the bank commenced an unbroken line of villages, stretching south along the river. Ten chiefs were given presents, messengers were sent to the reth, and two thousand Shilluk appeared bringing a few bulls and sheep in exchange. A few days later they halted before 'Dimak' (i.e. Denab), the reth's residence. Their efforts to obtain an interview with him were unsuccessful, but the following day men, women, and children willingly supplied the expedition with provisions in exchange for cloth.[4]

Beyond the Sobat junction, as they sailed westwards, the Shilluk villages receded to the north, the sunt trees disappeared, the papyrus, fringing the broad and sluggish river, thickened, deepened

[1] M. Thibaut, 'Expédition à la recherche des Sources du Nil (1839–1840)'. *Nouvelles Ann. des Voyages*, Paris, 1856, p. 15.

[2] Thibaut to Jomard, *Bull. Soc. Géog. de Paris*, 1843, p. 443.

[3] Thibaut, p. 28; Selim Bimbachi, 'Voyage aux sources du Nil Blanc', ed. E. F. Jomard, *Mém. Soc. Géog. de Paris*, 1842, p. 18. The nervousness of these Shilluk may well have resulted from a raid undertaken against them by the Governor in 1830; Hill, p. 63.

[4] Thibaut, pp. 36–38; Selim, pp. 19–26.

and made a landing practically impossible. The horizons of apparently uninhabited swamp dwarfed the tiny ships, and the men were delivered over to the attacks of an insect world which rendered life almost unbearable. The monotony, mosquitoes, stale air, and muddy waters were an ordeal which future travellers also were to experience, but in addition the first expedition faced the strain of the unknown. It was only after three frustrating days, during which they vainly attempted to discover a way westwards through the shifting maze of swamp which at Lake No obscures the entrance to the Bahr el Ghazal, that they turned south and entered the channel of the Bahr el Jebel.

Discouraged, tense and anxious, their first encounters with the few Nuer and Cic Dinka who were near the river were clouded by misunderstandings and fear; a chief refused to visit them, a goat received as a gift was thought to be poisoned and the donors were fired upon, their interpreter was quick to imagine hostility, Cic in four small canoes attacked them and some were killed, the soldiers got out of hand and ransacked several fishing villages. The prevailing mood was expressed by one of the Turkish officers in the words, 'it is necessary to sow terror; the route we follow will then be easier'.[1]

For nineteen days they sailed southwards, often delayed by the numerous windings of the river, sometimes in doubt as to which was the main channel, and always surrounded by lagoons and the vast, grassy, almost treeless plain.[2] Then, at one of the rare places where the bank was sufficiently firm to enable them to land, they rested near a large Cic village, repaired their boats, held a review of the troops and impressed the inhabitants with their firearms. The tension lowered as their self-confidence returned, and as they proceeded on their way the Cic, 'Bonderial', Aliab, and other Dinka tribes co-operated in the work of hauling the boats. Friendly contact was established with village chiefs, youths were accepted as voluntary recruits and, having finally reached wooded country, they were assisted by the Bor in collecting firewood. Some indication of the impression they created on the thunderstruck tribes is recorded by the fact that throughout their southward journey the expedition received continuous gifts of cattle, and in some

[1] Thibaut, pp. 55–65; Selim, pp. 30–48.

[2] A few years later a French trader described the scene as follows: 'C'est toujours autour de nous l'éternelle savane criblé de petits lacs comme un tapis vert semé de paillettes d'argent' (Vay. Mss. 14/XII/53.)

places cattle were sacrificed from afar to propitiate these messengers from the Gods. 'We were worshipped,' Thibaut remarked, 'and we had the good sense to respect them'.[1]

On 26 January 1840, confronted with yet another bifurcation of the river and able to obtain only the scantiest information about its subsequent course, they decided to return. They arrived at Khartoum, replenished their supplies, waited for the north wind and set sail for the south again in November 1840. After a fairly uneventful journey they arrived amongst the Bor and, leaving this southernmost Dinka tribe behind, they came into contact with the Sere, a section of the Bari-speaking Mondari. Here, surrounded by 'an incredible number of people dancing and singing on both shores', their progress was described as 'a constant triumphant march', and in January 1841, they moored their boats off the Bari village of Ulibari, a few miles north of Gondokoro.[2]

One of their first visitors was Nyigilo, brother of Lagonu the Belinian rain-chief. From the first his 'friendly-looking countenance and his handsome roman-like head' created a good impression, and he was to become a key figure in Bari history until his death in 1859. A few days later Lagonu himself arrived wearing a high bonnet of ostrich feathers, strings of blue glass beads and copper rings, and a long wide blue cotton shirt which distinguished him from the other naked Bari who crowded the banks in numbers of six to eight thousand. He went on board Salīm's boat, received presents, and seemed deeply impressed by the boats and the cannons which were fired. On their side a most favourable impression was received by the expedition. Compared with the distrust and reserve of the Shilluk reth, here was a ruler whose welcome reflected the contrast between this pleasant, rolling park-land and the dreary swamps to the north, and here was a pastoral people, yet skilled in iron-working and in agriculture, ready to exchange cattle and ivory for beads.[3] In addition it seemed possible that wider commercial horizons would open up, for it was discovered that Lagonu's glass beads, copper rings and cotton shirt had been

[1] Thibaut, pp. 65–83; Selim, pp. 48–60.
[2] F. Werne, *Expedition to discover the sources of the White Nile*, 2 vols., 1849, vol. i, p. 329.
[3] Werne, vol. ii, pp. 22–68; Thibaut, Khartoum, 28/IV/41 in *Bull. Soc. Géog. de Paris*, 1841, p. 128. In the light of later difficulties it is interesting to note that Thibaut qualifies his favourable impression with the remark 'tous ces peuples en général sont mendiants'.

obtained from the Pari, a small Luo tribe, who, it was rumoured, had trading connections with tribes further in the interior. This was in fact, however, only the merest trickle of trade. It had done nothing to modify the concept of economic self-sufficiency or to introduce a practice and experience of trading methods. Lagonu confessed that the copper was mostly plundered and that commercial intercourse with the Pari was constantly interrupted by the more customary methods of cattle raids.[1]

It was fortunate that the Bari seemed so prosperous, important, and friendly since the shallowness of the broad river with its shifting sandbanks prevented the expedition from proceeding further. The following year Salīm, leading a third expedition, pushed a few miles further south but it was only to find that where the river narrows and deepens beyond Rejaf the rocky passage and islands rendered any further progress impossible. Salīm's expeditions had discovered therefore, not the sources of the Nile, but a route which seemed to open up vast possibilities. The French Consul-General in Cairo reported to Paris that he found Muḥammad ʿAlī 'deeply pre-occupied' with the expedition's report of the friendly disposition of the Bari, with its rumours of gold, copper and iron mines, with its hopes that through the Pari they might be put 'in full communication . . . with the great Christian nations which inhabit the centre of Africa in the country of Sydame, Caffa and Narea', and, what was to prove much less illusory, with the fact that the area possessed 'ivory in great abundance'. Muḥammad ʿAlī ended by telling him that it was his intention to send further 'more important expeditions, but with a purely commercial object'.[2] The Nile was becoming a highway into tropical Africa.

[1] Werne, vol. ii, pp. 56–57. The Pari had traditional contacts both with the Anuak in the north and the Acholi in the south; see below p. 38.

[2] A. E. Corr. Consul. Alex. /14. de Rohan-Chabon to Guizot, 18/VI/41; ibid. Alex./15. Gauttier d'Arc to Guizot, 24/I/43.

II

MISSIONARIES AND MERCHANTS

1. The contest for the initiative, 1841–1850

THESE new opportunities were not exploited immediately by Egypt. A period of retrenchment and reaction marked the closing years of Muḥammad ʿAlī's reign and neither the resources nor the determination needed for an intensive development were available. The destruction of his fleet at Navarino in 1827 and his costly campaigns in Syria throughout the thirties had been a severe drain on Egyptian resources, and in 1840 the Treaty of London forced him to renounce his ambitions in Asia. Old and weakening he could no longer maintain the impetus and personal initiative which had sustained and controlled the expansion in the Sudan.[1] His hopes of large official commercial expeditions continuing to penetrate deep into the interior of Africa did not therefore materialize. Egypt's incapacity became Europe's opportunity, and European interest and activity in the southern Sudan rapidly developed.

The accounts of Thibaut, d'Arnaud and Werne, who accompanied Salīm's expeditions, aroused considerable interest in Europe. Jomard, the distinguished Egyptologist and member of the Société de Géographie de Paris, published a translation of Salīm's journal, entered into correspondence with Europeans in the Sudan, and published their letters in the Société's 'Bulletin'. In Berlin the German geographer, Professor Carl Ritter, published in 1844 'A Glance at the Source-territory of the Nile' with a map which incorporated d'Arnaud's and Werne's results. Werne's book was translated into English, and the newly-founded Royal Geographical Society focussed its attention on the problem of the Nile, as the mouth of the Niger had been discovered in 1830. For the next twenty years—and even when the major Nile quest was solved—a succession of colourful explorers attempted to penetrate south from the Bahr el Jebel and the Bahr el Ghazal, and their writings, of varied interest and accuracy, found a ready

---

[1] J. Heyworth-Dunne, *An Introduction to the history of education in modern Egypt*, 1939, pp. 223–30.

market. Typical of the wide interest aroused was Alexandre Dumas' preface to Louis du Couret's 'Voyage au Pays des Niam-Niams', a work which perhaps owed much to the novelist's own fertile imagination.[1] Yet unlike the earlier expeditions to the Niger and those later from Zanzibar and the East African coast, exploration in the Sudan was not as a rule subsidized by geographical societies and governments. Conditions on the White Nile encouraged local independent initiative: the explorers were able to rely on the assistance of local European traders, and often they were an integral part of the drive to introduce European commerce. The general distant interest aroused in the area by the accounts of travellers and explorers nevertheless formed a complement and a setting to the stronger, more immediate impulses of European commerce and evangelism, which in the decade following Salīm's discovery seized the initiative in the southern Sudan.

Although Muḥammad 'Alī was unable to sponsor further large expeditions to the White Nile, the Governor of the Sudan dispatched from Khartoum small annual trading enterprises consisting of four to seven boats,[2] which obtained ivory from the riverain tribes.[3] Their profits were sufficient to arouse the interest of the few European traders in Khartoum, who found themselves frustrated by the Governor's desire to maintain an exclusive control over the potential riches of the area. The traders, therefore, mobilized all available assistance to defeat this monopoly and precipitated a conflict which resulted in Europe gaining unobstructed access to the southern Sudan.

The traders' protagonist was Brun Rollet, a Savoyard who had come to the Sudan in 1831 in the service of a Frenchman reported to be engaged in the slave trade. In 1839 Joyce Thurburn and Company, a foremost British mercantile firm established at Alexandria, supplied him with credit and manufactures which were 'to be sold against Sudan products on joint account', and, obtaining 'satisfactory results', they renewed operations with him on 'a larger scale' in 1843.[4] Together with Lafargue, a French veterinary officer who had accompanied Salīm's second expedition, he was permitted to sail with the Governor's trading expedition in 1844

[1] c.p. Hill, *Biographical Dictionary*.
[2] Knobl. Ms. 13/XI/49.
[3] see below, pp. 34–37.
[4] F.O. 141/19 J. Thurburn & Co. to Murray, 15/IV/51 and Hill, *Biographical Dictionary*.

but found himself unescapably handicapped. At Gondokoro he contacted Nyigilo[1] and, realizing that he was potentially a most useful agent, he encouraged him to accompany them on a visit to Khartoum. In the course of the journey, however, the Turks insisted that Nyigilo should travel with them, and, according to Brun Rollet, it was only with difficulty that they were persuaded not to enslave him at Khartoum.[2] The following year Brun Rollet sailed from Khartoum on 10 October with two boats bound for the White Nile. Having collected over £1000 worth of ivory he was forced to hand this over to three government boats. He obtained no compensation; and the Africans with whom he had traded were attacked, two villages were burnt and some slaves were taken. He reported the incident to the Sardinian Consul-General and for the moment relinquished his attempt to open up the White Nile.[3]

The conflict was thus transferred to the plane of Consular action in Egypt, and the issue became merely an incident in that process of gradual encroachment by which the European Powers obtained extra-territorial rights and a privileged position in Egypt. In 1838 the Porte had been persuaded to sign a treaty regulating monopolistic practices,[4] but Muḥammad ʿAlī claimed that since Kordofan and Sennar had never been included in the Ottoman Empire they were unaffected by this treaty, and he maintained that he could legitimately continue to enforce a monopoly.[5] Palmerston at the Foreign Office insisted however that Muḥammad ʿAlī, being a subject of the Porte, could not make a conquest 'on his own account',[6] and when Murray, an energetic and capable Consul-General, reported that a merchant under British protection

---

[1] see above, p. 18.

[2] A.E. Mém. Egypte/I. Rollet to Reitz, 20/VII/51, (copy), and A. Brun Rollet, *Le Nil Blanc et le Soudan*, 1855, pp. 186–8.

[3] F.O. 141/16. Brun Rollet to Murray, 1/X/49. Brun Rollet's writings are full of extravagant description, but his account of the official attitude is corroborated by Knoblecher's later experiences, see below pp. 36–37.

[4] Robert Thurburn, H.M. Consul at Alexandria and partner of the 'well-known house of Briggs and Co.', strongly complained about monopoly practices to Bowring, who considered them to be obstacles in the way of a 'a considerable trade' which 'might be made instrumental in suppressing the slave trade'. F.O. 78/381, Bowring report, March 1839, pp. 213 and 232–3.

[5] Very occasionally he gave permission for a European to buy gum on a licence, but Thibaut, who was doing this, experienced great difficulty at the Egyptian Customs. A.E. Corr. Consul. Alex./17. Barrot to Guizot, 29/X/45.

[6] F.O. 78/381. Note by Palmerston on draft of Bowring's report, p. 351.

had suffered through the monopoly, he was instructed to state that H.M. Government regarded this as an infringement of the treaty and required that it should 'cease forthwith'.[1] Throughout 1848, while the other European powers were distracted by revolutions, Palmerston and Murray intensified the pressure. A Firman was obtained from the Porte enjoining Muḥammad 'Alī to desist from these practices, and eventually in November it was agreed to abandon the Sudan monopolies after three months.[2]

Theoretically the victory had been won, but the validity of the decision had yet to be demonstrated to the Government at Khartoum, and in the depths of the Sudan European individuals had as yet no Consul to protect them. In the summer of 1850 several European and other traders at Khartoum were making preparations to sail for the White Nile when the Governor, 'Abd al-Laṭīf Pasha, intervened. He forced them to form a society and provided a company of soldiers to 'protect' them on condition that the Government received a third of the ivory. They agreed reluctantly and the expedition left Khartoum in November.[3] Only the previous month, however, Brun Rollet had denounced Laṭīf Pasha for his continual attempts to retain a monopoly of Kordofan gum.[4] Determined not to submit to this fresh intervention, he sought the aid of the Roman Catholic mission to Central Africa, which by 1850 was a factor of considerable importance.

As early as 1844 the attention of the Congregation of Propaganda Fide had been drawn by the Prefect Apostolic of Tripoli and Mgr. Casolani, Canon of Malta Cathedral, to the discovery of a highway into central Africa. It was rumoured that a Protestant Bishop was intending to send missionaries to this virgin field, and since there was an obvious possibility that Islam might quickly spread over the area Pope Gregory XVI created the Vicariate Apostolic of Central Africa in 1846 and Propaganda sent out a

[1] F.O. 141/12. Palmerston to Murray, 31/VIII/47 and 9/XI/47. Murray, a Scottish nobleman previously in the Queen's Household, spoke fluent Arabic and Turkish. 'Son esprit est cultivé'. A.E. Corr. Consul. Alex./22. Le Moyne to M. le Min. 20/V/50.

[2] F.O. 141/15 Palmerston to Murray, 4/II/48 and 23/VI/48; Murray to Palmerston 4/XI/48. The order was ratified by 'Abbās I (installed 7/XII/48) with whom Murray had great influence. Heyworth-Dunne, op. cit., p. 288.

[3] A.E. Corr. Comm. Alex./34 Le Moyne to M. le Min. 24/XII/51, enclosing Massaja to Le Moyne 12/XI/51 and Massaja's journal dated 10/XI/51.

[4] F.O. 141/19 Cerruti to Murray 8/IV/51, enclosing Brun Rollet to C. 16/X/50.

small reconnaissance party. Ryllo, a Polish Jesuit whose interest
in the area had been aroused by his experience of the slave trade in
the Levant, was appointed pro-vicar, and with three other priests he
reached Khartoum on 11 February 1848. Four months later he
died leaving as successor Knoblecher, a Slovene aged twenty-
eight of delicate build and fair complexion, an accomplished
linguist with cultured and scientific interests. He was supported
by Angelo Vinco, a young priest from the Institute of Don Nicola
Mazza at Verona, and Pedemonte, a Jesuit of advanced age.[1]

The mission made no attempt to proselytize Muslims for their
efforts were to be concentrated on the pagans.[2] They created a
headquarters and base at Khartoum, but with their meagre
resources the prospects of establishing themselves in the pagan
south seemed slight. Vinco re-visited Italy to seek financial aid but
in the year of Garibaldi's defence of the Roman Republic his
troubles seemed relatively insignificant and by October 1849 he
had returned to Khartoum unsuccessful.[3] At this juncture they
were given an opportunity to accompany the Government's annual
trading expedition, Brun Rollet lending them a boat.[4]

After a journey the physical discomfort of which was mitigated
by an almost universally friendly reception,[5] they reached Bari
territory and on 9 January 1850 Nyigilo with a numerous crowd
hailed the expedition from the bank. On the 11th they met
Shobek, Lagonu's son and successor as rain-chief at Belinian,

---

[1] M. Grancelli, *Mons. Daniele Comboni, e la Missione dell' Africa Centrale*,
Verona, 1923, pp. 22–26; C. Tappi, *Cenno Storico della Missione dell' Africa
Centrale*, Turin, 1894, pp. 26–29; E. Toniolo, 'The First Centenary . . .', *S.N.R.*,
1946; B. Taylor, *Life and Landscapes from Egypt to the Negro kingdoms of the
White Nile*, 1854, p. 284, for a description of Knoblecher.

[2] 'Die dortige Mission hat den Zweck, das Christentum unter den heidnischen
Negerstämmen auszubreiten und somit dem Sklavenhandel entgegen zu wirken.
Den Mohammedanern das Christentum zu predigen und Proseliten zu machen
ist tractatwidrig; jeder Versuch dieser Art würde die unangenehmsten Folgen
haben' O.S. (A.V.) Handelsministerium 1851, zl. 1572. 'Provisorische Amtsinstruction für das k.k. Konsulat in Chartum', Huber, 24/XII/50.

[3] E. Crestani, *Don Angelo Vinco*, Verona, 1941, p. 63. His visit to Verona
however aroused Comboni's interest in the area.

[4] Brun Rollet, pp. 193–4.

[5] Knoblecher wrote in his diary that 'die Durchfahr der Schiffe der Expedition
ist ein Fest für die Eingeborenen': the Sere crowded the banks, some followed
the expedition for three days, and while they helped haul the boats through one
of the many difficult passages, he climbed to the masthead and scattered glass-beads
amongst the workers (Knobl. MS. 4–7/I/50). The exceptions to this friendliness,
which throw light on the problems of the ivory trade, are discussed below,
pp. 36–37.

while Nyigilo with twenty wives established himself in Knoblecher's boat. Reacting favourably to the suggestion that two
missionaries should settle with him, Nyigilo asked for means to
defend himself against the neighbouring Lotuko; and Knoblecher,
anxious that Nyigilo should not again have to 'come to Khartoum
and seek Turkish aid', promised to send him some firearms.[1]

Knoblecher accompanied by some of the Turks then made a
brief excursion to Rejaf, climbed the small mountain from which
he saw the Nile disappearing to the south, and returned to Gondokoro only to find that Shobek, influenced by the Turkish officials,
had overruled Nyigilo and refused to allow Pedemonte to settle.
The missionaries were prevented from settling at two other Bari
villages, and subsequently Knoblecher learnt that the Governor
had given orders that they were all to be brought back to Khartoum.[2]
Besides being an unfortunate introduction to Christianity for the
Bari, the journey revealed to Knoblecher the absolute necessity
of asserting the independence of the mission. On his return to
Khartoum he decided to visit Europe in order to obtain political
and financial support.

The leader of the mission was therefore absent when in November
1850 Laṭīf Pasha forced the European merchants to accept his
terms and Brun Rollet sought its assistance. Knoblecher however
authorized Angelo Vinco to make an independent journey to
Gondokoro provided that it cost the mission nothing; and Brun
Rollet put his two boats, servants, and merchandise at Vinco's
disposal. In January 1851, evading the vigilance of Laṭīf Pasha,
Vinco and the two boats managed to sail for the south. Three and
a half months later the boats returned bringing £600 worth of
ivory for Brun Rollet and the news that Vinco was remaining with
the Bari.[3] Brun Rollet was jubilant:

> This happy return which has astonished the population of this
> country, the two voyages which I have undertaken with M. Lafargue,
> and the hospitality which Don Angelo, my friend, has found among the
> Bers (Bari), are a proof that the sources of the White Nile are no
> longer inaccessible to the 'savants' and industrialists of Europe.[4]

[1] Knobl. MS. 12/I/50.   [2] Knobl. MS. 13-24/I/50.
[3] A.E. Corr. Comm. Alex/34. Le Moyne to M. le Min. 24/XII/51, enclosing
Massaja to Le Moyne 12/XI/51 and Massaja's journal dated 10/XI/51. The
five European merchants who accepted Laṭīf's terms had only obtained £150
worth of ivory.
[4] A.E. Mém. Egypte/I. Brun Rollet to Reitz, 20/VII/51 (copy).

In the midst of these events an Austrian Consular Agent arrived in Khartoum. Knoblecher, a subject of the Austrian Empire, had gone to Vienna, had obtained an audience with the Emperor Franz Josef, and the *Marien-Verein zur Beförderung der katholischen Mission in Zentral-Afrika*, a committee of influential supporters, had been founded.[1] As a result of his visit it was also decided to establish a Consular Agency whose duties, besides rendering the customary consular services in the Levant, were to include the protection of the Catholic Mission and the liberation of Austrian trade from the Egyptian monopoly. Important developments were expected. The Agent was instructed 'to give an expert opinion . . . whether and where it would be possible to found profitable Austrian trading establishments in the interior of Africa', keeping in mind both Darfur and 'the independent Negro races of the White Nile which are rich in ivory'.[2] The Austrian Consul-General in Egypt was confident that the 'indefatigable' Dr. Reitz, the new Agent, would:

> further the interest of the Mission in all directions under his control, and therefore we hope will best promote both the fame of Austria, and the spread of Christian civilization in the Sudan.[3]

Generous, brusque, and eccentric, an intrepid horseman and hunter, Reitz played an important part in the closing stages of the conflict. Laṭīf Pasha, having failed to force Brun Rollet to surrender a third of his profits, had placed the latter under a ban and was threatening to bring Vinco back by force, when in November 1851 Reitz, trusting in his Consular powers to defeat Laṭīf's threats, ran two vessels past the guard at Khartoum and Brun Rollet was allowed to proceed.[4] At the same time, following the protests of the Consuls General in Egypt, 'Abbās I, who succeeded Muḥammad 'Alī in 1849, recalled Laṭīf, formally instructed his successor

---

[1] Grancelli, p. 26: 'L'imperatore dava al Knoblecher 25 mila lire della sua cassa privata . . .'

[2] O.S. (A.V.) Handelsministerium 1851, zl. 1572. 'Provisorische Amtsinstruction für das k.k. Konsulat in Chartum' Huber, 24/XII/50).

[3] O.S. Ad. Reg. F. 27/6. Huber to Schwarzenberg, 6/X/51.

[4] Brun Rollet, pp. 178–82; Taylor, pp. 387–94. An English traveller who visited Khartoum in January 1851 had several conversations with Laṭīf Pasha, who 'found himself in the midst of a circle of enterprising Europeans every one assuming the authority of a Consul, and talking in a style as if he commanded a prodigious force . . .', G. Melly *Khartoum, and the Blue and White Niles*, 1851, i. p. 158.

that private expeditions were not to be obstructed, and issued letters of recommendation assuring Brun Rollet and other merchants 'the most absolute freedom to navigate the White Nile'.[1]

It was hardly a noble conflict. In Egypt Muḥammad 'Alī, an aged adventurer, vainly resisted the remorseless and acquisitive diplomatic pressure of the European Powers. In the Sudan there was the somewhat strange alliance between Vinco, the missionary, and the thrusting, speculative Brun Rollet intent on breaking the Governors' illegal efforts to preserve a traditional system which they respected and which they found considerably to their personal advantage. It was however a conflict fraught with significance for the immediate future of the southern Sudan. Europe had forced a way into Central Africa and, for a crucial decade, the initiative passed from the Egyptian Government to the European community at Khartoum.

2. The development of the deadlock, 1850–1859

It seemed that the forces of Christianity and commerce were at last free to bring European civilization to the isolated pagan tribes. The new Vicariate of Central Africa, stretching from Abyssinia to the Guinea coast and southwards, somewhat vaguely, to Ptolemy's 'Mountains of the moon', was the most extensive in the world.[2] It is not surprising that its early fortunes were followed with considerable interest in influential quarters. In September 1851 Knoblecher returned to Cairo with the good wishes and financial support of the Emperor Franz Josef, the Austrian episcopate, and the Congregation of Propaganda Fide. In an interview with 'Abbās I, who showed 'a lively interest in the negro tribes of the White Nile', he was welcomed 'with the friendliest goodwill', which included a firman for the Customs and an order to obtain a good 'dahabiah' (a Nile sailing-boat) at a cheap price

---

[1] A.S.T. Con. Naz. Aless./1851. Cerruti to Min. 5/XII/51 & 4/I/52; F.O. 141/19 Cerruti to Murray 26/XI/51. Thurburn & Co. had urged Murray to obtain 'a satisfactory guarantee against the recurrence' of these past grievances, having 'little doubt but a speedy development of the trade will follow equally remunerative to all interested'. F.O. 141/19. Chas. Thurburn to Murray 18/XI/51.

[2] Grancelli, p. 24.

from the Ministry of Transport.[1] This boat gave the mission independence from both traders and government and it was decided to found a station amongst the Bari. At that time, when Christian missions were restricted to the mere fringe of pagan Africa, this represented a unique attempt at penetration. If a flourishing mission had been successfully established it might well have radiated its influence deep into the interior and have become a permanent factor of decisive importance.

The commercial opportunity seemed as great. Ivory was the prize which attracted traders to the area. The products manufactured from it, chiefly knife-handles, combs, billiard-balls, and piano-keys, had an assured and rapidly expanding market in the many Western countries which could increasingly afford a wide distribution of such middle-class luxuries. Between the eighteen-forties and the eighteen-seventies both the price of ivory on the London market and the quantity imported more than doubled, and the trade obtained a recognized and valuable place in the world's economy.[2] In 1882 it was thought that 'an enormous trade could be done in a really satisfactory substitute' but as long as ample supplies were forthcoming there was little danger that a substitute would succeed.[3]

Africa was by far the most important source of these supplies and the most valuable kind—soft, opaque, easily-worked yet climate-resisting—came mainly from the central and eastern half of the continent.[4] Before the opening of the Congo route in the eighteen-eighties this area could be approached only from Zanzibar and the Nile. Sultan Sa'īd's dominion at Zanzibar provided a secure base for the Indian creditors who financed the Arab traders in their progressive penetration to Lake Tanganyika, the upper reaches of the Congo, and Buganda. But this system, like that of the

[1] O.S. Ad. Reg. F.27/6. Huber to Schwarzenberg, 6/X/51. Five years later when Prince Ḥalīm Pasha was appointed Governor General he promised 'dieser österreichischen Humanitätsgestalt jede thunliche Unterstützung angedeihen zu lassen' (ibid. Huber to Buol-Schauenstein, 29/IV/56). Sa'īd Pasha during his visit to the Sudan in 1856-7 'subscribed largely to this mission, and made them a grant of land on the Island of Philae' (F.O. 84/1120 Colquhoun to Russell, enclosing Memorandum on the Slave Trade by Mr. Coulthard, Colquhoun's secretary, 8/VI/60).

[2] A. Somborn, *Die Elfenbein und Beinschnitzerei*, Heidelberg, 1899.

[3] *J. Soc. Arts.*, June 1882.

[4] W. Westendarp, 'Das Gebeit der Elephanten . . .', *Mitt. Geog. Gesell. Hamburg*, 1878-9.

Muslim caravan routes in the Sudan, effectively excluded European enterprise,[1] with the result that the opening of the White Nile trade presented a unique opportunity to the small group of European traders at Khartoum. Here, it was thought, Europe would be able to establish a flourishing commerce deep in the interior of Africa; here was a test case for Bowring's and the humanitarians' belief[2] that an extensive 'legitimate' trade, effectively supplanting the slave trade, would follow the abolition of the Egyptian monopoly.

Exeter Hall, however, would hardly have chosen as its emissaries the Khartoum traders of the early 'fifties. They possessed some of the virtues and most of the vices of a speculative 'frontier' community. Cordial, hospitable, adventurous, several of them shared the lively scientific curiosity which attracted throughout this period a stream of distinguished travellers and explorers to Khartoum and the White Nile.[3] Most Europeans lived in comfortable cool houses built in an Egyptian style, and several traders brought their wives out with them while others were married by the Catholic missionaries to Abyssinian women. Their boats were constantly bringing in unfamiliar birds and beasts, many of which were sent to zoological gardens in Europe, and later when their expeditions were penetrating into the Congo basin the sight of Pygmies caused a good deal of astonishment. Years later the explorer and administrator, Sir Harry Johnston, enviously noted that there seemed 'to have been little, if any, international jealousy in this wonderful field of exploration between 1840 and 1860'. The partitioning of Africa had not yet begun. 'The tyranny, social and administrative, of the British military officer and his dame was not to come for many years; the 'smart' hotel was absent; provisions were good, plentiful, and cheap'.[4] On the other hand, casting off the restraints imposed by European conventional morality, the traders were determined, often to the point of an unscrupulous use of force, to gain their profits. Many of them

---

[1] In the 'eighties agents of the German firm, Meyer & Co., attempted to break into this system but failed disastrously. F.O. 84/1773 Kirk to Sec. of State, 11/III/86.

[2] See above, p. 22, n.4.

[3] Vayssière's diaries, for example, reveal a keen curiosity and appreciation of nature, and Brun Rollet, whom Melly considered to be 'by far the most agreeable man we have met' (op. cit. vol. ii, pp. 95-96), had a notable ethnographic collection.

[4] Johnston, pp. 109-10.

kept slaves in their households, and an insight into their general attitude to the people of the south is gained by Brun Rollet's words, closely echoing the remark of the Turkish official on the first expedition: 'beyond el-Eis it is necessary to distrust all those who do not fear us'.[1]

By no means all of them were the 'riff-raff' of Europe as has sometimes been supposed. In addition to the Austrian Consular Agent, Europe was officially represented by Petherick and Vaudey, the British and Sardinian Vice-Consuls. Both were typical examples of the European traders. A Welsh mining-engineer, John Petherick had been specially engaged by Muḥammad ʿAlī to investigate reported supplies of coal in Kordofan. The search was unsuccessful and, on the death of Muḥammad ʿAlī, Petherick became interested in the gum trade. In May 1850 he was appointed Vice-Consul, his 'most important duty' being that of 'protecting British trade against local monopoly'.[2] By June 1851 he was hoping to join in the ivory 'rush' on the White Nile.[3] After several successful expeditions to the Bahr el Ghazal, he returned to England in 1859 to obtain full Consular powers which he thought 'would be of incalculable (use) in promoting commerce'.[4] The powers were readily granted since they cost the Foreign Office practically nothing; but his further request for support in an attempt to import five hundred muskets, eighty elephant-rifles, and two tons of lead, for his two hundred men located 'amongst turbulent and warlike tribes', evoked from Lord John Russell, the Foreign Secretary, the observation that 'Mr. Petherick has a wild Arab sort of manner, fitter for those districts than St. James's Street . . . a fourth of the number should suffice'.[5]

Alexandre Vaudey, a Savoyard like Brun Rollet, had, as secretary to Clot Bey from 1837 to 1849, been intimately connected with one of the most progressive developments in Egypt: Muḥammad ʿAlī's attempt to introduce a new system of military education and

[1] Brun-Rollet, p. 47; see above, p. 17.

[2] F.O. 78/2253 Murray to Petherick 6/V/50, enclosed in Petherick to Stanley 26/III/68.

[3] F.O. 141/19 Petherick to Murray, 1/VI/51, 'It is my intention to send an expedition on the White River this year in research of Ivory etc., good boats are scarce, yours would be the thing . . . . Latif Pasha will no doubt protest against the measure, but "nous verrons".'

[4] F.O. 78/1465. Petherick Memo. 17/VIII/59.

[5] F.O. 78/1612 Petherick to Russell, 29/III/61 and minute by Russell.

health.[1] On the latter's death, like Petherick he found himself unemployed, and joined Brun Rollet in the Kordofan gum-trade. After a visit to Europe during which he was appointed Sardinian Vice-Consul to the Sudan, he returned to Cairo bringing his two young nephews Ambroise and Jules Poncet,[2] with a letter of support from Palmerston obtained through his Ambassador in London, and a promise of credit from Joyce Thurburn and Company.[3] His attention was focussed on the ivory trade, and while he was in Cairo he drew up a 'project for the commerce of the White Nile', which is a good example of the hopes which ivory aroused.

> Each year, [he wrote] when the north winds begin to blow at Khartoum, towards the middle of November, an expedition of a dozen boats ascends the White Nile as far as 4.30′ Lat. north. . . . These boats bring back annually about 400 quintals of ivory, which brought to Cairo represents a value of approximately 100,000 francs. To procure this ivory they give beads whose value does certainly not exceed 1,000 francs.
>
> In order not only to monopolise this product, but also to increase it considerably and perhaps even to double it each year, it would suffice to have a steamer based on Khartoum.[4]

Although the steamer did not materialize, the hopes were to some extent fulfilled. By 1856 the dozen boats had increased to over forty,[5] and in 1859 about eighty left Khartoum for the White Nile.[6] The increase in the quantity of ivory collected was at first correspondingly rapid: by 1856, Petherick reported that the 400 quintals

[1] Hill, *Biographical Dictionary*.
[2] 'Zweier strebsamer Männer", Heuglin, p. 10.
[3] F.O. 141/19. C. Thurburn to Murray, 18/XI/51. The Sardinian Consul-General had previously suggested the need for a Consular Agent. A.S.T. Cons. Naz. Aless/1850 Cerruti to Min., 5/XII/50.
[4] A.E. Mém Egypte/I. 'Projet pour le commerce du fleuve blanc', A. Vaudey, Cairo, 27/II/52. Vaudey failed to raise the necessary capital (c. £4,400), and it was not until 1858 that Lafargue took a steamer to Gondokoro (Morlang MS. 26/XI/58).
[5] O.S. Gen. Con. Alex/1857. Huber to Buol-Schauenstein, 16/I/57.
[6] de Pruyssenaere to his parents, February 1859, in 'Vingt-six lettres d'Eugène de Pruyssenaere', *Bull. Soc. Roy. Géog. d'Anvers*, 1930, p. 194. (Of a noble Flemish family, de Pruyssenaere came to the Sudan in 1857 to satisfy a desire for adventure and to undertake geographical and botanical research. He made several voyages up the White Nile in company with ivory traders and his letters are of considerable interest.) On 1/XII/60 Morlang noted in his diary that more than eighty boats had already left Khartoum in the season just started.

of 1851 had increased to '1400 cantars (quintals) or upwards, and I believe the annual imports will increase, the traffic being now better understood and more vigorously prosecuted than before.'[1] It was possible in these early years to meet people who had made 'almost a fortune in ivory', and reports of 'very good profits' were fairly common.[2]

Yet, although a prospect of great and hopeful progress beckoned both missionaries and traders, the history of their subsequent contact with the south is one of almost unrelieved tragedy. Historians have attributed this to the influence of the slave trade: 'vast regions hitherto untouched . . . were thus opened up to the rapacious slave-dealers. . . . The government did not attempt to administer the southern Sudan; but traders flocked there . . . driving ever deeper inland as the negroes fled from the more accessible areas'.[3]

This interpretation is due partly to the humanitarian pre-occupation with the slave trade, and is based almost entirely upon the observations of three British explorers, Speke, Grant, and Baker, who, arriving on the scene relatively late, witnessed scenes of large-scale violence and concluded that they were the result of slave-trading. The diaries, letters, and published accounts of earlier European observers reveal however a far more complex process, in which the decline of peaceful contact into conflict and violence is seen primarily as the result of an unbridled clash between widely differing societies and cultures. The total unpreparedness of the southern tribes to encounter the impact of the outside world was matched by a complete ignorance on the part of the missionaries and traders of the values of tribal society. The early welcome rapidly degenerated therefore into suspicion and finally open hostility. The demand for slaves was but one of the factors which exacerbated these fundamental difficulties, and on the Bahr el Jebel it had but a minor and secondary influence. The 'myth' of the rapacious Arab slave-traders has continued to embitter relationships between north and south;[4] it has also ob-

---

[1] F.O. 141/30. Petherick to Bruce, 5/XII/56.
[2] de Pruyssenaere to his parents, 17/V/56, *Bull. Soc. Roy. Géog. d'Anvers*, p. 151; O.S. Admin. Reg. F. 27/6. Gostner to Huber 16/IV/55, enclosed in Huber to Buol-Schauenstein, 4/VI/55.
[3] A. B. Theobald, *The Mahdiya*, 1951, p. 11. See also Shukry, p. 67.
[4] e.g.: *Report of the Commission of Inquiry into the Disturbances in the Southern Sudan during August 1955*, Khartoum, 1956, pp. 4, 5, 123–4.

scured the fact that the deadlock which developed between tribesmen and intruders illustrates in microcosm the difficulties of communication and understanding which still confront multi-racial Africa.

The contact passed through two main phases. At first the traders and the Africans faced each other with roughly equal forces. In their boats the traders had an unchallenged technical superiority and security, but on land both they and the missionaries were completely dependent on the co-operation of the Africans. On the coasts of West Africa a similar equilibrium became stabilized and endured for a considerable period while the immediate hinterland was developed through African middlemen. In the southern Sudan however various factors prevented the development of any co-operation. A deadlock developed, and the brief, uneasy period of equilibrium was followed by the second phase in which the traders, bringing in large numbers of armed Arab servants, founded their own stations in the interior and the ivory trade became dependent on widespread violence.

The early phase was practically restricted to contact with the Bari and the Shilluk. These tribes, easily accessible from the river, represented two foci of powerful, settled populations, separated by the nomadic Dinka and Nuer. Arab traders quickly established a *modus vivendi* with the Shilluk, and Kaka, the first large group of Shilluk village settlements to be reached from the north, was rapidly drawn into the orbit of Sudanese trade to the exclusion of the Europeans. In 1840 the Jellaba (small itinerant traders) from Khartoum were already visiting the Shilluk to barter cotton goods and beads for ivory, cows, and honey,[1] and a missionary visiting Kaka in 1858 described how Egyptians, Berberines, and Arabs from the Blue Nile, Darfur, and Kordofan, mingled with the local Shilluk many of whom were wearing cotton clothes. 'Immediately on the arrival of the "Stella Matutina" people stream forth from all quarters to trade with the ship's crew. The Shilluk women bring eggs and beautifully branded gourds for sale, and the Arab women bring *merissa*, cotton-cloth, harnesses, beans in plate-like baskets, etc.'[2]

Groups of the Arab traders and their families, sometimes fugitives from the Government, settled and formed small colonies

[1] Werne, ii. 288.
[2] Kir. MS. 30/I/58 and 25/IV/58.

amongst the Shilluk even as far south as the large village group of Wau.[1] This contact however hardly affected the traditional pattern of Shilluk life or its range of influence. Mounted on their small canoes, the Shilluk continued to undertake their annual raids ranging two hundred miles to the north.[2] Islam, despite its 'many contacts', was unable even 'to strike one root' according to one attentive observer;[3] and, most important of all, the reth rigidly refused to have any official or trading contact with Khartoum.[4] It was only later that this equilibrium was destroyed and these settlements became the source of quarrels disastrous for the Shilluk.

The European traders were not unduly perturbed by their exclusion from Shilluk territory. There was little ivory in the country and, secure in their boats which represented a capital outlay quite beyond the means of any Jellab, they stopped only to obtain a fresh supply of provisions before they pressed on to the south. Contact with the Dinka and Nuer was restricted both by the vagaries of seasonal migration and by the fact that the river, surrounded by shifting swamp and backed by tall savannah grass, offered only a few opportunities for trading stations. It was therefore the Bari who occupied the decisive point in the early development of the ivory trade, and it was amongst the Bari that the missionaries established their first station. Here if anywhere the traders might have succeeded in establishing an equitable, legitimate commerce. Salīm's exploratory expeditions had received a warm welcome, prospects for trade were good, and the area seemed almost prosperous in comparison to the dreary swamps.

The situation, however, had begun to deteriorate even before the traders and missionaries gained unobstructed access to the area in 1850. Salīm's discovery, it will be remembered,[5] was followed by small government trading expeditions during the 'forties. By the time this monopoly was broken the original friendly attitude of the

---

[1] Ibid. 2/II/58.

[2] Sometimes 'in revenge' the Baqqara were able to surprise and kidnap these marauding Shilluk (MA. MSS. Comboni to his fàther, 5/III/58, my italics). Kaufmann records that Shilluk joined the Arab settlers in raids on the Dinka, p. 62.

[3] Heuglin, p. 94.

[4] Miani, an Italian explorer, attempted to visit the reth but failed even though he was accompanied by a certain 'Mohamet-Uod-Adan' of Dongola who claimed to be 'il segretario o confidente del re', Mi.MS. 21–22/XII/59.

[5] See above, p. 21.

Bari was already turning into hostility, and their mendicant tendency, noted by Thibaut during Salīm's expeditions,[1] was assuming formidable proportions. We have little record of their contact with the early official expeditions yet it seems that three factors were mainly responsible for this change. The substantial profits of the ivory trade were throughout partly dependent on gaining access to accumulated 'stores' of ivory, the remains of elephants which had previously been hunted solely for their flesh. In some cases this ivory had been collected and was used as cattle-pegs or ornaments, but generally it had been left at the place of killing, and, though some of it had deteriorated, a large proportion was still of excellent quality. Small though they were, the government expeditions, restricted to the use of a few landing-places, must have purchased fairly rapidly the immediately available supplies. As the value of beads depreciated,[2] the Bari demanded higher prices for less ivory, and, at the same time the Turks became dependent on these riverain Bari to act as middlemen in the search for and purchase of further supplies.

It would seem that it was precisely at this point that the second factor became operative. If anyone among the Bari had been likely to become a successful middleman, that person was Nyigilo. It will be remembered how he had impressed the first expeditions, how he had travelled as far as Khartoum, and how he had at first welcomed Knoblecher.[3] He had well-established connections amongst the Pari, the small Luo tribe who had contacts with the Anuak to the north and the Acholi to the south,[4] and as trade developed he even travelled 'in the direction of the Lutuche (Lotuko) to buy cattle, sheep and other objects with a few beads'.[5] His early attempts, however, to co-operate with Europeans were suppressed by the Turks, and the subsequent subterfuge and

---

[1] See above, p. 18, n.3.

[2] In the beginning of 1854, 'les matrons et les petits maitres du lieu ont decidé que les verroteries adorés jusqu'ici étaient maintenant de mauvais gout. Ceci fait, que nous n'aurons pas que rien à leur offrir en échange des défenses qui cette année sont en plus grande quantité que jamais. Nous apprenons avec plaisir que la barque de M. Lafargue . . . est littéralement charger d'ivoire. Il séra le seul à avoir fait de bonnes affaires', Vay. MS. 6/I/54.

[3] See above, pp. 18, 22, 25.

[4] See below, p. 38.

[5] Crestani, p. 79, Knoblecher spoke with five Pari ('aus Berry') who came to visit Nyigilo, Knob. MS. 19/I/50.

intrigue to which he was driven[1] destroyed what respect the Bari might have had for either European or Turkish prestige and technical superiority. At the same time Nyigilo was prevented from exploiting to the full the benefits—for example the rifles with which Knoblecher was willing to supply him—which he would otherwise have obtained from his position as their agent. It is of course only too possible that the external chaos of tribal hostilities, and the myriad jealousies within Bari society, would have prevented him from ever becoming a really powerful and effective middleman, but it is certain that the unfortunate dichotomy between Turkish sovereignty and European commerce in these crucial early years prevented the only experiment which might have changed the subsequent pattern of events.

The third factor was the attitude of the officials and their Arab soldiers and crews towards the southerners. It is indisputable that the prevalent attitude of scorn towards the savage, naked 'abids' (slaves), which then existed in the northern Sudan, has been one of the most important and disastrous influences governing the contact of the southern Sudan with the outside world. The sharp division between Islam and the pagan world contibuted to this attitude,[2] but it is significant that it was completely shared by many of the nominally Christian traders of Khartoum, and it is a common-place that the European myth of the 'noble savage' was, in the course of the nineteenth century, only too often replaced by a complacent and ignorant dismissal of all African values. The Arabs' consciousness—however dim—of being heirs of one of the great languages and literatures of the world, their wider economic and political horizons, and above all their technological superiority constituted so marked a cultural contrast as to seem to confer on the northern Sudanese almost an inherent racial ascendancy.

It is impossible, in the absence of fuller records, to assess this factor adequately in these earliest years of contact. It is glimpsed only occasionally and one can but hazard some suggestions as to its influence. Knoblecher recorded the welcome generally given to the last government trading expedition,[3] but in some places he noticed that friendliness was already being replaced by fear. On

---

[1] Knoblecher records how Nyigilo had carefully hidden a large supply of ivory for them, Knob. MS. 14/I/50.

[2] See above, p. 7.

[3] See above, p. 24.

13 December 1849 the expedition reached an 'emporium' where it was expected to find a large number of Cic Dinka with a considerable supply of ivory from the interior; instead they were told that a prophet had forbidden the Cic to sell ivory to the 'Turks', and for the next two days, although Cic were assembled along the banks in great crowds, practically no ivory was forthcoming, while on the third day they came to a village almost deserted 'from fear of the Turks.'[1] On the 20th they bought ivory from a separate section of Cic further to the south who fled away after receiving their beads. Knoblecher wrote a weighty protest against the 'Turks'. 'I know no other reason for this timidity than the way in which the Turk treats everyone who is not a Turk. He wants all people in the world to become his servants and slaves.'[2] Knoblecher realized the next day that the difficulties were not all caused only by the 'Turks' when he learnt that the expedition of the previous year had been forced to fight in order to break a monopolistic attempt on the part of this section of the riverain Cic.[3] But it was not only the Cic who were afraid. On the return journey Knoblecher noticed that the Aliab were 'much more nervous towards us than on the outward journey', and, enquiring the reason, he was told by the boat's crew that previous expeditions had seized their women and children on the return journey.[4] Amongst the Bari Knoblecher reported no similar incidents, but as the other difficulties developed this scornful attitude of the intruders—Turks, Arabs and Europeans —made it increasingly probable that a violent solution would be sought by both sides.[5]

[1] Knob. MS. 12–16/XII/49. Since this is a most interesting example of the prophets who were later to play an important part in the Dinka's reaction to the outside world, I quote Knoblecher's account in full: '. . . die Nachricht von einem begeisterten Schwarzen, der vorgibt, wunderliche Zauberkräfte zu besitzen und den Landsleuten unter der Drohung eines plötzlichen Todes und der Versiegung des Flusses verbiethet, den Türken Elephantenzähne zu bringen. Er findet unter diesen einfachen Leuten zum Theil Glauben und benützt die Gelegenheit, um eine Menge Rindvieh, die einzige Habe dieser armen Leute, an sich zu bringen.'

[2] Knob. MS. 20/XII/49.   [3] Ibid. 21/XII/49.

[4] Ibid. 22–27/I/50, 'Sie hatten dieses Jahr dies nicht zu befürchten, da die Türken durch meine Gegenwart in derlei Unternehmungen geniert wurden, indem ich verschiedene Knaben, die man ergriffen hatte, mit Trotz in Freiheit setzen liess'.

[5] I have quoted extensively from Knoblecher as his diary bears all the marks of a reliable eye-witness account. It is supported by the few other records available, e.g. D'Arnaud to Jomard, 1/VIII/48, in H. Déhérain, Le Soudan Egyptien sous Mehemet Ali, Paris, 1898, p. 346.

Thus a complex and delicate situation faced both missionaries and merchants when at last, with the overthrow of the Government's monopoly, they obtaned direct untrammelled contact with the Bari. The missionaries' experience vividly illustrates the clash of cultures which followed, the difficult adaptation which was demanded of the Bari and the tensions which rapidly developed. Angelo Vinco was the first missionary to settle amongst the Bari. With Brun Rollet's boats he arrived near Gondokoro in February 1851[1], and he eventually established himself with a few servants at Nyigilo's village on Belinian. In Nyigilo's company he visited the Pari where he discovered that this splinter Luo group was obtaining its trickle of 'luxury' goods not only through the 'Gnaghi' (i.e. Anuak?) from the Beni Shanqul country and Abyssinia to the north, but also through the 'Cioco' (i.e. Acholi) from the Lacustrine kingdoms on the equator and ultimately from Zanzibar.[2] Prevented both by fever and by a war between the Bari and the Pari from visiting these equatorial tribes, he attempted later to reach them by following the Nile southwards. Welcomed at Shindiru, the chief rain-maker's shrine, he passed through several Bari groups but was finally frustrated by the reputedly implacable hostility of the Madi to the south. Finally in June 1852 he had to return to Khartoum, partly in order to report to Knoblecher, but also because the Bari threatened him with death if he did not help them in a war against the Lokoya.[3] Thus even at this early date the chaos of small tribal divisions presented a barrier to any great expansion.

Vinco returned to the Bari and died in January 1853 in the presence of Knoblecher and three other priests who had arrived to establish the permanent station. Their first action—the purchase of some land from a local chief—was the source of serious misunderstanding, for, as one of the missionaries later realized, Bari law recognizes only 'the transfer of movables'.[4] Thus although

[1] See above, p. 25.

[2] The Missioni Africane possess at Verona Vinco's ms. account. It has been published by R. Almagia, 'Angelo Vinco; Relazione delle sue esplorazione sull' alto Nilo (1849–1853)', Ann. Lateranensi, 1940, and by Crestani, pp. 71–134. In 1863 Baker reported that the Lotuko had trading connections with Bunyoro, Sir. S. W. Baker, The Albert Nyanza, Great Basin of the Nile, edition of 1867, pp. 326–9.

[3] Crestani, p. 121; Brun Rollet, pp. 201–2.

[4] M.A. MSS. Uberbacher to Mitterutzner, 28/I/58. For this account I have also drawn on a typescript by C. Tappi, 'Due Parole d'Introduzione', (s.d.) which quotes extensively from unpublished correspondence.

the 'sale' had, as the missionaries thought, been duly witnessed; there were continual arguments on the subject, and attempts to sow crops, to use stone and wood for building, and to bury a missionary were the signals for united demands for further beads and presents.[1] It was also incomprehensible to the hungry[2] Bari, with their system of communal kinship assistance, that the mission should attempt to reserve for its own use the scanty provisions brought from Khartoum. The missionaries realized that the Bari attitude to 'hospitality' was a great hindrance to the mission which was stigmatized as 'mean and hard-hearted', and against a background of incessant thefts it became a struggle to survive.[3]

Having settled the missionaries at Gondokoro Knoblecher returned to fetch fresh supplies from Khartoum, but when the first boats reached Gondokoro the following year, a French trader records how they found the mission in a 'very critical position': their supplies were exhausted, the Bari in stealing their cows had wounded a servant, and they were 'demoralized' by the dangers they had undergone. 'Their mission, they say, has not the least chance of success and Don Ignace (Knoblecher) must abandon it if he listens to them. They have not made the slightest Christian impact.'[4] When shortly after this two of the missionaries died, Mozgan, the survivor, abandoned Gondokoro and founded 'Holy Cross', a station amongst a few Cic riverain fishermen a hundred and fifty miles to the north.[5] For a year the few huts at Gondokoro remained in the charge of a Muslim servant, and then in April 1855 Knoblecher arrived with Uberbacher and several brick-layers who built a chapel, houses, and 'a strong encircling wall to defend the mission from the invasions of the Bari'.[6] The following year Uberbacher was joined by Morlang. Their efforts were almost entirely confined to translation work and a school, but, in the face of strong protests from the parents, it proved impossible to discipline the pupils. The robberies increased until in May 1858,

---

[1] Tappi, 'Due Parole', p. 16; A. Kaufmann, *Das Gebiet des Weissen Flüsses und dessen Bewohner*, Brixen, 1861, pp. 192–7; Kir. MS. 1–4/III/58.

[2] From April to July the Bari suffered a period of famine. 'Man hört da nichts als von Raub und Einbrüchen, von Diebstahl und Todschlag', Kaufmann, p. 169.

[3] Kaufmann, p. 90.

[4] Vay. MS. 6–14/I/54.

[5] Tappi, 'Due Parole', p. 18.

[6] Ibid. p. 20.

surrounded during the night by 'a veritable band of brigands', Morlang thought that 'the thefts would endanger the existence of this station'.[1] Dependent on Khartoum even for its supplies of corn, the station led a self-contained life and was only occasionally visited by Nyigilo or other chiefs who 'according to the custom of the Bari asked for presents'.[2] On the one occasion when the missionaries ventured alone beyond Gondokoro, they rode three or four miles to Belinian, and Morlang thankfully noted that they were 'not much molested for beads as we had none with us'.[3]

Similar difficulties, though possibly not with such intensity, have confronted other pioneer missionaries and elsewhere they were overcome. In some areas a powerful ruler, like Mutesa of Buganda or Mirambo of Unyamwezi, realized that their presence provided a protection against other alien intruders; in others, the missionaries were valued as distributors of trade goods; and nearly all pioneer missionaries could rely on the prestige and 'magic' of the white man.[4] At Gondokoro however their influence was compromised by the presence of the European traders. The missionaries were not the sole representatives of Western technical superiority and were therefore denied the prestige and advantages enjoyed by others elsewhere. Their own Muslim servants enjoyed the confidence of the Bari to a greater extent than they themselves, while, since these servants traded on their own account, Morlang did not wonder that the Bari 'do not know how to distinguish clearly between our house and the traders' establishments'.[5] Behind the story of vexations, robberies, and hostility, there lay the Bari's increasing suspicion of the ultimate intentions of all these alien intruders, and as the relationship between the traders and the tribes deteriorated the mission's contact with the Bari became increasingly difficult.[6]

The barrier to penetration caused by inter-tribal warfare, the difficulties springing from the Bari's almost total ignorance of trading methods, and the gulf of misunderstanding and mutual

[1] Morlang MS. 5–7/V/58.
[2] Ibid. 29/IX/57.
[3] Ibid. 15/III/58.
[4] Oliver, pp. 66–73. For the support which Mutesa obtained from missionaries, see below, Chapter 6.
[5] Morlang MS. 26/V/58; Kaufman, pp. 197–8, who adds that these servants were necessary 'weil zwei Menschen sich nicht ein Jahr lang gegen solches Raubgesindel halten konnen'.
[6] See below, p. 44.

scorn were thus partly illustrated by the experience of the missionaries. The traders, when confronted with similar difficulties and
demands, soon had recourse to force. In 1854, as Vayssière and
de Malzac, two French traders, approached the Bari they were met
by disquieting news: the mission was beleaguered; one of Brun
Rollet's boats was involved in a fight near Rejaf and two of his
men were killed and several wounded;[1] at the mooring place of
Ulibari there was but little security and one was 'continually under
the menace of an attack which could be evaded only by an ample
distribution of beads'.[2] It was decided therefore to convert their
boat into a fortress, with screens as a protection against arrows,
and in the morning of 14 January they reached Ulibari.

> A comic scene took place. The blacks came on board our boat; one
> demanded tribute, another the toll for his land, etc. We started by
> putting everybody at action stations and showed the muzzles of our
> rifles. There followed an explanation in which we declared that we
> would in no way give forced gifts and that we would reply by bullets
> to any hostile demonstration. Our attitude dismayed the other
> traders . . . and infuriated the inhabitants of the place who withdrew,
> gratifying us with the epithet *d'Aloron* (wicked people). All the Arab
> sailors and all the servants were filled on the contrary with ad-
> miration.[3]

At Gondokoro the scene was re-enacted. Assailed by the Bari
with demands for a landing fee they dealt with them in a similar
manner: 'we threatened immediately to hang them at the yard-arm
of our boat, then we gave them a handful of beads promising to
burn down their village if a single grain of our pile of durra was
missing.' On the 16th they left Gondokoro and at a village a little
further to the south three frustrating days culminated in the
'exorbitant pretensions' of a chief, 'whom Habib had imprisoned
for some days last year'.[4] It was decided to return to the north,
and on the way they killed forty men in a quarrel with the Sere.[5]

Vayssière's account of these incidents reveals the deeper causes
of the conflict. It was not merely a question of trading difficulties

---

[1] Tappi, 'Due Parole . . .', p. 18 states that Beltrame at Khartoum was told
that Brun Rollet's men had killed seventy Africans.
[2] Vay. MS. 6–12/I/54.
[3] Vay. MS. 14/I/54.
[4] Ḥabīb was a Syrian trader of unscrupulous character, see below p. 49.
[5] Vay MS. 7/II/54.

and economic incompatibility, exploited or aggravated on both sides by unscrupulous cupidity. At a deeper level it was a failure of imaginative understanding, an inability to recognize the strain and turmoil of a clash of cultures. Vayssière was not an unscrupulous blackguard. Later, when conditions had disastrously deteriorated, he strongly condemned the slave trade.[1] But in these early days not once did he pause to consider the consequences of his actions, or attempt to understand the fears and uncertainties which lay behind the aggressive demands of the Bari. There is no hint in his diary that it ever occurred to him that in relying upon a blatant use of force to solve an economic impasse, he was inevitably intensifying and not depleting the tension inherent in the situation. He relied, naturally and yet disastrously, upon an interpretation based entirely on a rigid western scale of values which made no allowance for the immensely difficult adjustment demanded of the Bari. Firmness was doubtless necessary and justifiable, but the roughshod impatience of the European traders mingled inopportunely with the scornful attitude of their Arab servants towards the 'abids' of the south.

Shortly after Vayssière's visit the conflict intensified to a pitched battle. After a successful season in 1852-3, Vaudey, the Sardinian Vice-Consul, with his two nephews, three boats, and more than a hundred cantars of beads for barter, sailed for the south again in December 1853.[2] The following months he spent trading in the neighbourhood of the Bari, and towards the end of March 1854 he was training oxen for transport in an attempt to reach, with Nyigilo's help, the Lacustrine Kingdoms first reported by Vinco.[3] On the 4 April Knoblecher's boat passed him at Ulibari, and the following day disaster occurred. Vaudey had lent his smallest boat to Muḥammad Effendi, a Turkish trader, who returning by Gondokoro fired the customary salute to Knoblecher. The rifles of some of his men were loaded and a child was killed amongst the crowd of Bari, to whom Knoblecher was distributing beads.[4] In the confusion which followed the boat was assailed with arrows and more

[1] See below, p. 49, and Lejean, p. 72.
[2] Vaudey to his mother, 11/XII/53 in Buet, *Les premiers explorateurs français du Soudan Equatorial*, Paris, s.d., pp. 25–30.
[3] Lejean, p. 78; Buet, p. 47.
[4] 'Avec une prodigalité tout à fait singulière'—Ambroise Poncet to Folco, 18/V/54 enclosed in Leardi to Min. 7/VII/54 (A.S.T. Con. Naz. Aless./1854). Buet, pp. 49–51, is based on Poncet's report.

shots were fired. Hearing the firing, Vaudey dashed to the rescue and 'an extremely violent battle' on land between him and four to five thousand Bari developed, in which Vaudey, Muḥammad, and many of his men were killed.[1] It was later suggested that Vaudey had been thirsting for 'a favourable opportunity to give the Bari a trenchant lesson',[2] and, although the eye-witness accounts show that Vaudey had no part in the opening stages of the quarrel, it is evident that once the incident had started he was fully determined to assert his prestige. Knoblecher, who turned the mission into 'a veritable field-hospital' for the Bari, and whose mediation enabled Vaudey's nephews to withdraw their boats, considered that although the way still remained opened for the mission, henceforth no other boat 'would dare to anchor there'.

The trader's boats, however, continued to arrive, and Vaudey's death was not the cataclysmic event imagined by Knoblecher,[3] but it did much to destroy the faint hope of equal and harmonious co-operation with the Bari. For the next few years an uneasy tension prevailed. The traders were restricted to a few weeks of bartering with the riverain Bari. There was a steady succession of incidents, difficulties and frustrations;[4] the hopes of reaching new sources of wealth beyond the Bari disappeared; and the final failure of co-operation was clearly revealed in the downfall of Nyigilo. His attempt to become the agent of the Europeans brought him a relatively impressive increase in wealth, but it did not provide him with sufficient power to overcome the envy and antipathy of his fellow Bari, who resented this attempt to under-take functions which were in no way sanctioned by his traditional status.[5] As the ally of the outside world, he became a scapegoat on

[1] O.S. Pol. Archiv. Kons. Ag./1854. Knoblecher's account of the incident dated 8/IV/54 is quoted in Gostner to Huber, 17/V/54, enclosed in Huber to Buol-Schauenstein, 30/VI/54.

[2] Hansal, *Neuste Briefe aus Chartum*, Vienna, 1855, p. 127.

[3] and by Shukry, op. cit. p. 100.

[4] Morlang's diary mentions several incidents: e.g. 16/III/57. The Vakil of Lafargue killed ten or eleven Africans to the south of Gondokoro, who had refused to let him sit under a tree. The Duke d'Aumont, 'Du Caire à Gondokoro et au Mont Redjaif', *Bull. Soc. Khédiviale Géog.*, 1883, records his hostile reception among the Bari, and of all the tribes on the White Nile they were the most feared. 'Die Nuer sind am meisten gefürchtet *nebst* den Bari und scheinen besser genährt als alle Neger'. (Kir. MS. 19/IV/58, my italics.)

[5] Nyigilo was but the brother of the Belinian rain chief (cf. A. C. Beaton, 'A Chapter in Bari History', *S.N.R.* 1934), and this fact accentuated the lack of traditional sanction.

which the Bari focussed their fear and hatred of the intruders.
In January 1854, Vayssière heard that 'Nygilo, chief of the
mountain and protégé of the mission, had been robbed by his men
under pretext that the rain did not come'.[1] Throughout this
period of tension he continued to be in a precarious position until
in May 1859, during a time of famine, his huts were destroyed, his
cattle slaughtered and he was forced to flee to a relative near
Gondokoro in an attempt to hide and to escape eventually by boat
to Khartoum. Hunted by numerous gangs of armed youths he
was killed on 21 June 1859.[2]

Thus, instead of laying the foundations for a mutually advantageous commercial co-operation, the first phase of contact finished
in a complete deadlock between the Bari and all the alien intruders.
The missionaries found themselves completely frustrated. Inter-
tribal rivalries prevented them from reaching tribes further into
the interior, and seriously compromised by the presence of the
European traders and their Arab servants the mission made
virtually no impression on the Bari at Gondokoro. Added to all
this the climate entailed a fearful loss of life. Between 1851 and
1857 more than half of the many recruits sent out by the mission
died, and in 1858 the deaths of Mozgan and Uberbacher, of
Oliboni, leader of a fresh party from Verona, of Gostner the Vicar
General at Khartoum, and of Knoblecher himself, made a withdrawal
almost inevitable.[3] Nyigilo's assassination also destroyed all hopes of
establishing an equitable relationship between traders and tribesmen.
The crucial moment in the contact of the southern Sudan with the
outside world had passed. A peaceful fusion was now impossible.

In this first phase of contact the slave trade played an insignificant
part in the creation of the deadlock between the traders and the
peoples of the southern Sudan. During the development of the
ivory trade slaves continued to be 'the most profitable' export
from the Sudan,[4] but the opening of the White Nile had little
influence on this slave trade. It remained far easier and cheaper to
continue to capture slaves from the Nuba mountains, the Blue

[1] Vay. MS. 6/I/54.
[2] Mor. MS. May and June. Seligman, op. cit., p. 293, quotes a shortened
account of Nyigilo's death by Morlang published in Petermann's Mitteilungen
as an example of the fate which overtakes rain-makers if they fail to produce
rain; but in this case there were other, and more important factors at work.
[3] O.S. Ad. Reg. 27/6. Huber to Buol-Schauenstein, 17/VI/58.
[4] O.S. Pol. Archiv. Kons. Ag./1854. Huber to Buol-Schauenstein, 30/VI/54.

Nile and the border-lands of Abyssinia, in the constant reprisal raids on tribes beyond the bounds of Turkish administration or on those which refused to pay their taxes.[1] Compared with these traditional sources the contribution of the Bahr el Jebel was insignificant. The soldiers and boats' crews of the early government expeditions captured or purchased the occasional woman or child[2] and they continued this practice under the European traders; by 1855 many of the boats which arrived in Khartoum from the White Nile carried from ten to thirty slaves who would possibly fetch about £7 each, and there was little doubt that the European traders connived at these proceedings even if they did not actually sell the slaves on their own account.[3] But this was a very small total. The Sudan counted its slaves in thousands, and at this time the profits gained by the servants from the sale of a few slaves were completely dwarfed by the profits of the ivory trade.

It is important also to realize that in this early phase the slave trade on the White Nile was almost entirely confined within the traditional pattern of tribal life. The slaves were generally purchased from a friendly tribe by whom they had been captured in the normal course of tribal raids. The demand for slaves was not, at first, an exacerbating factor greatly intensifying these raids. Thus while Vayssière was helping de Malzac to carry out a reconnaissance in the interior he bought from one of the Rol Dinka a 'Djour' boy. Youths like this one were taught Arabic and they became not slaves 'bien entendu' but 'interpreters and commercial agents'[4]. In 1855 Knoblecher was able to free several 'of the unlucky children of the Jur, Arol, Gok, etc. tribes living to the west of Holy Cross, who had been reciprocally robbed and then sold to the many-coloured Khartoum traders of all Confessions'.[5]

1 Ibid. for an example of a large-scale raid on Taka and Abyssinia.
2 See above, p. 37.
3 Hansal, p. 20, letter dated 25/VII/55. For rumours that Europeans were taking part, cp. Huber to Buol-Schauenstein, 30/VI/54, in O.S. Pol. Archiv. Kons. Ag./1854.
4 Vay. MS. 20/III/54.
5 O.S. Ad. Reg. 27/6. Knoblecher to Huber, 9/VIII/55, enclosed in Huber to Min. 24/X/55. Knoblecher added that the Muslim traders acquiesced in his action and were content to receive a small compensation, but 'die Leute des Herrn Lafargue und des Herrn Rollet haben eine bedeutende Anzahl solcher armen Geschöpfe in ihren Niederlassungen, ohne sich an die Reklamation der Mission zu kehren. Einer der Agenten des Rollet hatte sogar die Frechheit, ein Kind, welches sich in der Station befand, während der Abwesenheit des Missionärs mit Gewalt aus dem Missionshause zu ziehen.'

The flourishing slave trade in the northern Sudan and its Islamic sanction undoubtedly contributed to the contemptuous attitude of the northerners to the pagan south.[1] Indirectly therefore it helped to make a reliance upon force seem the natural and inevitable way to overcome the difficulties encountered in the search for ivory. The slave trade, however, does not appear to have been one of the primary difficulties which embittered the relationship between the southerners and the outside world in these early years. It was only later that its direct influence was heavily felt in the southern Sudan, and even then in a large part of the area it remained merely a facet of the ivory trade.

3. The sequence of violence, 1857–1863

The deadlock was broken only when the traders decided to undertake direct expeditions into the interior and to establish permanent and powerful stations with the aid of a large number of armed Arab servants. This decision profoundly altered the relationship of traders and tribes, and inaugurated the second phase of contact. The difficulties arising from tribal divisions and the gulf of social customs were henceforth overcome by an immediate application of force, and the foundation of numerous fortified stations involved the permanent intrusion of an alien community. The Arab servants settled, obtained wives and slaves from the neighbouring tribes, and established themselves as a ruling caste transcending the barriers of tribal society. The trading 'frontier' began to create a plural society. Henceforth adaptation to the outside world took place through a forced mingling of blood and a harsh turbulent disruption. The clash between pagan southerner and Arab northerner has dominated the subsequent history of the area; but it was the decision and actions of European traders which inaugurated and intensified the conflict, and although the search for ivory continued to be the dominant purpose of their activity, it became ever more closely bound to the extension of violence and the capture of slaves.

The impasse between tribesmen and traders was first overcome amongst the riverain Dinka tribes to the north of the Bari. As early as 1852 Brun Rollet and Vaudey left agents at the few landing places amongst the Cic and the Sere. These men collected small

[1] See above, pp. 7, 36.

quantities of ivory but they were dependent on the good will of the local tribal section and the range of their activities was severely limited. The supplies of ivory were quickly exhausted and beyond the riverain area it was impossible to penetrate without armed force.[1]

It was de Malzac who broke through these barriers and initiated the intensive exploitation of the interior. Returning with Vayssière from their frustrating visit to the Bari, they stopped at Shambe, the northernmost landing place amongst the Cic, and in March 1854 they carried out a reconnaissance. After several days in the interior they contacted the Rol Dinka tribe, but local tribal wars caused the abandonment of a second expedition and provided an ominous background for de Malzac's subsequent activities.[2] There is no record of the events of the crucial two years which followed, but by the end of 1856 de Malzac owned a flourishing station eight days' march into the interior. He employed interpreters for five different languages, and needed five hundred tribesmen to transport his ivory to the river.[3] He became known as the King of the White Nile[4] and his contemporaries quickly recognized that his success was achieved only by deeds of wide-spread cruelty and injustice. Eye-witness reports of whole tribes fleeing from his neighbourhood were fairly common while, amongst the missionaries at Khartoum, it was believed that the heads of his victims surrounded his settlement 'in order to instil terror into the neighbourhood'.[5]

It is most important, however, to realise that his influence was by no means wholly dependent upon terror and a direct use of armed Arab troops. He simply stimulated the existing tribal rivalries and stabilized their shifting antagonisms by forming alliances with certain tribal sections. His use of force was completely unscrupulous but not indiscriminate. The chaos of tribal warfare, which previously had appeared as an obstacle to any penetration and expansion, was exploited and transformed into the means of

[1] A.S.T. Con. Naz. Aless./1854. Brun Rollet to Cerutti, October 1853, enclosed in Cerutti to Min. 24/II/54; Vay. MS. 26/XII/53–6/I/54.

[2] Vay. MS. 21/III/54.

[3] F. de Lesseps' MS. report on his visit to Khartoum with Saʿīd Pasha in January 1857, dated Paris, 26/IV/57, and kept in the archives of the Société de Géographie. He had a long conversation with de Malzac at Khartoum.

[4] Mi.MS. 20/VII/59, and Kir.MS. 11/II/58; 'König der Schwarzen.'

[5] Mor. MS./IV 25/60 ando./6 31/XII

extending his power over a vast region. A firm pattern of alliances, subjection and hostility was established.

This was clearly revealed when, on de Malzac's death in April 1860, his stations were bought and visited by Franz Binder, a Transylvanian trader. Arrived at Shambe, Binder at first had difficulty in re-assuring the Cic chiefs that his three boats and one thousand armed attendants would only be directed against their rivals the Lau Dinka. Soon however he received daily visits from the Cic, and he was accompanied into the interior by 'the great chief Ariodetch' who seemed genuinely distressed on hearing of de Malzac's death. When after a week Binder reached the settlement at 'Ronga' (Rumbek) he was greeted 'by many chieftains who came here from two days' journey . . . to lament with me over the death of my "brother"'. A few days later at 'Ronga' four chiefs of the Cic, Agar and 'Agjel' Dinka tribes came to complain that other hostile Dinka tribes had declared war on them. The trader's alliance was invoked and one hundred and ten armed men accompanied by one thousand tribesmen were sent out to undertake extensive raids. Other expeditions subsequently collected over 100 kantars of ivory, and eventually nine hundred porters were summoned by three cannon shots to carry the ivory to the river.[1]

The policy of divide and rule is a fairly common phenomenon in the process of colonization, but in the southern Sudan this exploitation of tribal hostilities was peculiarly destructive. The political supremacy of the traders was not used to produce an ever-widening sphere of constructive, stabilizing influence in which to establish commercial relationships; instead trading was fused with robbery. The raids on 'hostile' tribes became an integral, indispensable part of the ivory trade as they produced the two 'commodities', cattle and slaves, which began to occupy an essential place in the traders' profits. Cattle supplied all the basic needs of the nomadic Dinka and Nuer and possessed for them a supreme and exclusive value. Once the restricted demand for beads had slackened,[2] these people with a proud repugnance for

[1] E. Kurt. Binder, *Reisen und Erlebnisse eines Siebenbürger Sachsen um die Mitte des vorigen Jahrhunderts im Orient und in Afrika'*, Hermannstadt, 1930. Dr. Walter Hirschberg of Vienna kindly lent me a copy of this book and there is now a microfilm copy in the Royal Commonwealth Society. It contains Franz Binder's autobiography.

[2] E.g. de Pruyssenaere to his mother, 20/IV/60, *Bull. Soc. Géog. d'Anvers*, p. 270.

clothing[1] had no wants which could easily be supplied by the traders
in return for further ivory or, what for the traders was equally
important, their services as porters. Perhaps with patience market
demands might have been stimulated,[2] but so delayed a turnover
would have demanded more capital than any trader possessed.
It was far easier and cheaper to accept the suggestion of a friendly
chief that a portion of a neighbouring herd of cattle would be an
acceptable reward for ivory or services.

De Malzac clarified this situation into a well organized system of
'razzias' or raids. 'The methods of de Malzac's people (170 men),
who engage in formal robbery, have this year been extended to
Njerkani. They raid the natives for cattle, a part of which is
needed for food and a part as barter for ivory.'[3] Others followed
his example, among them the Syrian Ḥabīb who on a trumpery
excuse attacked the Bor, killed nine men, caused 'hundreds of
women' to drown while attempting to escape, and took two thous-
and cows 'free of charge in order to obtain ivory with them'.[4] This
conduct was severely criticized by several traders, including
Vayssière who had broken with de Malzac and established another
river station at Agorbar to the south of Shambe; but raided cattle
soon became the universal and indispensable medium of exchange
and even Vayssière himself became involved in the consequences.
Early in 1860 having purchased about four hundred cows which a
Syrian trader, Ibrāhīm Bās, had seized from the Bor, Vayssière was
attacked by the latter and forced to escape to the deserted mission
station of Holy Cross.[5] In 1862 Petherick was told by Jules Poncet,

[1] A Dinka chief once told Kaufmann 'um 30 Kühe würde ich nicht immer
gekleidet gehen', op. cit., p. 83.
[2] 'In lieu of the introduction of more valuable and civilising merchandise,
such as cutlery, or cloth for wearing apparel, as articles of barter, of which the
negroes are very fond—when the value of glass beads and copper ornaments
began to decline and lose their charm—the traders disgraced themselves by
descending ... to enrich themselves by the plunder and destruction of tribe after
tribe', Petherick to Murchison, 20/XII/63, in *Proc. R. Geog. Soc.*, 1864, p. 139.
[3] Kir. MS. 17/IV/58. Piaggia (*Le Memorie di Carlo Piaggia*, ed. G. A.
Pellegrinetti, Florence, 1941, p. 110) and Miani were also witnesses: 'La barca
di Scenuda ... racconta che gli armati di Malzac distrussero un intero villaggio
per rubare le vacche. Siccome ogni quattro bovi hanno un "biringi" (bel dente)
uccidono impunemente il genere umano per avere i loro armenti e fare così un
(dicono loro) onorato commercio', Mi. MS. 6/III/60.
[4] Kir. MS. 9/IV/58. Lejean, p. 73, tells how the Bor revenged themselves by
killing Cheho, Ḥabīb's successor, and by completely routing a reprisal raid.
[5] Mor. MS. 25/IV/60; Mi. MS. 27/II/60; de Pruyssenaere to his mother
23/I/60, *Bull. Soc. Roy. Géog. d'Anvers*, p. 236.

who had established several trading stations in the same area, that the Cic would not act as porters unless the Aliab were raided for cattle, and amongst the Rol Petherick was 'compelled to yield a reluctant assent' to a cattle razzia which Poncet's men evidently regarded as a regular event.[1]

Slaves, the other 'commodity' produced by the exploitation of these tribal raids, began in this second phase of contact to have an important function within the structure of the ivory trade. In order to understand this connection it is necessary to study the structure of the ivory trade and to examine the sources and distribution of its profits. The traders' capital expenditure steadily increased. The use of force, both to break through the difficulties originally posed by tribal divisions and also to supply the southerners' demand for cattle, inevitably resulted in a dependence on an increasing number of armed servants. In the summer of 1857 de Malzac, who previously had about sixty soldiers at his station, prepared at Khartoum 'the greatest expedition made until then'. It consisted of three boats and about three hundred armed men and involved a capital outlay of over 120,000 francs (c. £4,800).[2] This burden of increased expenditure coincided with seriously diminished returns. As the easily accessible supplies became exhausted, the export of ivory by no means kept pace with the rapid increase in the number of boats which continued to be attracted by the hopes of considerable profits: between 1851 and 1856 the number of boats and the quantity of ivory collected had both more than trebled,[3] but by 1863 although the number of boats had again trebled, rising to 120, the quantity of ivory had merely increased from 1400 kantars to 2000.[4] The results of this growing scarcity of ivory were to a slight extent offset by a gradual rise in its price at Khartoum, but this was not sufficient to modify the striking decrease in the overall profits gained directly from the purchase of ivory.

---

[1] J. Petherick, *Travels in Central Africa*, 1869 (2 vols.), vol. i, pp. 168–229.

[2] Piaggia, pp. 106, 124. The need for these soldiers was dramatically demonstrated the following summer when his station was attacked by hostile tribes, who lost over 100 men but wounded many of the soldiers with poisoned arrows, ibid., p. 126.

[3] See above, pp. 31–32.

[4] F.O. 84/1246. Joyce to Egyptian Trading Co., 19/XI/64 for the figure of 120 boats; A.E. Corr. Consul. Alex./31. Taska to Drouyn de Lhuys, 30/VI/63 enclosing Thibaut to Taska 27/IV/63 for figure of 2000 kantars.

The difficulties of the White Nile traders were enhanced by the fact that the principal beneficiaries of the trade were the creditors who advanced the capital and the middlemen who dealt with the ivory after its arrival in Khartoum. Franz Binder, for example, arrived in the Sudan in 1852 with a puny capital of about £100. After a few years dealing in the transport and sale of ivory and other Sudan exports in Egypt, he became one of de Malzac's principal creditors. He obtained the latter's stations and 'trading rights' for the paltry sum of £500 on his death, and by 1862 he was considered to be the richest European in Khartoum with a capital of at least £8000.[1] He was but a typical example of those creditors who flourished in a place where there was but 'little money or credit', where the legal rate of interest was 36 per cent. and the rate usually demanded was 60 per cent., where the majority of fortunes had their origin in usury and where it was commonly thought that the White Nile traders 'instead of enriching themselves, enrich their creditors'.[2]

With this background of added expenditure, decreasing overall profits and ruinous credit, the majority of the White Nile traders would have been forced to abandon their activity had it not been for the capture of slaves, which enabled them to obtain the services of their armed servants at a very reduced actual cost, and even in some cases practically free of charge. The average nominal wage of these servants was about ten shillings per month, but they were obliged to receive a large proportion of their wages in merchandise supplied to them by the trader at 'a most exorbitant price', and a part of the 'merchandise' so supplied was slaves captured in the raids on hostile tribes.[3] The profits of the traders thus became dependent not only on the export of ivory but also on their position as traders with their own servants and stations— with the centres of the new plural society. Again it was de Malzac who first systematically exploited this situation. Carlo Piaggia, who was engaged by him as his chief elephant hunter for the season

---

[1] Binder, p. 30; O.S. Ad. Reg. 27/9. Natterer to v. Siknell, 30/X/62.
[2] de Pruyssenaere to his mother, 20/IV/60, *Bull. Soc. Roy. Géog. d'Anvers*, p. 269. Miani supports this observation: 'In generale le casse di questi signori che trafficano sul Fiume Bianco sono sempre vuote. Tutti gli anni fanno debiti per poter fare le loro spedizioni e vendono anticipatamente l'avorio (che forse porteranno) al 50 per 100 di ribasso, ricevendo parte denaro e parte generi', Mi. MS. 20/VII/59.
[3] F.O. 84/1246. Joyce to the Egyptian Trading Co., 10/XI/64.

1857–8, relates how, in a market opposite to the station at Rol, de Malzac sold the women and children, taken in cattle raids, to his soldiers. Each slave cost the equivalent of about three months' pay. Many of the women became wives of the Arabs, some of the children were trained as their assistants, and others were sold to traders and taken northwards on the Nile to be sold at more than double the price at which they were acquired.[1] In this, as in cattle-raiding, de Malzac's example was followed by others and by 1864 it was thought in Khartoum that all traders on the White Nile permitted their agents 'to seize and sell slaves being well aware of the fact and indirectly partners in the profits'.[2]

Some traders also exported slaves directly on their own account. In May 1859 Jules Poncet anchored near an Arab merchant who was selling into slavery a considerable number of men who had acted as porters for him from the interior,[3] and there is evidence that by 1860 several White Nile traders had a large stake in the slave trade. In letters to his Consul-General in Egypt, Josef Natterer, the Austrian Consular Agent at Khartoum, described at great length and with detailed eye-witness accounts several examples of their activity. In 1860 the trade was, indirectly and perhaps unwittingly, fostered by the highest authority. Sa'īd Pasha, the Viceroy of Egypt, placed an order for a bodyguard of five hundred Negro soldiers with 'a great trader in Cairo with whom he stood in friendliest relationship', Mūsā Bey al-'Aqqād. The latter's brother, Muḥammad Aḥmad al-'Aqqād, came to Khartoum, and in the early summer of 1860, his agent's first boat brought in ninety-two slaves from the White Nile direct to the city, where they were marched naked through the streets to the Government barracks.[4] On his accession Sa'īd had 'instructed the Governors of the Southern Provinces to prevent in future the introduction of slaves from Abyssinia, Dongola, etc. into Egypt across the Southern frontier'.[5] This abolition of the public slave markets had brought Egypt into line with Turkey where since 1847 steps had been taken to suppress the slave trade,[6] and during a visit to Khartoum

[1] Piaggia, p. 124.

[2] F.O. 84/1246. Joyce to the Egyptian Trading Co., 10/XI/64.

[3] Jules Poncet, 'Excursions et chasses à l'éléphant au Fleuve Blanc', *Nouvelles Ann. des Voyages*, 1863–4, pp. 209–10.

[4] O.S. Ad. Reg. 27/9. Natterer to Schreiner, 15/VIII/60 enclosed in Schreiner to Rechberg-Rothenlöwen, 21/III/61.

[5] F.O. 84/974. Bruce to Clarendon 17/I/55.   [6] Shukry, p. 111.

in 1857 he had reiterated his desire to suppress the slave trade. Now, three years later, Saʿīd maintained that his new bodyguard would consist of conscripts and not of slaves,[1] but the episode revealed a tragic discrepancy between apparently good intentions and the actual state of affairs.

The only tangible result achieved by Saʿīd's efforts to abolish the slave trade had been to cause the slave trade in the Sudan to operate beneath a flimsy veil of secrecy. The open slave market at Khartoum had been abolished and transferred to centres a little further removed from the eye of authority, and the Shilluk village of Kaka had become the market for slaves from the White Nile, whence they were marched northwards to Kordofan and then across the desert to Dongola and Egypt or to Darfur. Natterer thought that by 1860 an average of 2000 slaves were sold at Kaka each year and a considerable number were still smuggled into Khartoum by boat. Europeans were amongst the foremost participators in this trade. Delphin Barthélemy, a Frenchman whose brother had left him a fortune of £4000 gained in trading in beads between Cairo, Khartoum and the White Nile, was accused by reliable eye-witnesses who included Lejean, a well-known French explorer, and Marchese Antinori, a founder of the Italian Geographical Society. Another European trader who combined the export of slaves with that of ivory was Andrea de Bono, a Maltese who had much experience of trading on the White Nile. One of his four boats in 1860 carried 550 slaves, of whom the greater part died in transit, while another of his boats was reported to be making five or six journeys to Kaka.[2]

The figures might have been exaggerated but the outline was corroborated by Morlang when at the end of 1860 he returned to the mission station of Holy Cross for a brief period. From 6 April to 23 May 1861 twenty-five boats passed the mission returning northwards, about half of which were carrying slaves, including four belonging to de Bono whose men had seized 150 slaves at a riverain village to the south. At other times, Morlang notes specific instances of slave-dealing by Barthélemy and Genuda, a wealthy Coptic trader.[3] In most places the friendly welcome of the riverain

[1] F.O. 84/1120 Colquhoun to Russell, 29/IV/60.
[2] O.S. Ad. Reg. 27/9. Natterer to Schreiner, 15/VIII/60 encl. in Schreiner to Rechberg-Rothenlöwen, 21/III/61.
[3] Mor. MS. 26/XII/60, 4/II/61, 8/IX/61, May 1862.

H.S.S.—E

tribes had given way to bitter hostility, while groups of desperate men took the offensive and defied any attempt to re-establish contact with them.[1] Missionaries were not the only witnesses: in 1860 the Italian explorer Miani passed two boats crowded with slaves,[2] and in 1863 Petherick while sailing up the Bahr el Jebel intercepted his own vakil (agent) with slaves who had been captured on a joint raid with de Bono's men.[3]

Thus from the late 1850's the ivory trade on the White Nile brought the slave trade in its train. The slave trade was, however, merely the last factor to be brought into a complex situation of increasing violence, and, although it undoubtedly added to the total misery, it was not the primary cause of this tragedy. The stages in this disastrous development have been demonstrated by de Malzac's career. Frustrated by the growing deadlock between the Bari and the traders, he had returned northwards to the Dinka in 1854 and had concentrated his efforts on penetrating into the interior.[4] Restricted at first by local tribal wars, his ruthless use of force had then converted the obstacle of tribal rivalries into an asset, which he had soon realised could be exploited in an attempt to solve his economic difficulties.[5] Stolen cattle had become his standard currency[6] and finally the sale of slaves had partly covered him against increased overheads,[7] until on his early death his stations, boats, and contracts had passed into the hands of his principal creditor. His example was imitated by many of the White Nile traders until a crucial part of their profits became dependent on trade in goods and slaves with the ruling-caste of Arab servants which they had established. The quest for ivory supplied the momentum to this vicious spiral of violence, expeditions were continually driven deeper into the interior, and when in 1859 the traders decided to break the deadlock between them-

[1] Mor. MS. 16–18/II/61. A certain Nyaciual, who was living in a large fishing village which had been raided for slaves, asked Morlang to intercede with the traders for him in June 1862. Finding Morlang powerless, he stole two small boats belonging to the mission, and returned to his village where, with numerous followers, he ambushed the traders' boats. Eighteen months later Morlang passed the place and two of his servants were badly wounded, but to the disgust of his men, he forbad any retaliation. 26/II/63.

[2] Mi. MS. 6/I/60, 24/IV/60.

[3] F.O. 84/1181 Petherick to Colquhoun, 24/V/63.

[4] See above, p. 41.

[5] See above, pp. 47–48.

[6] See above, p. 49.

[7] See above, pp. 51–52.

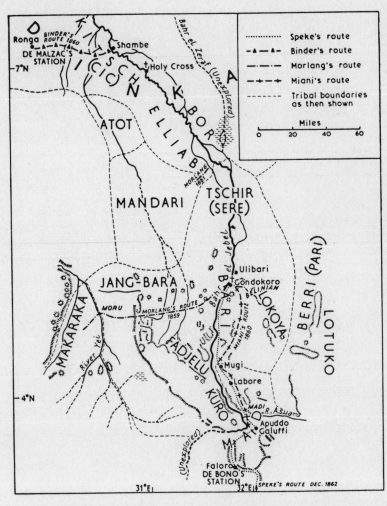

Map 3. GONDOKORO AND SURROUNDINGS 1859–1862

(from M. T. von Heuglin, *Reise in das Gebiet des Weissen Nil*)

selves and the Bari they employed these methods with similar consequences.

A few months before Nyigilo's death on 21 June 1859,[1] the traders, returning as usual to Khartoum at the end of the season, left behind them agents in charge of small groups of northern Arabs, who built encampments near Gondokoro and, during the succeeding months, undertook expeditions into the interior. At first they were most successful in the west. Crossing the Nile, a small band penetrated through the Bari-speaking Nyangbara to the river Yei and returned with reports of cheap ivory and corn in abundance. A larger expedition was quickly dispatched, and as it was a period of famine amongst the riverain Bari there was little difficulty in persuading many of them, 'of every age and sex', to act as porters in the hope of being able to purchase some grain.[2] In October Morlang, in search of a more congenial centre for the mission than Gondokoro, accompanied a similar expedition of more than a hundred men. Already in some districts the market for beads was exhausted, villagers were hostile or 'beggars', and the 'ferocious aggressiveness of the merchants', combined with the cut-throat rivalry of the different trading groups, were causing difficulties. Some chiefs, however, enthusiastically collected ivory for the expedition and the aggression by no means always came from the traders. During the return journey they were attacked by a large number of Nyangbara; Morlang had no doubt that the latter were to blame, and the hostile and rival chiefs even confessed that they had hoped to plunder the heavily laden caravan.[3]

The westward drive continued. Early the following year the traders' expeditions were in hostile contact to the west of the Yei river with the Makaraka, the eastern-most spearhead of Zande speaking people whose cannibalistic reputation and military prowess caused terror to the surrounding tribes.[4] By 1861 de Bono and other traders had established stations on the Yei River, and were starting to subdue the Makaraka. De Bono described the process in the following words:

[1] See above, p. 44.

[2] Mor. MS. May–August, 1859.

[3] Ibid. 20/X/59 to 9/XII/59. On another occasion an equally trustworthy observer considered that the Nyangbara were the aggressors (Peney, 'Les dernieres explorations . . .', *Bull. Soc. Géog.*, 1863, p. 14).

[4] Mi. MS. 22/II/60 to 5/III/60.

Scarcely had my nephew arrived at Macraca when the drums beat in sign of war and immediately men and women joined together to open the attack. My nephew signalled to them that he had not come with warlike intentions, but rather to barter beads for ivory. Seeing that conciliation was useless he was forced to open fire.[1]

There is no record of the subsequent events by which the Makaraka were induced to accept the domination of the traders; but their intelligence, industry and adaptability, which was later to convert them into invaluable allies of the Egyptian administration, was already apparent to a sympathetic observer.[2]

The traders were not so fortunate towards the east. Beyond Belinian the mountain ranges sheltered the small yet powerful and independent Lokoya, who commanded a pass which led east towards the Lotuko. In 1859 small trading expeditions were sent to the Lokoya, but they were coldly received,[3] and in January 1860 five men were killed while trading with them. The traders then combined their forces and 150 soldiers were sent 'to revenge their fallen comrades' and 'to pursue the enemy in order to capture their cattle'. Two days later thirty badly wounded survivors returned with the news that they had been attacked in a wood and that 120 soldiers with several Bari interpreters had been killed.[4] The incident had widespread repercussions and marked another serious step in the spread of violence. Both sides became more embittered. Far to the north, at Holy Cross, the crew of one of de Malzac's boats on hearing the news 'of the death of their comrades uttered violent war-cries'.[5] South of Gondokoro the Bari became 'much emboldened' at the news of the victory,[6] and at Gondokoro itself the Bari, filled with 'hatred against all strangers', refused to allow the missionaries to keep any of their catechumens.[7]

Having suffered this check in the east, the traders were all the more anxious to penetrate to the south and at the same time to

[1] A. de Bono, *Recenti Scoperte sul Fiume Bianco*, Alexandria, 1862, p. 13.

[2] Peney, p. 21.

[3] Morlang accompanied one of the expeditions and after a frustrating day the caravan hastened away to avoid the molestations, Mor. MS. 24–28/VII/59.

[4] Mor. MS. 10–15/I/60; Mi. MS. 27/I/60, who lists 97 killed.

[5] Mor. MS. 2/II/60.

[6] Mi. MS. 3/II/60.

[7] Ibid. 16/I/60; The opposition was led by a Bari chief who had lost his son, a former pupil of the mission, who had been forced by the traders to accompany the expedition as an interpreter.

re-assert their prestige by a frequent use of firearms. A reconnaissance party to the south opened fire on four occasions, and on 16 March 1860 a band of a hundred of de Bono's soldiers and as many Bari porters set off on a further expedition. It was commanded by Wad al-Mak, a courageous villain, the son of an important chief from the Fazughli area of the Blue Nile who had been killed by Arabs in search of gold.[1] Outbursts of violence were numerous and, in the opinion of the explorer, Miani, who accompanied the expedition, they were often justified by provocation on the part of the tribesmen. The rearguard, on being asked to pay for their passage through a Bari section, opened fire killing three men and wounding many others; further south, menaced by tribesmen with spears, they defended themselves by killing and wounding several men; and later a Madi chief was killed after attacking the soldiers, his large village was left a smoking ruin and several 'prisoners' together with five hundred cattle and sheep were captured.[2] The expedition reached 'Galuffi' a point to the south of the river Asua and returned with ivory and the promise of future supplies and aid from several village chiefs. Penetration southwards was thus dependent from the beginning on a direct use of force in exploiting tribal divisions; and, a year later, in February 1861 Morlang on a visit to Gondokoro noted that the familiar pattern of cattle and slave raids was firmly established:

> An expedition has arrived fom Loki to the south bringing slaves and cattle; it is said that they have been amongst the Madi and Cucu (Kuku), that they have killed people, burnt huts, and seized ivory and slaves. With the stolen cattle they will buy ivory from the Liresi (Lokoya), and if a chief wants to keep a slave girl they give him one or two.[3]

As the central supply base for all this activity Gondokoro rapidly became a sprawling insanitary settlement of some seven hundred armed Arab servants, most of whom collected numerous wives and servants from the local tribes.[4] Less than a decade

[1] Mi. MS. 11–16/III/60.

[2] Ibid., 17/III/60 to 3/IV/60. It is interesting to note that Miani, who often denounced the slave trade, here uses the word 'prisoners'.

[3] Mor. MS. 12/II/61. In April de Bono traded these cattle with Legghe, chief of the Lokoya (Peney, pp. 50–7), who for a brief period became a successful middleman commanding the route to the ivory-rich Lotuko, until his monopoly was broken when the traders reached the Lotuko from the south (S. W. Baker, *The Albert Nyanza*, 1867 edition, vol. i, 166–9).

[4] de Pruyssenaere to Auguste, 1/III/62, *Bull. Soc. Roy. Géog. d'Anvers*, p. 291.

previously the isolated missionary outpost had struggled to survive
in the face of the Bari's threats and extortions; now a conquering
force was entrenched to crush opposition, slowly imposing a new
way of life on the area, and its influence reached deep into the
interior. In 1861 de Bono decided to establish a strong permanent
station far to the south among the Madi at Faloro, where a hundred
well-disciplined men under the command of Wad al-Mak 'collected
an immense store of ivory, purchasing it with plundered cattle, and
occasionally a few beads'.[1] The raiding squads were reaching forth
towards the sources of the Nile, and all pretence of legitimate
commerce had disappeared.

4. The zeribas in the Bahr el Ghazal, 1857–1869

While de Malzac was pioneering this ruthless exploitation on the
Bahr el Jebel, the area of the Bahr el Ghazal and its huge hinterland
was being opened up to a similar sequence of violence and conflict.
Here the process of subjugation by an Arab ruling caste was more
quickly and more firmly established. The discovery of the Bahr el
Ghazal in 1855, unlike that of the Bahr el Jebel and the equatorial
lakes, opened up no prospects of extensive river transport; instead,
meandering through a vast maze of practically uninhabited swamp,
the river's navigable course terminated at Meshra er Req, a small
patch of moderately dry ground surrounded by permanent swamp
and the vast grazing grounds of the Dinka. There was, therefore,
no period of equilibrium and there were no attempts to find
middlemen, but contact with the populous tribes of the interior
was dependent from the first on a series of zeribas maintained by
armed Arab servants.

Attracted by rumours of a great river flowing from the west,
Salīm's first expedition had entered Lake No but failed to find
amidst the maze of swamp a channel to the west,[2] and, with
attention diverted by the subsequent discovery of the Bahr el Jebel,
it was not until 1855 that one of Petherick's boats sailing under the
command of a Copt called Ḥabashī discovered the main channel
of the Bahr el Ghazal. Petherick then joined him in a journey up
the river in January 1856. 'After two or three days sail we closed
to the Northern Bank ... where the Natives came cautiously

---

[1] J. A. Grant, A Walk across Africa, 1864, pp. 324–38.
[2] See above, p. 17.

down to see us and were friendly enough inclined.' Then, guided by 'a clever Noowaer,' (Nuer), they entered 'an immense lake' and subsequently followed a winding channel eventually arriving at the place later known as Meshra er Req.[1]

In February 1856 Brun Rollet, hoping to find a way through to the kingdom of Wadai, entered the river with three boats, and these pioneers were followed by Syrian and Egyptian traders.[2] Arrived at Meshra er Req, the traders led small bands of armed men into the interior and, with a few Dinka to act as porters and guides, they reached the Luo and the Bongo. These tribes inhabited the outskirts of the ironstone ridges which rise almost imperceptibly from the vast swampy plains. Amongst these small and scattered agricultural communities it was safe and profitable to leave 'a score of armed servants' to purchase ivory while the merchants returned to Khartoum.[3]

Petherick's zeriba amongst the Luo was typical of these early settlements: a square of more than a hundred paces enclosing twenty-two huts, the magazine and stores, was surrounded by a large Luo village. Two sentries were posted each night, no armed tribesman was allowed inside, and the market for ivory and provisions was conducted in the village. The local chief was required 'to provide all the needs of the station' in return for the trader's support, which gave him an internal power and an external security hitherto unknown.[4] In a letter written from

[1] F.O. 141/30. Petherick to Bruce, 8/VI/56. The facts, as stated in this letter, completely contradict the account of his explorations which he published in *Egypt, the Soudan and Central Africa*, and which has been followed by subsequent writers, e.g. Lotar, 'Souvenirs del'Uele,' in *Congo*, 1938. In his book Petherick states that he left Khartoum on 19/XI/53 (p. 337), discovering Meshra er Req before returning to Khartoum. The following October he set sail again (p. 370), and after various adventures among the Luo and Dinka returned to Meshra er Req on 25/IV/55, waiting there three weeks before sailing for Khartoum (p. 385). That these early expeditions were merely a product of his imagination is proved not only by the account given in his letter quoted above, but also by the fact that from February to May 1855 Petherick was involved in a quarrel with the Governor General and was writing frequent letters from Khartoum (e.g. F.O. 141/19. 24/II/55, 6, 14, 19/III/55, 23/IV/55). Geographers queried his extravagant claim to have reached the equator (in fact Mundo, his southernmost point, was north of 6 degrees Lat. N., *Pet. Geog. Mit.* 1880, Tafel 4) but the acceptance of his account in its main details was probably due to the death of the principal Europeans who could have questioned it.

[2] *Peterman's Geog. Mit. Erganzungsband*, 1862. 'Brun Rollet's Reise in den Sumpfregionen . . .'

[3] A. Castlebolognesi, 'Voyage au Fleuve des Gazelles', *Le Tour du Monde*, 1862.

[4] Ibid. Castlebolognesi acted as an agent for Petherick.

Khartoum after his return Petherick gives a vivid picture of the opportunities and difficulties of the situation:

The only article of importance offered for traffic is Ivory, which is bartered for various kinds of beads, cowries and occasionally from one to four or five pairs of Copper Bracelets. The beads most in demand are large round white beads, known in commerce as 'Bered' or 'Pidgeons' Eggs,' from two to three hundred being given for a tusk according to the size thereof—the latter being the value of a fine tusk weighing one hundredweight or upwards. The value of the tusk having been decided as regards the 'Bered', the final purchase is easily concluded, as a pair or two of copper bracelets, and small quantities of different sorts of small beads viz. Blue, Black, White, Red and Green, the whole amounting to 3 or 4 lbs. weight, and a 1000 or 2 cowrie shells are deemed ample payment.

The purchase concluded and the Beads consigned it is different with regard to the ivory. Some 8 or 12 negroes, who carried it on their heads and shoulders alternately, slung to a long pole, immediately seize it and do not give it up until they each receive a 'Bacjshish' of Beads for their trouble, when the purchaser's men take hold of one extremity, and the negroes hold fast the other end of the tusk, and a good humoured struggle commences for the possession thereof, which is often only obtained by pelting off the Negroes with beads, when after a moderate shower amidst hearty laughter they abandon the contest to collect the beads and the purchase is concluded . . . . Although Ivory is purchased for a trifle, the 'Cantar' not costing as far as beads are concerned more than three to four thousand piastres, but few men have realised Profits on the White River in consequence of the great outlay for pay and nourishment of a considerable number of armed attendants, necessary to guard both life and merchandise whilst journeying on foot in the Interior. There a good complement of animal courage is required to daunt both Negroes and the rabble escort composed of far too numerous nationalities and colours to mention.

Although the Negroes are glad enough of an opportunity of a Market for their Ivory and Provisions they are in general insolent and overbearing in their conduct towards us, regarding us as just and desirable objects for plunder, and it behoves consequently to be always on our guard both by day and night.[1]

As elsewhere, however, the market for beads was quickly glutted; the sources of ivory became exhausted; the capture of

[1] F.O. 141/30 Petherick to Bruce, 5/XII/56.

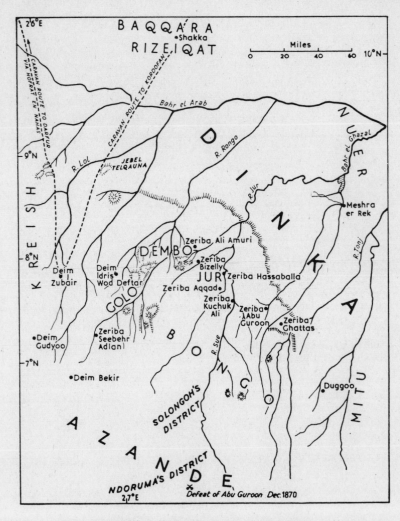

Map 4. THE PRINCIPAL ZERIBAS OF THE BAHR EL GHAZAL

(from G. Schweinfurth, *The Heart of Africa*)

cattle and slaves commenced;[1] the hostile incidents multiplied;[2] and Heuglin, a German explorer who visited various zeribas in 1863, reported that he came 'into little contact with the natives', many of whom were ready to seize any opportunity to attack the stations, and were 'shamelessly plundered' of all their corn to maintain the traders' communities.[3]

The results of this hostility and subjugation were described in detail by George Schweinfurth, another German explorer of wide scientific interests and acute powers of observation, who arrived in the area in 1869. Peaceful contact with the Dinka was restricted to a very few chiefs living near the regular routes into the interior. The rest of the vast clay plain, with its 'tracts of grazing ground' which took 'a whole day to cross' and its numerous cattle parks many of which contained ten thousand cattle,[4] was regarded solely as a source of cattle which could be robbed and then bartered for ivory in the interior. Ghattās, a wealthy Coptic merchant, carried out raids over the whole of the lower course of the river Tonj. In 1868 his company seized 800 oxen there, and Schweinfurth considered that a trading company needed 2,000 cattle a year.[5] Often, however, the Dinka were successful in retreating with their cattle to the inaccessible marshes and, accustomed to tribal raids, they were already becoming formidable adversaries capable of inflicting severe defeats on the raiding forces.[6]

Between the Dinka and the Azande, 'the whole country was occupied, at intervals of 5 or 6 leagues, with settlements of the Khartoomers in their palisaded Zeribas' and from the river Rohl north-westwards to the river Lol there stretched a series of more than eighty of these stations. The area was divided between a dozen wealthy merchants each of whom had several subsidiary zeribas linked with one or two principal ones. Ghattās' zeriba near the Tonj was typical of the larger stations. Rising in the middle of the plain the conical huts seemed to embrace 'almost the whole horizon' and in their centre a lofty square palisade was crammed full with

[1] Castlebolognesi, p. 391; Heuglin, p. 153; Piaggia, p. 175.

[2] Piaggia, pp. 179–171, 264–5, describes the growth of hostility between Zeriba Ghattās and Meshra er Req.

[3] Heuglin, pp. 193, 223.

[4] G. Schweinfurth, *The Heart of Africa*, 2 vols., 1873, vol. ii, p. 141.

[5] Ibid. vol. i, pp. 226–8.

[6] The chief zeriba on the river Rohl was abandoned in April 1869 'after nearly all their entire garrison of a hundred men had been killed during a raid against the Dinka tribe of the Agar', ibid. vol. i, p. 225.

huts of bamboo and straw. The resident armed force of about
250 men, with their numerous wives and attendants amounting to
at least a thousand souls, was surrounded by Bongo, Luo and
even Dinka villages, and the fertile land for two miles round the
station was partitioned into fields which supplied the greater part
of the grain needed by the garrison.[1] Throughout this long 'zeriba
country' the original agricultural communities had been faced with
the wretched alternative of flight to the powerful and dreaded
Azande or Dinka areas, or of submission to the exactions of the
traders. Those who chose the latter were reduced to a condition
of vassalage. They supplied the stations with food,[2] and, although
it completely disrupted their economy, they were forced[3] to act as
porters for long and arduous periods while accompanying the
traders, who from their zeriba bases thrust deeper into the interior.

In contrast to this subjugation, contact with the Azande was on
a more equal basis. Petherick established friendly relations with a
frontier group of Azande near Mundo in 1858, and a few years later
Piaggia spent two years alone with Tombo and other Zande
chiefs, having accompanied a trading company into their area.[4]
His vague reminiscences reveal a situation in which dynastic
rivalries were still of far more importance to the Azande than the
impact of the trading companies with whom they carried on a
barter for ivory; but the passage of these companies, whose armed
strength was constantly increasing, was already sometimes
punctuated with hostile incidents caused by the forceful seizure of
provisions or the occasional capture of a woman or child, and the
extent and intensity of the impact rapidly developed.

The traders established mutually recognized monopolistic 'rights'
over the various routes into the Zande country, and in some districts
the zeriba system was superimposed on the traditional tribal
organization which henceforth functioned in the traders' service.
In 1870 Schweinfurth accompanied a thousand men, porters, and
women attendants from the companies of G̲h̲attās and a Nubian,
Muḥammad 'Abd al-Ṣamad, on an expedition deep into the interior.
Proceeding through a Zande frontier territory ruled over by

[1] Ibid. vol. i, pp. 172–8.
[2] Amongst the Luo 'the Nubians every year carry off at least half the corn
that is grown,' ibid., vol. i. p. 211.
[3] Heuglin described how these porters were guarded as prisoners 'und Nachts
sogar gebunden', op. cit., p. 150.
[4] Piaggia, pp. 186–263.

Nganye, an ally chief of 'Abd al-Ṣamad, they reached a district
where 'Abd al-Ṣamad had deposed the former hostile ruler and
installed Surur, the younger brother of Nganye. Supported by
about fifty armed Arabs, Surur ruled over 'a populous area of
700 sq. miles' in which there was one main zeriba situated near
his homestead and three smaller enclosures in the charge of Zande
overseers. Many of his Azande had been initiated into the use of
firearms, and all his warriors obeyed the traditional summons of
the chief's Nogara (a drum) and undertook foraging raids on the
neighbouring tribes to obtain corn for the expedition and female
slaves for themselves and the Arab soldiers. Unlike the Bongo and
other tribes, these Azande could not be forced to act as porters,
and Schweinfurth summed up the contrast by remarking that 'at
present they hardly comprehend their state of subjection'; they
continued to furnish large supplies of ivory in exchange for beads,
copper and cloth for which there was a large potential demand.[1]

Beyond these districts, on the Nile-Congo watershed, lay a
strip of hostile Zande territory ruled over by Wando and Mbio
who easily repulsed an attack by 'Abd al-Ṣamad on the return
journey in May 1870.[2] On the outward journey the expedition
pressed quickly to reach, south of the Wele river, the territory of
Munza, King of the western Mangbetu. Of the tribes encountered
by the Khartoum traders from the Bahr el Ghazal, the Mangbetu
most resembled the powerful Lacustrine kingdoms of Bunyoro
and Buganda. They inhabited an extremely fertile, densely populated land which was rich with ivory.[3] Pomp and ritual surrounded
a powerful sovereign who ruled over a people skilled in the arts of
war and peace. 'Abd al-Ṣamad, a man of courage, considerable
tact, and a friendly disposition, was first invited by Munza to visit
his court in 1867. He quickly established good relations with
Munza and left a small number of Arabs with him, who were
allowed to build a small station and accompanied the king on
raids in search of ivory, slaves and goats.[4] This amicable

[1] Schweinfurth, vol. i, pp. 465–7, ii, pp. 202–22, 244.

[2] For a full account of Mbio's career see E. E. Evans-Pritchard, 'A History
of the Kingdom of Gbudwe (Azande of the Sudan)', Zaïre, x, 1956. Mbio (or
Yambio) changed his name later to Gbudwe.

[3] Schweinfurth considered that there were at least 250 inhabitants to the
square mile, making an aggregate population of about a million. ibid., vol. ii,
pp. 81–82.

[4] Ibid. vol. ii, pp. 37–149.

F

cooperation concealed, however, a source of tension. Munza, un-willing to relinquish a most profitable monopoly over the copper trade, would permit no further penetration to the south, and although in 1870 'Abd al-Ṣamad was prepared to comply with this restriction, he would become less amenable if the supplies of ivory began to diminish. Munza's position was also by no means as secure as it seemed. To the east, Degberra, a rival Mangbetu king, who had been in contact with other trading companies since 1866,[1] waited an opportunity to attack, while to the north and west hostile Azande were extending their conquests. In a later trial of strength these rivalries, exploited by the traders, were to destroy the flourishing Mangbetu regime.

To the north of the Wele river stretched the vast area inhabited by the rest of the Azande.[2] Several routes led into their territory from the 'zeriba country' of the Bahr el Ghazal. Some of the most powerful chiefs in the interior were ready to provide the traders with ivory,[3] but in some of the frontier districts tensions were already developing at the end of the 1860's. Ndoruma, one of these frontier chieftains whose stores of ivory were exhausted, attempted to prevent the traders from reaching the interior as he hoped to retain a monopoly over the traders' copper and cloth. Angered also by the seizure of some women and the depredations which 'the Nubians are accustomed ... to commence ... upon any land from which they have no longer anything to gain by an amicable trade,'[4] he attacked and overpowered a zeriba, which Abū Quroon, a former servant of Petherick, had established in his country. With the help of several rival trading companies, Abū Quroon led out an expedition of over two thousand men and women,[5] which at the end of October 1870 was ambushed by

[1] Poncets' men from their zeriba at Mvolo were able to make two expeditions to the Mangbetu each year, and the discovery of this great river flowing west-wards had aroused hopes of being able to open up communication with the River Niger, via Lake Chad. Buet, pp. 74–81.   [2] See map.

[3] E.g. Kanna 'whose enormous stores of ivory had ever constituted a great attraction', sent a deputation to 'Abd al-Ṣamad to invite him to visit his country in 1870. Schweinfurth, vol. ii, pp. 55–56.

[4] Ibid. vol. ii, pp. 287, 309. Evans-Pritchard in *Zaïre*, 1956, p. 480, suggests that, although this desire to protect a commercial monopoly may have been a consideration, Ndoruma's overriding motive was his anxiety to reassert his authority by revenging the outrages committed against his subjects.

[5] The expedition included numerous women for 'it was with some difficulty that these undisciplined soldiers could be prevailed upon to join the arduous enterprise at all', ibid., vol. ii, p. 308.

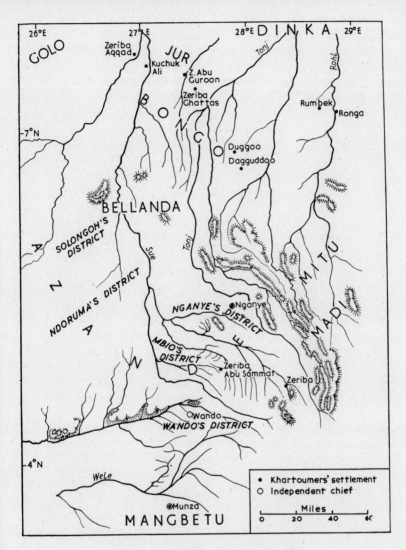

Map 5. THE ROUTE TO MUNZA
(from G. Schweinfurth, *The Heart of Africa*)

Ndoruma. Abū Quroon and many of his men were killed, the expedition was completely routed, and a hundred loads of ammunition were captured by Ndoruma. The defeat vividly demonstrated that the Azande, with their powerful military organizations, could still easily protect themselves against the traders, until at a later date the latter discovered that here also dynastic rivalries could be exploited.[1]

The events in the area of the Bahr el Ghazal so far described bore a fairly close resemblance to those on the Bahr el Jebel. The nature of the country and the hostility of the Dinka necessitated, it is true, a quicker and fuller evolution of the zeriba system than on the Bahr el Jebel, and this development was aided by the ease with which the Bongo and other tribes were subjected. But the same search for ivory dominated the ever-increasing expansion, attracted the necessary capital, and brought in its wake a similar pattern of violence, although the Azande and Mangbetu had yet to feel its full force. In the north-west of the Bahr el Ghazal, however, south of Darfur, the outside world had been in contact with the fringe of these vast pagan lands long before the discovery of the river route. On this western frontier between the northern and southern Sudan the slave trade was a dominant factor, and from this fringe its influence gradually bit deeper into the southern Sudan.

To the south of the ancient, independent, Muslim Kingdom of Darfur, in the midst of an arid sparsely populated wilderness lay the celebrated copper mines of Hofrat en Nahas. Here in the eighteenth century lived a mixed Muslim population of 'Furanjs, Jellabas, Bornouese, Dajo, Nuba, etc.' under the nominal suzerainty of Darfur.[2] Most of the copper passed, via Darfur, into the network of Muslim trade[3] but some of it was traded to the pagan peoples to the south. Contact with these people was slight, but when at the end of the eighteenth century the first European succeeded in reaching Darfur he learnt that small expeditions were penetrating into their lands via Hofrat en Nahas.[4] Sometimes these expeditions

[1] Solongoh, another frontier Zande chief to the north of Ndoruma, was at war with Kuchūk ʿAlī's men even stealing guns from their zeriba at night, ibid., vol. ii, p. 389.

[2] H. Barth, 'Account of two expeditions in Central Africa by the Furanys', *J. Roy. Geog. Soc.*, 1853; Heuglin, p. 371.

[3] In the middle of the nineteenth century Barth found that 'a considerable supply' was imported annually into Kano (*Travels*, vol. ii, p. 141).

[4] W. G. Browne, *Travels in Africa*, 1800, Appendix.

were full scale military raids whose profits in slaves were dependent
on large scale plunder;[1] but usually they consisted of Jellaba, or
petty itinerant traders, who exchanged a small supply of beads,
copper, and blue Egyptian cottons for ivory and slaves with the
Kreish and the northernmost Azande. Markets became established
and their fame spread so that Salīm's expeditions up the Bahr el
Jebel heard rumours of Muslim traders to the west,[2] while later a
Rol Dinka told Vayssière how he had travelled twenty days to the
'Korek' (Kreish) where he sold slaves and ivory to 'black and red'
merchants who rode donkeys and camels.[3] Some idea of the
extent of this trade between Darfur and the pagan countries can
be gathered from the fact that in 1859 the caravan from Darfur was
expected to bring to Asyut 1,000 kantars of ivory,[4] and although
there are no reliable estimates of the slave trade at this date it must
have been very considerable.[5]

The interest in this overland route widened and in 1853 Heuglin,
the Austrian Consular Agent at Khartoum, reported the existence
of 'a new trade way into the interior of Africa' recently opened up
by Jellaba from Kordofan. Skirting the southeast boundary of
Darfur, they had settled in Telqauna to the southeast of Hofrat en
Nahas and 'carried on a very good business through the import of
cowries, cotton and beads'.[6] The activities of these Jellaba involved
no direct large-scale subjugation of peoples, and penetration was
not dependent on armed force. As in the Beni Shanqul, the Galla
country and East Africa, the Arab trader was forced to pay the
local chief a toll for every load of goods which he wished to pass
through the territory.[7] This situation, however, was completely
altered by the opening of the Bahr el Ghazal to river-borne trade
from Khartoum.

In 1856 some Khartoum Jellaba, who had fled from Darfur and
had been held almost as prisoners for more than a year at Hofrat en
Nahas, succeeded in joining the traders on the Bahr el Ghazal.[8]

---

[1] Barth, 'Account, etc.,' *J. Roy. Geog. Soc.* 1853. They reported a large river
flowing to the west probably the Mbomu, if not even the Wele.

[2] Werne, i, p. 335.   [3] Vay. MS. 27/II/54.

[4] Meyer MSS. C. Westendarp. Cairo, November, 1859.

[5] Lauture, *Le Desert et le Soudan*, 1853, p. 303, saw 945 slaves arrive with the
caravan of 1850. The Sultan of Darfur was reputed to possess more than a
thousand eunuchs: Tunisi, *Voyage au Darfour*, 1845, p. 252.

[6] O.S. Pol. Archiv. Kons. Ag./1854. Heuglin to Huber 5/XII/53 encl. in
Huber to Buol-Schauenstein, 13/1/54.

[7] Heuglin, p. 217.   [8] Castlebolognesi, p. 391.

Soon afterwards Idrīs wad Daftār, a former Berberine servant of the Catholic mission who later became a partner in 'Aqqād's firm, established a zeriba near the sources of the river Pongo.[1] Other traders quickly followed him. By 1862 reports were reaching Khartoum that expeditions from that area had reached what was probably the Mbomu river,[2] and with the force which was at their disposal these traders rapidly subdued the Kreish chiefs, who had previously been able to tax the Jellaba.[3]

Under the security of the zeriba system the itinerant Jellaba were soon able to travel freely throughout the Bahr el Ghazal, effecting a rapid extension of the network of overland Muslim trade. Hundreds of them[4] descended from Darfur and Kordofan on the area, and Schweinfurth's encounter at Kuchūk 'Alī's zeriba with 'a speculative slave trader from Tunis' who was making 'a second journey over Darfoor' was but a striking example of the extent of this network.[5] Most of them invested their puny capital in a bullock or donkey which they loaded with cotton-cloth, cheap Belgian firearms and other goods needed by the Arab soldiers. When they arrived in the Bahr el Ghazal they sold the animal and their goods to the zeriba settlers for four or five slaves. They marched the slaves north across the deserts, and made a comfortable profit if the slaves survived the horrors of the journey.

Other Jellaba arrived as the agents of wealthy Kordofan and Darfur slave-traders. These settled in the stations where they acted as Fakirs or sellers of amulets and religious charms, and collected hundreds of slaves from every tribe for their employers. The Azande and Mangbetu women were the most valuable, but in 1870 only a few of them were as yet enslaved and hardly any were exported. Of the rest, the Bongo being docile and adaptable were much sought after, but the vast majority of the slaves that were exported were drawn from beyond the Dar Fertit, an

[1] Heuglin, p. 225.
[2] Letter from Heuglin, 8/XII/62 in *Petermann's Mit.*, 1863.
[3] E.g. Gudyoo previously a Kreish chief 'and a great patron of the slave traders had now settled down to the east . . . as an ordinary Sheik of Agahds possessions', Schweinfurth, vol. ii, p. 380.
[4] 2,700 arrived in 1870 and Schweinfurth estimated that a further 2,000 were permanent residents in the zeribas, op. cit., vol. ii, p. 356.
[5] Ibid. vol. i, p. 139. In 1874 Nachtigal reported that there were at least 5,000 Jellaba households in Darfur, most of whom came from Berber and Dongola but also from as far as Morocco, G. Nachtigal, *Sahara und Sudan*, Leipzig, 1889, vol. iii, p. 457.

uninhabited wilderness to the west of the river Lol. For decades this region had been the hunting ground of the Darfur slave-raiders, and the arrival of the Khartoum traders merely intensified the process. Some of the traders undertook direct slave raids on their own account; others, including Idrīs wad Daftār, obtained them through Mopoi, the northernmost Azande chief, who had used his previous contact with the overland traders to increase his power and wealth. Mopoi established a trading monopoly through-out his extensive domains and his officials reported to him the arrival of a trader, who was then escorted to his village.[1] He continued to receive firearms, ammunition and trade-goods in return for 'thousands upon thousands' of slaves which he obtained either from 'the slave tribes' that he had subjected or 'by raids organized against the surrounding nations'.[2] This overland route exporting, Schweinfurth estimated, about twelve to fifteen thousand slaves per annum, together with the other traditional sources of the Nuba mountains, the pagan tribes south of Sennar, and the Galla and other tribes to the south and west of Abyssinia, completely dwarfed the White Nile slave trade with its total export of about two thousand slaves in the peak years.[3]

The more far-sighted of the Khartoum ivory traders and the agents in charge of their zeribas were opposed to this slave trade, as they were 'extremely anxious' that the tribes whom they had reduced to serfdom should remain to serve the needs of the station and to supply them with porters.[4] They were, however, practically powerless to prevent their lawless Arab servants from selling slaves to the itinerant slave-traders who found 'snug quarters in every

[1] Heuglin, p. 212.

[2] Schweinfurth, vol. ii, p. 418.

[3] The figures for the Bahr el Jebel and Bahr el Ghazal river-routes (1,000 and 4–600 respectively) quoted by Schweinfurth (vol. ii, p. 429) are probably somewhat under-estimated (see above p. 53 for the figure of 2,000, which is partly confirmed by the fact that from June 1864 till February 1866 the river police seized over 3,500 slaves: G. Douin, vol. iii (i), p. 469.) It is impossible to check his estimate of the overland route, but it does not seem improbable. It agrees with Wylde's estimates made in 1878 (see below, p. 126), and is partly confirmed in a report by a British Consular Agent, who, disguised as an Arab, visited the Egyptian slave markets in 1867: 'It is a matter of public notoriety that from 10–15,000 slaves are annually brought down the Nile to Cairo, while an equal or even greater number find their way to Sowakin and the Red Sea'. The Agent thought that at any one time there were probably about 3,000 slaves on sale secretly at Cairo (F.O. 84/1277. Reade to Stanley, 9/VIII/67).

[4] Schweinfurth, vol. ii, p. 318.

zeriba',[1] while in the northwest the overland slave trade was one of the principal economic supports of the 'empire' which al-Zubair Raḥma Manṣūr was in the process of founding. A Ja'li Arab, educated at Khartoum, Zubair set out for the Bahr el Ghazal in 1856. After numerous adventures, including marriage to the daughter of a powerful Azande chief called Tikima, he built Deim Zubair, a zeriba strategically placed to tap this overland trade. In 1866 an alliance with the Rizeiqat Arabs, a cattle-owning tribe inhabiting the area north of the Bahr el Arab, secured the Kordofan route for his slave caravans.[2] He employed a thousand armed men; his zeriba, surrounded by hundreds of farmsteads, 'had the aspect of a town in the Sudan', and vividly reminded Schweinfurth of 'Matamma, the great market town in Gallabat, where all the inland trade with Abyssinia is transacted'. In one year he exported 'probably as many as 1,800 slaves,'[3] and the stage was set for a career of conquest which in the following decade was to place him and his son in the forefront of Sudanese history.

Thus throughout the southern Sudan, in Faloro and the other outposts of Gondokoro and in the zeribas of the Bahr el Ghazal, a new ruling caste of traders established itself during the 1860's. The early hopes and efforts of individual European missionaries and merchants were replaced by the power and exactions of increasing numbers of Arab settlers. The deadlock between traders and tribes was broken by a violence which cumulatively created a chaos of destruction. The search for ivory brought not legitimate commerce but robbery, and in some areas the slave trade was following in its train. Yet a fresh impulse towards penetration was developing and a new, imperial factor was preparing to enter the southern Sudan.

[1] Schweinfurth., vol. ii, p. 228. Earlier, Petherick had described his servants as 'a most disorderly set of Ruffians, who once out of reach of the jurisdiction of the Divan, few men can make anything of, their openly often defying their superiors and are but too frequently the ruin of speculations' .... F.O. 141/30 Petherick to Bruce, 8/VI/56.

[2] H. C. Jackson, *Black Ivory and White*, 1913. Although compiled solely from Zubair's reminiscences, there seems no reason to doubt this part of his account. By 1866 the river police on the White Nile (see below, p. 76) were increasing the importance of the overland route for slave trade, and the Rizeiqat Arabs, who had never been subdued by Darfur (cp. Tunisi, op. cit., p. 130) were his natural allies.

[3] These would have been worth about £8 each at Khartoum, or c. £14,400 compared with his export of ivory which was worth only £2,300 that year. Schweinfurth, vol. ii, pp. 355, 366.

III

EGYPT AND EQUATORIA

1. Ismā'īl's intervention, 1863–1869

AFTER the effective abolition of the government monopoly
in 1851 the southern Sudan occupied a unique position in
Africa: it was the one sphere in the interior readily open to
European enterprise. Yet although this was procured primarily
through the diplomatic pressure of the Great Powers,[1] Europe
had little success in exploiting the opportunity. Many years later,
in Nyasaland and in Uganda, missionary activity was to be a
dominant factor in European imperial expansion[2] and the Vicarate
of Central Africa might similarly have forged a vital and enduring
link between the southern Sudan and Europe. It enjoyed high
patronage,[3] and it might well have remained the spearhead of the
Vatican's interest in the interior of Africa. But the frustrations
faced by the missionaries amongst the Bari and the severe losses
caused by the climate discouraged the mission's supporters. By
1859 funds and recruits were scarce, and in 1860 the station at
Gondokoro was abandoned.[4] Morlang paid two brief visits to
Holy Cross and Gondokoro in 1861–1863 but he was merely a
helpless spectator of the spread of violence. In 1861 a large party
of Franciscans from Rome attempted to found a mission amongst
the Shilluk but they also were almost immediately forced to withdraw by the climate. Daniele Comboni, a young priest from
Verona who had accompanied Oliboni to Holy Cross, slowly
rebuilt the fortunes of the mission and after 1871 directed its
efforts towards the pagan inhabitants of the Nuba mountains, but
for the remainder of the nineteenth century the mission played no
direct part in the history of the southern Sudan.[5]

The search for the Nile's sources, another potential link between
Europe and the southern Sudan, encountered similar difficulties.

[1] See above, pp. 22–23.
[2] Oliver, pp. 94–163.
[3] See above, p. 26.
[4] At one time there was not even enough money to purchase the provisions
needed by the missionaries,—Tappi, 'L'Istituto Neri', typescript.
[5] Grancelli, op. cit.

Several explorers died of malaria and blackwater fever; the hostility of the Bari prevented others from penetrating to the south, and when after 1859 this barrier was broken explorers, like Miani,[1] remained completely dependent on the movements of the traders' cattle-raiding expeditions. There were however many travellers to the more accessible parts of the southern Sudan. Various traders including Brun Rollet, Petherick, and Jules Poncet published accounts of their travels, and a journey up the White Nile even became an attraction for the adventurous, wealthy, intelligent tourist. In 1850 Andre Melly, a prosperous Liverpool merchant, took his wife, two sons and a daughter to Khartoum in an attempt to visit the White Nile. A year later the American poet and diplomat, Bayard Taylor, ascended the river as far south as Kaka. They were followed by many other travellers: by aristocrats including Prince Muḥammad 'Abd al-Ḥalīm Pasha, Duc d'Aumont et de Villequier, Baron von Harnier, and Eugène de Pruyssenaere, by Liberals like Guillaume Lejean, a close friend of Lamartine, and by several Italian patriots including Marchese Orazio Antinori. The most spectacular expedition was organized by the young, noble, beautiful and accomplished Alexandrine Tinné, the richest heiress in Holland. Accompanied by her mother and her aunt, by two Dutch maidservants, by Baron d'Ablaing and the German naturalists and explorers Theodor von Heuglin and Hermann Steudner, she hired a small fleet of steamers and sailing boats and visited Gondokoro and the Bahr el Ghazal in 1862–4.[2] All these travellers increased Europe's knowledge of conditions in the area and consular reports often relied on the accounts they brought back, but the scientific results were not spectacular, penetration into the unknown interior was negligible, and the decisive attack on the problem of the Nile was to come from a different quarter.[3]

The commercial exploitation of the opportunity created by the opening of the White Nile was left to the small and relatively insignificant group of European merchants at Khartoum. Several factors prevented a further development of European commercial interests. The handling of the ivory trade in Egypt effectively excluded direct participation by firms based in Europe. In 1859

---

[1] See above, p. 57.
[2] Johnston, op. cit., and Hill, *Biographical Dictionary*.
[3] See above, p. 58.

Carl Westendarp, a young representative of the family which controlled the German ivory firm of H. A. Meyer of Hamburg, visited Egypt to investigate the possibilities of purchasing ivory on more advantageous terms than those provided by the London markets. He discovered that at Cairo the trade was 'practically monopolized' by Greek traders whose agents at Asyut and elsewhere bought up the ivory. As a result very little ivory came on to the market, and the little that was available was quoted at prices hardly cheaper than those in London. He was told that it would be possible to purchase ivory at Khartoum, but the irregularity and insecurity of communications made it necessary for all financial transactions to be conducted by private agents, and his informant was unable to recommend any 'respectable correspondent in Khartoum'.[1]

Similarly merchants engaged in the export of European goods had little incentive to establish themselves in the Sudan. Cairo, and not Khartoum, was the 'great market' where European cotton and iron goods, beads and firearms were sold to local merchants or their agents from the Sudan. Europeans exported only very slight quantities directly to Khartoum, and the European mercantile firms in Egypt seldom sent their agents to the south.[2] While there was therefore little inducement for metropolitan European firms to venture into the Sudan, the fortunes of the local European community at Khartoum were also declining. Brun Rollet, de Malzac, Vayssière and later Barthélemy, were victims of the murderous climate; Binder and Lafargue retired with a comfortable profit; and by 1862 the remainder were rapidly being eclipsed by Copts like Ghattās, by Syrians such as Ibrāhīm Bās the former agent of Brun Rollet, by Zubair and other Arabs, and above all by the Egyptian 'Aqqād, who, with his several agents and the support of the Government, was alone among White Nile traders in being able to manage without loans.[3]

This recession of European mercantile enterprise and the abeyance of missionary activity marked the loss of Europe's unique opportunity to dominate the development of the southern Sudan in the nineteenth century. Already the Egyptian Government was

[1] Meyer MSS. Westendarp. Cairo, November 1859.
[2] O.S.Ad. Reg. 8. Schreiner to Mensdorff-Pouilly, 20/III/65.
[3] O.S. Ad. Reg. 27/9. Natterer to Schreiner, 15/VIII/60, enclosed in Schreiner to Rechberg-Rothenlöwen, 21/III/61.

becoming determined to control the area. At first the advance was
hesitant and slow, but when later the possibility of a vast imperial
expansion was suddenly revealed Egypt was prepared to seize the
opportunity.

The opening of the White Nile to European enterprise had
coincided with the recession of Egyptian initiative which marked
the closing years of Muḥammad 'Alī's reign and those of his
successor, 'Abbās I 1849-1854. In so personal a regime developments in the Sudan were considerably influenced by the character
of the Viceroy. A cautious conservative by nature 'Abbās rigor-
ously retrenched expenditure, suspended the gold-mining south
of Sennar, neglected the solitary primary school at Khartoum, and
through lack of confidence shackled the administration by appointing five governors-general within six years. Taxation caused
several minor risings in the northern Sudan, some of the more
fertile riverain areas were depopulated, and by 1852 the permanent
garrison had increased to 18,000 men.[1] But his successor Muḥammad Sa'īd, a son of Muḥammad 'Alī, was educated by French
tutors, was considerably influenced by European culture, and was
anxious to develop both Egypt and the Sudan. He gave concessions
for the construction of the Suez Canal, and for the foundation of
the Eastern Telegraph Company and the Bank of Egypt.[2] He also
took steps to suppress the slave trade in Egypt, but slaves continued to be sold privately and his action had little effect in the
Sudan.[3] From November 1856 to January 1857 Sa'īd paid a spectacular visit to the Sudan with 8,000 men and 10,000 camels. He
reorganized the administration and attempted to reform taxation
by appointing advisory councils to assess and collect taxes, but
burdened with the problems of Egypt he was unable to control the
Sudan effectively or to introduce the permanent improvement
in communications which could alone radically change the
situation.[4]

Sa'īd did, however, initiate the first steps in reviving Egyptian
interest in the southern Sudan. His brother visited Gòndokoro
and the White Nile and he himself supported several attempts to
discover the sources of the Nile. In 1856 he spent £500,000 on a

---

[1] Shukry, pp. 95–7. Hill, *Biographical Dictionary*.
[2] Hill, *Biographical Dictionary*.
[3] See above, pp. 52–53.
[4] Shukry, pp. 113–17; Hill, pp. 90–104.

venture commanded by a Frenchman, Count d'Escayrac de
Lauture, but despite this fantastic expenditure the expedition
never even left Cairo.[1] His subsequent efforts were far less extravagant. In 1860 he encouraged Dr. Alfred Peney, the French chief
medical officer of Egyptian troops in the Sudan, and Giovanni
Miani, an exiled Italian patriot, to explore the upper reaches
beyond Gondokoro, but both these explorers were restricted to the
movements of the traders' raiding forays.[2] Sa'īd also tentatively
began to bring the White Nile within the military administration
of Khartoum. Brun Rollet, previously the most active opponent
of the Government's monopoly, was ironically one of the first to
advocate an expansion of Egyptian power. Having experienced
some of the difficulties and dangers of trading with the Nilotes,
and desiring a security less costly than that of servants armed at
his own expense, he suggested in 1853 that 'a battalion of infantry
and four hundred irregular cavalry camped near the mouth of the
Saubat would, together with ten gun-boats, suffice to guarantee
the submission' of the Dinka, Nuer, Shilluk and Baqqara.[3] Two
years later, after Sa'īd had forbidden the import of slaves into
Egypt, an expedition of over eight hundred soldiers was sent 'to
occupy the White Nile' and a resident Mudir of the new province
was appointed.[4] Their duties included a search of all boats in an
endeavour to suppress the slave trade,[5] and Sa'īd undoubtedly
hoped that the expenses of the undertaking would be partly
covered by a tax on the ivory trade.[6] Defended by a large enclosure,
a post was established at the mouth of the Sobat, but suffering
illness, lack of food, the accidental destruction of their powder-
magazine and the unabated hostility of the Shilluk reth, the men

[1] Hill, *Biographical Dictionary*.
[2] Ibid.
[3] A.S.T. Con., Naz. Aless/1854. Brun Rollet to Consul, October 1853.
[4] F.O. 141/19. Petherick to Green, 21/XII/55.
[5] D'Aumont, op. cit. In a few cases this had a successful result, and in March
1858 for instance two government boats arrived at Gondokoro returning rescued
slaves (Kir. MS. 24/III/58; Mor. MS. 26/III/58).
[6] In July 1855 an attempt to tax the ivory trade was renounced since Sa'īd
admitted that merchandise coming from Darfur and the White Nile was subject
only to 3% at port of export as 'ces deux provinces ne sont part de l'Egypte'.
But in 1857 the Viceroy, having despatched his expedition and 'considering the
White River as an Egyptian dependence', ordered that 'a duty of 12% shall be
paid on all imports therefrom'. With the withdrawal of the expedition the matter
was allowed to drop (F.O. 141/19 Petherick to Bruce, 8/VII/55, and P. to
Green, 21/XII/55. F.O. 141/33. P. to Green, 24, 26/XII/57).

were withdrawn early in 1857.[1] With the failure of this intervention, the initiative remained with the traders until the first steps towards decisive control were eventually undertaken in response to insistent demands for action against the slave trade.

When the missionaries, disheartened by the final outburst of hostility among the Bari and the ever-increasing difficulties which the traders' use of force placed in the way of any peaceful contact, returned to Khartoum in March 1860 they persuaded the Austrian Consular Agent to take action. Josef Natterer, recently appointed to the post, immediately wrote a strong letter to his Consul General in Egypt condemning all traders—'there are no longer merchants but only robbers and slavers on the White Nile,'— and three months later submitted a thorough survey of the situation on the White Nile as it appeared from reports reaching Khartoum.[2] At the same time the Provicar Apostolic bitterly protested against the occupation by the traders of the mission stations left temporarily in the charge of local chieftains, and asserted that Christian children from the stations were among the slaves sold at Khartoum. He demanded therefore 'direct orders from the highest authority, which would produce an enduring impression and redress against this open evil'.[3] Since it was impossible to take effective action while the Egyptian Government continued its system of army 'recruitment' by giving contracts to notorious slave-dealers, the matter was brought before the Viceroy's Cabinet, but there was no tangible result[4] and Natterer's position at Khartoum became precarious. No one dared to transact business with him or even to enter his house for fear of being persecuted by the Governor and the Egyptian trader, Muḥammad al-'Aqqād. Convinced that his life was endangered, Natterer fled to Egypt in March 1861, accompanied by the Sardinian Consular Agent.[5] In response to the representations of Schreiner, the Austrian Consul-General, the

[1] Castlebolognesi, p. 395; Brun Rollet to Jomard, 3/II/56, in *Bull. Soc. Géog.* 1856. A few huts built by the soldiers at Ulibari were immediately destroyed by the Bari on their withdrawal. Mor. MS. 22/1/57.

[2] O.S. Ad. Reg. 27/6. Natterer to Schreiner, 5/IV/60 enclosed in Schreiner to Rechberg-Rothenlöwen, 31/V/60, and see above pp. 52–53.

[3] Ibid, Kirchner to Schreiner, 8/VIII/60, enclosed in Schreiner to Rechberg-Rothenlöwen, 2/IX/60.

[4] Ibid, Schreiner to Rechberg-Rothenlöwen, 2/IX/60, 19/IX/60.

[5] O.S. Ad. Reg. 27/9. Natterer's report enclosed in Schreiner to Rechberg-Rothenlöwen, 1/IV/61.

Governor was recalled and Natterer, honoured by the Porte with the Medjidie Order, returned in triumph to Khartoum.[1]

In his survey of the situation written in August 1860, Natterer maintained that the only way to deal radically with the slave trade was to establish a strong military garrison on the White Nile with the right to search all boats and the power to seize any slaves.[2] In the course of the negotiations which followed Natterer's arrival in Egypt, Schreiner strongly recommended this proposal to the Viceroy, and the following year the British Consul-General, having received similar suggestions from Consul Petherick,[3] added his support with the result that the Governor-General was instructed to take action. In October 1862, a small detachment of soldiers was despatched to inspect the traffic on the White Nile, while all merchants were required to furnish a list of their servants and to pay a tax equivalent to one month's salary for each employee.[4]

While these official deliberations were taking place, events on the White Nile increased the need for an intervention. The power of the Arab traders and settlers at Kaka the northernmost Shilluk settlement had steadily developed. By 1860 seventeen of the twenty-one large groups of homesteads were inhabited exclusively by Arabs, the northern Shilluk mixed with them and aided them in expeditions against the Dinka, and some Shilluk openly expressed their desire to be 'emancipated from the tyranny of the reth and his counsellors.'[5] This disruptive influence and the high-handed acts of some of the White Nile traders[6] evoked a violent reaction from the reth, and in September 1860 many Arabs were expelled from Kaka. Among them was Muḥammad Khair, a Dongolawi, who after several years of petty trading at Kaka had purchased a boat from the Syrian, Ibrāhīm Bās, and had made excursions against the Dinka, selling their women as slaves and pasturing their captured cattle on islands in the middle of the river.[7] On his

[1] O.S. Ad. Reg. 27/9. Natterer to Schreiner, 3/III/62.

[2] O.S. Ad. Reg. 27/9. Natterer to Schreiner, 15/VIII/60, enclosed in Schreiner to Rechberg-Rothenlöwen, 21/III/61.

[3] F.O. 84/1144 Petherick to Russell, 25/XI/61.

[4] Douin, vol. iii (1) p. 103.   [5] Beltrame, p. 86.

[6] E.g. Morlang in March 1860 while passing the Shilluk heard that Darawī, Barthélemy's Vakil, had on two occasions taken corn by force and killed some Shilluk. Mor. MS. 8–10/III/60.

[7] Mor. MS. 14/XII/60. Morlang adds that before his departure from Khartoum a few days previously three Shilluk, sent by the Dinka, had come to seek aid and protection against Muḥammad Khair. Their request was apparently unheeded.

expulsion from Kaka, Muḥammad Khair collected two hundred Baqqara cavalry and over one thousand riflemen. With these and thirteen boats, equipped with money borrowed from Europeans at Khartoum, he attacked the Shilluk in February 1861. The reth's capital at Denab and sixty other villages were burnt, in two pitched battles severe casualties were inflicted, and Muḥammad re-established himself near Kaka, defending his position with earthworks.[1]

A few months after this attack Muḥammad Khair sent a message to the Governor-General offering to pay a tribute of a thousand cattle a year in return for recognition of himself as ruler of the Shilluk,[2] and in 1862 he sent his brother to Khartoum to negotiate a settlement. There followed a lengthy period of intrigue with creditors and other applicants, until finally in March 1863 the Governor-General decided to appoint him as ruler over the Dinka, and to re-establish a Province of the White Nile with a garrison based on the Shilluk. Fortunately however for the Dinka this decision arrived too late, as Muḥammad Khair, uncertain of his position, had already retreated into the interior, where he was subsequently killed. The garrison amongst the Shilluk was only established at the end of the year,[3] and in the meanwhile the area continued to be ravaged. In March 1863 Morlang, returning from his final visit to the Bahr el Jebel, saw on the bank amongst the Shilluk

12 boats moored, and a number of Baggara Arabs with their small horses, tents and recuba. The first said that they were from Khartoum, under the command of Wad Ibrāhīm, to whom the Pasha (Governor-General) had consigned the Shilluk country for an annual payment of 200 purses (i.e. *c.* £1000). He wanted to collect the tax primarily in tusks, but foreseeing that these would not be sufficient to supply the desired money, he had brought with him during his voyage many Baggara, promising them a share in the booty of war. These men, thirsting after rapine, came here by land, and finding on the way 170 comrades killed shortly before by the Shilluk they redoubled their demonstrations of hostility. The boats have already been here

---

[1] Lejean, pp. 94–95; Mor. MS. 11/III/61. 'They said the captives taken amounted to 500 and the cattle to some 12,000 . . . Mahommed Cheir receiving two-thirds for his share,' Petherick, *Travels*, vol. i, p. 96.

[2] F.O. 84/1144 Petherick to Russell, 25/XI/61.

[3] Heuglin, p. 87; Douin, vol. iii (1) pp. 104–5.

12 days, the tribute consisting only of tusks, and the whole expedition wishes to proceed southwards to fight the Shilluk.[1]

Thus, the first steps of the Egyptian Government to reassert control over the White Nile were hesitant, cautious and largely ineffective, while when Ismā'īl, who succeeded Sa'īd as Viceroy in 1863, heard of the plans for the new Province he considered them to be premature.[2] Suddenly, however, all doubts as to the importance of the White Nile disappeared. In an interview with Ismā'īl on 1 June 1863 Speke and Grant, returning down the Nile after their historic journey from Zanzibar to its source at Ripon Falls on Lake Victoria, were able to disclose the nature of their achievement. They had accomplished a great feat of discovery; they had also grasped its significance in the task of opening up tropical Africa to the outside world, and they brought with them an idea which for more than a decade placed the southern Sudan in the forefront of African history.

Livingstone's return in 1856 from his great journey across Africa from Angola to Mozambique aroused public enthusiasm for his call to make 'an open path for commerce and Christianity', and it heralded a spate of exploration which within seven years laid bare the broad geographical aspects of East Africa and the Nile basin. From 1857 to 1863 the British Government entrusted Livingstone with an expedition up the Zambezi during the course of which he explored the Shire Highlands and Lake Nyasa. Meanwhile in its search for the sources of the Nile the Royal Geographical Society, under its President Sir Roderick Murchison, had turned its attention to attempts to penetrate inland from Zanzibar and the east coast of Africa. To the scientific interest in exploration was added the strategic importance of East Africa which was already becoming apparent to the rulers of India. In 1856 the Foreign Office, the East India Company, and the Royal Geographical Society provided funds for two Indian Army officers, Burton and Speke, to investigate the rumours of a huge inland sea reported in 1848–9 by Krapf and Rebmann, two C.M.S. missionaries who had first sighted the snow-capped mountains of Kenya and Kilimanjaro. Burton and Speke reached Lake Tanganyika and on the return journey Speke broke off to the north and

---

[1] The following day south of Kaka he passed another expedition of 14–20 boats going to rob the Dinka. Mor. MS. 17–18/III/63.

[2] Douin, vol. iii (1) p. 105.

became the first European to reach the southern shores of Lake Victoria. In 1860, again assisted by the Government and the Royal Geographical Society, Speke returned accompanied by Grant, another Indian Army officer, and in 1862 finally reached the Ripon Falls and then pushed north to Gondokoro and Cairo.[1]

The reports of these explorers revealed that beyond the arid plains which confine the narrow coastal belt of East Africa there existed 'a fertile and well-watered crescent'[2] stretching from Lake Nyasa to Lake Victoria. In the north, around the western shores of Lake Victoria, lay the Bantu kingdoms of Buganda, Bunyoro and Karagwe. Densely populated, with well-established, ancient and despotic dynasties, these kingdoms through contact with Arab merchants from Zanzibar had already developed a considerable market for European goods. 'Their sovereigns,' Speke reported, 'evinced a keen desire for commercial intercourse with civilised countries, while the climate appears far superior to, and the soil more promising than those of any region adjoining, either to the north or south.'[3] Approaching the area from the southern Sudan, the Victoria Nile 'appeared to be the limit of utter savagedom'. Beyond it, in these kingdoms, clothing was valued and not despised, so that printed cottons and not stolen cattle could easily take the place of beads when the market for these slackened.[4] Once again seemingly bright prospects of legitimate commerce were displayed to the outside world.

The routes into this fertile area were, however, difficult and dangerous. In the far south Livingstone discovered that shoals, sandbanks and rapids destroyed his hope that the Zambezi might be a navigable highway, while fever and the slave trade frustrated a missionary settlement in the Shire Highlands. When therefore the Zambezi expedition was withdrawn in 1863 it had achieved little, and the plans for an approach from the south remained in abeyance for more than a decade.[5] From Zanzibar the route followed by Speke and Grant was described by Murchison as 'long and somewhat circuitous . . . through a country held by a

---

[1] Coupland, *The Exploitation of East Africa*, 1939, pp. 102–34.

[2] Oliver, p. 29.

[3] F.O. 78/1839. Murchison to Russell, 28/IV/64.

[4] S. W. Baker, *The Albert N'yanza, Great Basin of the Nile*. 1867 ed., vol. i, pp. 362–3, vol. ii, pp. 45–52.

[5] R. Coupland, *Kirk on the Zambezi*, 1928; Oliver, pp. 11–15.

variety of petty chiefs, each able to cause vexatious delays to travellers, but none powerful enough to keep the line open for regular traffic'.[1] Another route further to the north though shorter passed 'through the territory of the Masai, a tribe reported to be so very warlike and inhospitable as to forbid the possibility of traversing their country'.[2] On their return therefore Speke and Grant carried Murchison with them in their conviction that 'the east coast of Africa does not offer a proper base of operations' for opening up the equatorial kingdoms, and as a result they focussed attention on the situation in the southern Sudan.

> The other line of communication, and indeed the only natural one between the regions in question and the sea, is from Egypt by ascending the great White Nile. . . . Between Gondokoro and the equatorial kingdoms lies a belt of country less than 200 miles in breadth, which at present offers the only considerable difficulty on the route. This difficulty arises from the lawlessness of certain Bari tribes, who in addition to their being under no powerful king or ruler, have of late years been utterly demoralized by the ivory traders . . .'[3]

Private enterprise could not attempt to grapple with these difficulties. Although Speke himself was anxious to return being fully convinced that much good would result if he could 'meet the natives on equitable terms', and although 'friends in trade, the honest merchants of England', begged him to ascend the Nile valley, nothing would induce him to do so unless he was 'armed with authority to put the trade on a legitimate footing'. It was indeed also a matter of urgency for unless the 'armed gangs' of de Bono and others were checked, they would 'annihilate the Kings of the Equator . . . in the same way as the Zanzibar Arab traders have dethroned the chief of Unyamyembe and established a colony of their own at Kaze'. Only the firm assertion of imperial control could solve these problems, and the immediate necessity was the occupation of Gondokoro by an 'organised force' capable of preventing the import of firearms. 'For although the tribes situated at a distance from either bank might only partially feel the benefits of a settled government, still the power in possession of the river would virtually hold the country, and the natives would gladly trade with the established depots.' Having established this

[1] F.O. 78/1839 Murchison to Russell, 28/IV/64.
[2] Ibid.
[3] Ibid.

station at Gondokoro, an embassy should be sent to the court of Bunyoro 'and the finest lands in the world would be open to Europe'. It was suggested that ivory, together with considerable exports to the equatorial kings, 'who would hail an opening for the products and manufactures of the world', should make it a most profitable venture, and it was hoped that the undertaking would suppress 'that infamous traffic in slaves, which is at present carried on to an enormous extent upon the White Nile'.[1]

There was but one power, Egypt, which could conceivably be willing at this date to attempt such an extension of imperial sovereignty. As a result of Speke's conversation with Ismā'īl in June 1863 Murchison believed that the latter would 'readily appreciate the commercial advantages arising from such a policy', and that he would be more willing to implement it 'if he received the slightest encouragement from the British Government'. Murchison and Speke suggested that the encouragement could take the form of a scientific expedition which would act 'as a prelude to future commercial settlements', and the Royal Geographical Society was willing to contribute £1,000 towards its expenses.[2] But Speke's death in September 1864 prevented him from pursuing these ambitious proposals, and the Foreign Office was unwilling actively to encourage the extension of Egyptian power in the southern Sudan.[3]

Ismā'īl, however, had inherited Muḥammad 'Alī's interest in imperial expansion. Educated in Egypt, Vienna and Paris, he continued Sa'īd's work of introducing European institutions and technology into Egypt and the Sudan. The postal service was improved, the telegraph was extended in the Sudan, surveys for a railway in the Sudan were undertaken and the construction of a line southwards from Wadi Halfa to Dongola was begun in 1873. Considerable agricultural expansion took place in the Sudan. Since the Egyptian conquest fruit trees, sugar cane, and indigo were introduced, and Ism'āīl encouraged several ambitious attempts to expand the cultivation of cotton. With the growth of trade— and particularly that of the White Nile—Khartoum expanded, and in 1863 it had an estimated population of about 30,000. There was a prosperous boat-building industry under the direction of

[1] F.O. 78/1839. Murchison to Russell, 28/IV/64. Speke to Russell, 28/V/64.
[2] Ibid.
[3] On the attitude of the Foreign Office, see below Chapter VI.

Admiralty-trained Maltese, and besides the imposing brick and stone buildings of the Governor's palace and the Catholic Mission the town possessed a military hospital, an arsenal, large barracks and a soap-factory. The regime however continued to be dependent on the army, recruitment increased, and by 1865 over 27,000 men were stationed in the Sudan.[1]

Although in 1863 no expedition was sent to Gondokoro, Ismā'īl proceeded in the following years to take a series of measures designed to extend Egyptian control over the area. Soon after his interview with Speke four steamers were sent to the Sudan, six boats armed with cannon were ordered to provide a police for the White Nile, and in November 1863 Mūsā Pasha Ḥamdī, the Governor-General, after returning from a hurried visit to Cairo, trebled the tax on the trade of the White Nile.[2] Although in principle the tax could be defended as an essential means of financing the new security measures, it was arbitrarily imposed at the worst possible moment. The traders had already prepared their annual expeditions involving a large capital expenditure, and it evoked strong protests from the European community. Abandoning his business, Petherick retired to seek legal redress in Egypt and England;[3] de Pruyssenaere reported various examples of discrimination against Europeans;[4] and it was commonly believed that the tax was designed to destroy the few remaining European traders.[5] In 1865 de Bono sold his assets, valued by himself at £25,000, to the Government for £5,000,[6] and two years later Ambroise and Jules Poncet, the sole surviving European traders, sold theirs for a quarter of their real value.[7] Henceforth Ismā'īl was free to pursue his plans without fear of local European rivalry.

The downfall of most of these traders was by no means a disaster for the unfortunate tribes whom they had terrorized. Samuel Baker, a British explorer and big-game hunter who had met Speke and Grant at Gondokoro, returned to Khartoum in June 1865

[1] Shukry, pp. 134–5; Hill, pp. 122–34.

[2] O.S. Ad. Reg. 27/9 Hansal to Schreiner, 28/XI/63, enclosed in Schreiner to Rechberg-Rothenlöwen, 1/II/64; Douin, vol. iii (i), p. 106.

[3] F.O. 78/2253 is devoted solely to Petherick's complaints.

[4] De Pruyssenaere to Auguste, 6/XII/63, and to Aubert, 20/VI/64 in *Bull. Soc. Roy. Géog. D'Anvers*, 1930.

[5] O.S. Ad. Reg. 27/9. Hansal to Schreiner 28/XI/63, enclosed in Schreiner to Rechberg-Rothenlöwen, 1/II/64.

[6] F.O. 84/1246 Colquhoun to Russell, 10/VII/65.

[7] Buet, p. 115.

having discovered Lake Albert and bringing with him reports of the chaos being caused by the traders based on Gondokoro and Faloro. Two bands belonging to de Bono and 'Aqqād were beginning to exploit the rivalries of the Lacustrine kingdoms. In January 1864 when Baker, accompanying a band of 'Aqqād's men, had arrived at the confines of Bunyoro he had experienced great difficulty in assuaging the suspicions of Kamrasi, ruler of Bunyoro, and he had discovered that the latter was interested only in enlisting the support of 'Aqqād's men against his brother Rionga and Wad al-Mak, de Bono's agent. 'Aqqād's men had been only too ready to comply with Kamrasi's wishes and the attack being successful they had been rewarded with a magnificent supply of ivory, which, together with some collected amongst the Acholi, was worth just under £10,000 when delivered in Egypt and represented 'a perfect fortune' for Khūrshīd, 'Aqqād's agent.[1]

As Baker had returned northwards he had been able to observe the devastation which accompanied these profits. Within the ten months that he had been absent from Faloro and the Acholi 'a great change had taken place in the neighbourhood. The rival parties of Khurshid and Debono . . . had leagued themselves with contending tribes, and the utter ruin of the country was the consequence.' Extensive raids were undertaken to seize the four thousand cows required as payment for porters; tribes hitherto mutually hostile were now desperately united against the Turks; 'the entire camp was a mere slice from the infernal regions'; and on the march to Gondokoro they were persistently attacked by the Moogie, a section of the Bari tribe.[2]

When Baker reached Khartoum he informed the British Consul-General in Egypt that 'Gondokoro was *swarming* with slaves this year. Many thousands were there . . . Debono's people are about the worst of the lot, having utterly destroyed the country; of course their zareeba is full of slaves. . . . I have much to say to you on this matter, as I have myself been a witness to the atrocities of the White Nile trade'.[3] Elsewhere he states that there were three thousand slaves at Gondokoro.[4] Baker had a distinct tendency

---

[1] Baker, *Albert N'yanza*, vol. ii, p. 263. The extent to which Baker himself was forced to accept these violent methods can be seen in his advice to Kamrasi that 'if he would give them a supply of ivory, he might always reckon upon them as valuable allies'. ibid., p. 195.   [2] Ibid., pp. 248–77.

[3] F.O. 78/1871. Baker to Colquhoun, 21/VI/65.

[4] Baker, *Albert N'yanza*, vol. ii, p. 283.

towards exaggeration, but even if his figure is accepted, it must be
remembered that it was an exceptional year as a Government
blockade had recently been established on the White Nile[1] with
the result that the slaves had accumulated at Gondokoro, and of
these three thousand a very large proportion were certainly the
wives and attendants of the Arab soldiers. His emphasis on the
slave trade was unfortunate as it resulted in a serious misconception.
The impression given to those who directed policy both in Egypt
and Europe was that the misery of the situation on the White Nile
was solely due to the operations of the slave trade, with the result
that their subsequent efforts to suppress it led them to overlook
the more serious sources of this trade elsewhere and to ignore the
fundamental factors which were creating the disaster on the White
Nile. These factors have been described above and in part they
were recognized by Baker himself,[2] but with others he assumed far
too readily that the sole problem was that caused by a demand for
slaves. In his book, which influenced both contemporaries and
historians, he framed his challenge in this wise:

> What curse lies so heavily upon Africa and bows her down beneath
> all other nations? It is the infernal traffic in slaves. . . . Thus is Africa
> cursed: nor can she be raised to any scale approaching to civilisation
> until the slave-trade shall be totally suppressed. The first step neces-
> sary to the improvement of the savage tribes of the White Nile is the
> annihilation of the slave-trade. Until this be effected, no legitimate
> commerce can be established; neither is there an opening for
> missionary enterprise;—the country is sealed and closed against all
> improvement. . . . Should the slave-trade be suppressed, there will
> be a good opening for the ivory trade.[3]

His future experience and that of his successors proved the
fallacy of his wishful thinking. In the meanwhile, although the
European traders were removed, official intervention unfortunately
did not improve the situation. Muḥammad al-'Aqqād, who took
over de Bono's stations, paying the Government £3,000 p.a. for
monopolistic rights south of Gondokoro, continued to employ the
customary methods of 'trading'. In June 1868 the French Consul,
reporting the arrival of fifteen of his boats from the White Nile
bringing 800 kantars of ivory, commented 'beau produit s'il n'était

[1] See above; p. 82.
[2] E.g. his description of the ivory trade, *Albert N'yanza*, vol. i, pp. 17–23.
[3] Op. cit., vol. ii, pp. 294–7.

point taché de sang humain'.[1] The Governor-General himself, in
order to maintain his army of 27,000 men of whom over 20,000
were 'Negroes', conducted recruiting raids on a scale larger than
ever before,[2] and the prospects of the new Mudirieh founded
among the Shilluk in 1863 were ruined by this same fatal necessity
for recruiting.

At first some of the Shilluk were prepared to barter cattle and
corn with the new stations at Kaka and Fashoda, and Heuglin
found the Bimbashi in charge of Kaka at pains to convince them
that the Government would act as an effectual guard against the
raids of their Baqqara enemies. The Shilluk, however, could
hardly be expected to view with equanimity the arrival of a
thousand soldiers, and the majority of them withdrew from the
vicinity. In this tense situation the Mudir apparently attempted to
exact a tribute of cattle, and in the process seized fifty Shilluk who
were immediately despatched to regiments in the north. The
consequences were disastrous. The troops, henceforth dependent
on Khartoum for all provisions, lived 'continually on the qui vive
among a cruel People'. Discipline and morale were impaired by
the fact that the new Mudirieh became staffed with several hundreds
of criminal and political exiles from Egypt.[3] The situation deteriorated and by 1866 the reth, having seized several traders' boats, led
hordes of Shilluk against the Government. The attack was defeated,
but the garrisons hardly managed to survive and the major sections
of the tribe remained implacably hostile.[4]

While this unhappy experiment was proceeding, Ismāʿīl, who
never visited the Sudan, was preparing for the decisive advance.
Having obtained from the Porte the lease of the Red Sea ports
of Suakin and Massawa, he was seriously considering the construction of a railway to link Suakin with the Nile at Berber. At the
same time he effected a major re-organization of the administration
of the Sudan by dividing the country into the provinces of Taka,
Khartoum, and the White Nile, and Berber, Kordofan, and

[1] A.E. Corr. Consul. Alex./43. Thibaut to Poujade, 22/VI/68. Muḥammad
al- Aqqād had over thirty ships serving the needs of ten stations.
[2] Ibid. Alex./35. Garnier to Tasta 29/VI/64 and Alex./37 Garnier to Outrey
28/X/65. The mortality amongst these black soldiers was very great: in 1865
2,500 out of 4,000 at Khartoum died in an epidemic. Ibid., Alex./36. Garnier to
Tasta, 5/V/65.
[3] A.E. Corr. Consul. Alex./34. Thibaut to Tasta, 18/X/64, enclosed in Tasta
to Drouyn de Lhuys, 26/XI/64; Heuglin, pp. 242–3.
[4] Douin, vol. iii (1), pp. 316–17, 446–8.

Fazogli, whose Governors would henceforth be directly responsible to himself. 'All these facts,' concluded the French Consul-General, 'indicate the extent to which Ismail Pacha is preoccupied with the countries situated to the extreme south of Egypt'.[1] In 1868 the death of Theodor, Emperor of Abyssinia, removed a power which had threatened the security of the Sudan throughout Mūsā Pasha's tenure of office, and by 1869, with the revenues of Egypt and the Sudan seeming relatively stable, Ismā'īl, who during a visit to Paris in 1867 had reiterated his intention to combat the slave trade, was prepared to embark upon the ambitious project of an equatorial empire.[2]

2. Baker's Expedition, 1869–1873

Baker had returned to England after his discovery of Lake Albert filled, like Speke, with ideas for the future development of the Upper Nile Basin. For him 'the primary object of geographical exploration is the opening to general intercourse such portions of the earth as may become serviceable to the human race. The explorer is the precursor of the colonist. ...'[3] Unlike Speke however, his thoughts did not at first run in the direction of Egyptian intervention. For him there had been no interview with Ismā'īl; on the contrary his book published in 1866, and even more his letters, were full of bitter complaints against what seemed to him the hopeless incompetency of Egyptian rule. His interest in imperial strategy had already led him to conclude that 'there are no countries of the earth so valuable, or that would occupy so important a position in the family of nations, as Turkey ... and Egypt under a civilised and Christian government. As the great highway to India, Egypt is the most interesting country to the English'.[4] He discussed his plans with Murchison, and in his book brought forward at this early date the idea of development through a concessionaire Company,[5] but, with British interest in northeast Africa focussed in this period on Abyssinia,[6] his ideas evoked no concrete response.

[1] A.E. Corr. Alex./37. Outrey to Drouyn de Lhuys, 1/VI/65.
[2] Douin, vol. iii (1), pp. 475–80.
[3] Baker, *Albert N'yanza*, p. xxi.
[4] Ibid., p. xxix.
[5] Ibid., II, p. 296; and T. D. Murray & A. S. White, *Sir Samuel Baker, a memoir*, 1895, pp. 131, 263.
[6] See below, Chapter VI.

Knighted for his 'laborious researches in Africa', Baker settled down to the life of a country squire, until at the end of 1868 he received an invitation to accompany the Prince of Wales on an official visit to Egypt which would mark the opening of the Suez Canal. He owed the invitation to the fact that his brother, Valentine Baker, was an intimate friend of the Prince, and it was intended that Sir Samuel should introduce the latter to the delights of crocodile shooting on a brief excursion up the Nile. Ismā'īl seized the opportunity to discuss his ideas with Baker; the Prince of Wales considerably aided the final negotiations; and on 5 April 1869 Baker informed his brother John that he had 'after much consideration accepted the Viceroy's offer of the command of the greatest expedition of modern times'.[1]

In his late forties Baker still possessed remarkable physical strength and powers of endurance. Fearless, and an outstanding shot, he was one of the foremost big-game hunters in his generation: a man who respected and believed in the use of force, and was as ready to use it in the southern Sudan as most of his trading predecessors had been—though of course for rather different ends. It is quite false, however, to think of Baker solely as a blood-thirsty soldier ruthlessly leading his men into successive struggles with tribe after tribe caused primarily by a total misunderstanding of the nature of the task entrusted to him. His attitude to Africa was far more constructive, and it closely resembled that of many 20th century settlers. From Bristol ancestors his family had inherited estates in Jamaica and Mauritius, but his own experience of the Tropics before his journey up the Nile had been centred on Ceylon. Attracted there by the prospects of sport, he discovered in the remote highlands an area lying undeveloped which aroused in him the desire to create there an 'English village' with the whole of Ceylon for his 'manor, and no expense of gamekeepers'. Returning to England he persuaded his brother to assist him in this undertaking and for seven years, together with an English bailiff, groom, yeomen, and a pack of hounds, they had laboured to realize this idea. They succeeded, and, although he realized that the southern Sudan and the Equatorial Kingdoms were unsuitable for white

[1] B.MSS. S.W.B. to John Baker, 5/IV/69. He added—'it would be folly to decline such a splendid offer which presents both fortune and prestige upon a path that I know well'. See also Chapter XIII in Murray and White and B.MSS. Kanne to S.W.B., 9/XII/68.

settlement, he brought to his task in Africa a deep and optimistic belief in the potentialities of tropical development.[1]

Proclaiming himself, in a letter written to an influential Conservative friend shortly before the departure of the expedition, to be no 'nigger-worshipper', he yet hoped to effect 'a vast improvement among the tribes by the suppression of the Slave Trade, and by the introduction of agricultural and commercial enterprise. I have large quantities of seeds of all kinds that will be well adapted to the climate and soil of Central Africa, and that will confer a great blessing on the country. No man shall be idle under my rule. If I free them from slavery, I shall insist upon their working for themselves. They will then desire to exchange their surplus produce for our manufactures; but, unless by a vigorous authority compelled to work, they would quickly relapse into hopeless apathy and indolence; a desire for slaves would result from habits of idleness, and the Negro would enslave the Negro as before, should the paternal but strong arm be withdrawn from them.'[2]

The principal objects of the expedition, 'after *crushing the Slave Trade*', (his italics), were to secure for Egypt the Equatorial Nile Basin,[3] to establish 'a powerful government throughout all those tribes now warring with each other,' and, having opened the Lakes to steam navigation, to found a chain of trading stations, 'on the system adopted by the Hudson Bay Company' throughout the territory linking the north with the southern-most point. 'The natural productions are ivory, native flax, beeswax, and cotton; but I take seeds of the finest quality of the latter from Egypt. Every tribe will be compelled to cultivate a certain amount of corn and cotton, in proportion to the population. No wars will be permitted. Each chief will be held responsible for the acts of his tribe. Tribute will be exacted in labour to be performed in opening-out roads, on the same principle as the road-tax in Ceylon.'[4]

[1] Readers of E. Huxley's *White Man's Country*, 1935, will see the parallel with Delamere. Murray and White, Chapter IV re Ceylon. For a modern and most readable assessment of Baker's character and career, see D. Middleton, *Baker of the Nile*, 1949.

[2] Baker to Lord Wharncliffe, 22/X/69, in Murray and White, pp. 150–3.

[3] In his first report to Ismā'īl, quoted by Douin, vol. iii (i), p. 479, Baker clearly stated Egypt's permanent interest in the Nile waters: 'as the prosperity of all Egypt depends on the Nile it has become indispensable to annex for Egypt the two Lakes from which it takes its source'.

[4] Baker to Lord Wharncliffe, 22/X/69, in Murray and White, pp. 150–3.

Thus the first European administrator of any area in the interior of tropical Africa brought what was in some ways a remarkably modern attitude to his duties, at any rate when compared with the lack of interest in economic development displayed by many of his official British successors in this and other parts of Africa. Yet at that date his interest in development was by no means unique. His own attitude was determined primarily by his experience as a pioneer settler, but in the guise of 'legitimate commerce' a deep concern over economic development was shared by the few of his contemporaries who were interested in tropical Africa. It was of course proclaimed by the Exeter Hall which he often despised, and was re-echoed in the experiment of Chartered Company rule.[1] Since, however, he was in the service of a State, he envisaged the State as being intimately connected with economic development, and in this, as also in his impatience, he was followed by those who later directed the policy of the Congo Free State; while since the State which he served was not a European one, the civilization which he and his successors would bring to Equatorial Africa would be by no means predominantly European.

Despite these plans he himself was, in fact, able to bring but little commerce or civilization of any kind to the White Nile Basin. This failure was hardly due to lack of initial expenditure: the expedition was equipped on a scale sufficient to satisfy Baker's exacting requirements and Ismā'īl's lavish conceptions. 'I am to have any number (thousands if required) of troops as re-inforcements,' wrote Baker, 'and I have a "carte blanche" for all expenses, appointments and everything pertaining to the expedition'.[2]

From England three steamers of 251, 107 and 38 tons were commissioned. Together with two 10 ton steel lifeboats, they were to be conveyed from Cairo in sections by boat to Kurusku, across the Nubian Desert by camel, by boat again to Gondokoro, and then, it was hoped, by camel to a point above the Fola Rapids where they would be launched on the Albert Nile and could open up the unexplored extent of Lake Albert. Steam saw-mills, rockets and snider ammunition, and £9,000's worth of tools, necessities and trade goods were also ordered, and a train of forty-one railway wagons was needed to bring this equipment from

---

[1] Goldie however thought through the problems of African administration at a deeper level than Baker. C.f., M. Perham, *Native Administration in Nigeria*, 1937, p. 35.   [2] B.MSS. S.W.B. to John Baker, 5/IV/69.

Alexandria to Cairo, despite the fact that the largest steamer had yet to arrive. 1,500 troops, consisting of Egyptian and Sudanese infantry, artillery and irregular cavalry, were to accompany this material, together with Arab boat-builders and servants. There was also a British doctor and seven engineers, Baker's nephew, Julian who was a young naval lieutenant, and Lady Baker, still in her twenties, who had accompanied her husband on his previous exploration. The permanent acquisition of a large territory in the interior of tropical Africa was an undertaking unprecedented in character, and the scale of this enterprise rendered it unique even amongst subsequent pioneering expeditions.[1]

To some extent the lack of positive results achieved by the expedition was due to circumstances wholly beyond Baker's control. The difficulties of assembling transport at Cairo were great. The resources of the country were burdened with the extravagant festivities accompanying the opening of the Suez Canal, so that, although the troops started their journey in time, the equipment did not leave till well into the autumn and all the larger boats were unable to ascend the cataracts.[2] At the same time from Khartoum Ja'far Pasha Mazhar, the Governor-General, informed Baker that fifty boats would be needed to transport merely the durra (Indian millet) which had been ordered for the expedition. He asked Baker to consider how many other boats would be required for the camels, horses, donkeys, soldiers and equipment, pointing out despairingly that only two of the four steamers, sent to the Sudan by Isma'il in 1863, would be available, while the Government only owned fifteen sailing boats with the possibility of hiring ten more.[3]

---

[1] S. W. Baker, *Ismailia. A narrative of the expedition to Central Africa for the suppression of the Slave Trade organised by Ismail, Khedive of Egypt.* 1874, vol. i, pp. 9–16. For the impression created by the expedition on contemporary Europe, see below, Chapter VI.

[2] Ibid. vol. i, p. 26. B.MSS. Lady Baker to Edith, 25/VI/69.

[3] B.MSS. Ja'far Pasha to S.W.B., 16/VII/69. Ja'far's protests were to some extent weakened when it was discovered that he was at the same time organizing a large expedition to the Bahr el Ghazal (see below, Chapter IV), but Baker in *Ismailia*, vol. i, pp. 24–26 takes no account of these genuine difficulties confronting the Sudan authorities, and wholly ascribes the delay to a secret desire on their part to support the slave trade, apparently forgetting that Ja'far Pasha, with no reply to his earlier letter, had spent the month of August waiting for him at Berber (B.MSS. Giaffar Pasha to S.W.B. 30/VIII/69), while Lady Baker writing from Taufikia thought that 'Giaffar Pasha was very kind to us all,' B.MSS. Lady Baker to Edith, 15/VI/70.

Eventually, on the 8 February 1870, after a busy month at Khartoum, Baker set out for the White Nile with a preliminary force of 800 men, 2 steamers and 31 boats, leaving Higginbotham, the chief Engineer, to follow with the rest. Beyond the Shilluk he came into contact with an obstacle which he himself considered to be 'the greatest enemy to the expedition'. In 1863 masses of floating vegetation had formed a barrier across the White Nile in the area between the Bahr el Ghazal and the Sobat mouth, and, although for a few years the traders had managed to keep a minute passage clear, by 1870 this passage was completely closed. A solid growth of papyrus swamp formed a dense barrier of unknown extent, while the river ran through innumerable small subterranean channels. The broad navigable highway had ceased to exist. As an alternative the traders were using the Bahr el Zeraf, a twisting shallow channel which leaves the Bahr el Jebel north of Shambe, flows through the swampy, savannah plains inhabited by the Nuer, and rejoins the main river to the west of the Sobat mouth.[1] Up this channel Baker was forced to lead the expedition on the 17 February, despite the fact that due to the delays in starting the season was so advanced that the water level was already beginning to fall, while there remained but a few weeks of the north winds which alone could take the sailing vessels to Gondokoro.

Gradually as they went southwards amidst the vast shifting mass of swamp the channel narrowed until by the end of the month they were forced to cut their way through. It was a loathsome task for the men, who often were 'up to their necks in water all day',[2] and the whole of March was spent in vainly attempting to force a way through the wilderness. By the 20th the wind was from the south, thunderstorms were starting, and on 1 April, a year after Ismā'īl had signed Baker's contract, it was decided to abandon the attempt.

> There is no help for it. We shall be obliged to return and make a settlement in the Shillook country. It would take at least 6 weeks to get over these three bad places, by which time the rainy season would be in full force wetting all our corn and stores. We only have 5 months provisions, only having started with 7. We intended to have sown a large quantity of Dourra on our arrival at Gondokoro for the support of the troops when our present store should have been expended. This

[1] For a description of the sudd, see Baker, *Albert N'yanza*, vol. ii, pp. 329–30.
[2] J.B. MS. 27/II/70.

it will now be impossible to do as the ground could not be cleared in the wet season. It would also be impossible to procure a fresh supply of corn from Khartoum, as the boats could not get up again in time. The result would be starvation. Again, Higginbotham is behind us bringing up the remainder of the troops, that we were unable to do on account of the want of boats. All the strongest men were sent with us, thus he is bringing up all the invalids. If we are unable to get on with a force of nearly 1000 men, including the sailors, what would be his position, travelling much later in the season, with a force of only about 300 or 400? We now have 170 men sick and have lost 7. Now, supposing we go back to the Shillook country, we shall meet Higginbotham, we shall be able to sow our corn, reap it just in time to start early next season when the river is high, procure a fresh supply of stores from Alexandria, and go up together, the men having recruited their health, and there being plenty of time to do the work in.[1]

The expedition returned therefore and established a temporary station at Taufikia amongst the southern Shilluk, where Baker witnessed the further disintegration of Shilluk society under the impact of the garrisons at Fashoda and Kaka. Having defeated the reth's attack in 1866,[2] the Mudir resorted to the measure, adopted by the British administration in somewhat similar circumstances in the 20th century, of arbitrarily appointing a new reth who succeeded in rallying some of the northern sections of the tribe to the support of the administration. The south however remained intransigent and in November 1868 Ja'far Pasha ordered 2000 men to be enrolled against them, at the same time ordering the Shilluk and Dinka to pay an annual tribute of about £15,000.[3] The force proved incapable of pacifying the area; the oppressive levy provided further grounds for bitterness; and the southern Shilluk told Baker that the Mudir 'was constantly in the habit of making razzias upon them.' Baker himself was an eye-witness of one raid carried out by three government boats and five hundred men. He liberated 155 slaves captured by them and contacted the southern reth, Katcare, in an attempt to make peace between him

[1] J.B. MS. 1/IV/70.

[2] See above, p. 85.

[3] Douin, vol. iii, (i), p. 448. From May to November 1868 £4,000 had been taken. The figures should be compared with the £3,000 paid by 'Aqqād for his far greater holdings on the Upper Nile.

and the Mudir. The situation however was beyond his control and the disturbances continued to destroy Shilluk prosperity.[1]

Baker's stay at Taufikia also brought him into contact with the slave trade. When he had been in Gondokoro in 1865 he had overestimated, it will be remembered, the importance of the slave trade as a factor in the established pattern of violence between traders and tribes.[2] As a result of his and Speke's reports it was believed in England and Cairo that the Bahr el Jebel was the principal source of the thousands of slaves who were being smuggled into Egypt, or sent openly to Arabia, from the Sudan. Consular reports from Khartoum, read in the light of this preoccupation, did little to rectify this impression; but they aroused the anxiety of European governments and added weight to the representations which the latter increasingly placed before Ismā'īl.[3] Anxious to win European approval of his regime and sincere in his dislike of the horrors caused by slave raiding, Ismā'īl realized, like his grandfather, that a frontal attack on the institution of slavery itself was impossible for a Muslim ruler in his position. He thought, however, that it might be possible to reduce the evils by stopping the trade at its source. He hoped, therefore, that a decisive reduction in the volume of the slave trade would be one of the results brought about by the costly expedition entrusted to Baker, while Baker himself regarded the suppression of the slave trade as his primary objective and principal difficulty.[4]

[1] J.B. MS. 19/IV/70—5/V/70. An incident noted in Julian Baker's diary gives an insight into the conflicting situation: 'June 4th. "The Mek (reth) arrived in the evening. It seems that the Mudir of Fashoda had been giving his party guns and encouraging them to attack the Mek's people. They had just killed ten men and the Mek had come to complain, and as he said to take up his quarters close to us. We shall send a steamer to Fashoda tomorrow to inquire into the case." June 9th. "The steamer returned today. It appears that the Shilluk had killed two of the Mudir's soldiers for which he held Jahng, the man whom he had made king, responsible. Jahng went to take the men who had killed the soldiers but was met by the other party. There was a fight and Catcare's people got beaten".'   [2] See above, p. 84.

[3] Especially that of Great Britain, see Chapter VI.

[4] The veteran trader, Lafargue, at his home in Berber, also shared and supported this delusion. 'Papa had a letter from Mr. Lafargue, and he writes that the slave trade is worse than ever upon the White Nile, but we shall quickly extinguish it. The slave traders are already in a great fright about our expedition.' (B.MS. Lady Baker to Edith, Cairo, 29/X/69.) Ismā'īl's intentions regarding the slave trade were adroitly disclosed in conversation with Sir Bartle Frere (F.O. 84/1389. Frere to Granville, 1/I/73). See below, Chapter VI for the importance of the slave trade in determining the attitude of the Foreign Office towards Ismā'īl's imperialism.

This delusion was strengthened by an encounter with one of Kuchūk 'Alī's stations on the Bahr el Zeraf. It was one of three stations recently founded by the traders to protect the new route, and, by the date at which Baker arrived, they were conducting with the aid of some Nuer clans a fairly extensive slave trade, whose victims were easily smuggled past the garrison at Fashoda to be sold to Jellaba south of Khartoum.[1] Baker as he passed the station learnt that 'the place was full of slaves' and that his officers had been purchasing some for themselves; while after the expedition had returned to Taufikia a boat from this station was intercepted sailing northwards with 150 slaves on board.[2] This experience confirmed Baker in his preoccupation with the slave trade. He did not realize however that this was an exceptional situation confined to the limited area of the Bahr el Zeraf, and that, even in this case, the ivory trade, or rather the need to protect its lines of communication, and not the slave trade, was the basic *raison d'être* for the new stations' existence. The extent to which it was an exceptional situation is shown by the results of a search conducted by Baker from April till December 1870 on all boats passing Taufikia. Of these boats, nine carried a combined total of only 106 slaves, and four, together with an unspecified number of 'Aqqād's boats, had no slaves on board, while Julian Baker notes in his diary that many of these boats were carrying large quantities of ivory.[3]

Apart from the exception of the Bahr el Zeraf stations, the ivory trade was still the dominant factor in the situation on the White Nile. The slave trade remained but an incidental concomitant to this activity, and its suppression had comparatively little relevance to the complex problem of introducing ordered government and a legitimate commerce into the area of the Bahr el Jebel and that south of Gondokoro. In this vital task Baker's belief that the slave trade was the major obstacle to economic development proved sadly mistaken, and when confronted with the actual situation he

[1] An eye-witness account of their activities is contained in E. Marno, *Reisen im Gebiete des blauen und weissen Nil'*, Vienna, 1874.

[2] J.B. MS. 14/IV/70 and 18/V/70.

[3] Ibid. June–December, 1870. Higginbotham kept a journal which after his death was sent to the British Consul-General in Egypt. The Chaplain to the Consulate read it, and writing to Gordon, Baker's successor, said that it contained 'A good deal that is very damaging to Sir Samuel Baker.... As for suppressing the slave trade—to judge from Higginbotham's book he did not find very much of it to suppress.' (G. MSS. Davis to Gordon, 15/VI/74.)

found himself forced to adopt the violent expedients of his mercantile predecessors.

The expedition left Taufikia in December 1871 and reached Gondokoro on 15 April 1872 after 'a fearful struggle and a weary journey' up the tortuous channels of the Bahr el Zeraf. In many places they had to cut a passage through thick swamps and their success was to a large extent due to Baker's tireless and relentless persistence. On the day when all appeared hopeless he spent five hours dragging a small boat over high grass and mud with about fifteen men until he discovered a large lake of deep water 'into which by means of a dam, it was possible to drag the steamer and boats'.[1] When at last Baker reached Gondokoro he was a man in a hurry. As a result of circumstances beyond his control, two years of his contract had passed with practically no result and but two years remained in which to complete his ambitious programme. To his natural belief in force was added an understandable impatience; neither were qualities calculated to effect a peaceful transition to Egyptian sovereignty.

At Gondokoro they found that 'a great change' had taken place. The local riverain Bari under Alloron their headman had become the allies of al-'Aqqād, the sole owner of trading 'rights' in the area. Some of them had accompanied the trading parties to the permanent stations among the Makaraka in the west, the Lotuko in the east, and the Acholi in the south, where they acted as porters, herdsmen, and mercenary soldiers. The remainder, forced by the attacks of the Belinian Bari to abandon their villages on the east bank, had taken refuge on islands in the centre of the Nile or on the west bank where they awaited the annual arrival of 'Aqqād's boats.[2] Just as de Malzac and other traders had constructed alliances within the pattern of tribal hostilities, so at Gondokoro and in the area of the outlying stations the interests of small sections of the surrounding tribes had become integrated with those of the new ruling caste of Arab soldiers permanently settled in the south; but beyond the restricted radius of these alliances the great mass of people remained, in varying degrees of intensity, hostile to all intruders. On the one hand, therefore, Baker was confronted with the task of securing the transfer of allegiance of these semi-detribalized elements, and on the other with that of reaching forth

---

[1] B. MSS. Lady Baker to Edith, 19/V/71.
[2] Ibid. See also, *Ismailia*, vol. i, pp. 221–6.

and establishing confidence amongst the suspicious and alienated tribes. In both tasks he encountered attitudes hardened by the experience of the past thirty years, which, together with his own shortcomings and those of the men under his command, prevented him and to a certain extent his successors from creating anything like an ordered and prosperous development throughout the territories under their command.

On arrival at Gondokoro, Baker explained to Alloron and a few other 'headmen' that in return for the protection he offered them they would be expected to supply the expedition with building materials and a certain amount of corn. At first Alloron seemed satisfied with this, but difficulties rapidly developed, and within six weeks of his arrival Baker was in a state of open hostility with the Bari, which persisted throughout his stay at Gondokoro. Soon after the expedition had established itself at Gondokoro, Alloron's men started to drive their cattle over for grazing on to the pasture lands near the station which they had been unable to use previously for fear of the Belinian Bari and the Lokoya. When, however, Baker asked if he could purchase with his trade goods some of these cattle to feed his men, Alloron refused to sell them, questioned Baker's rights to settle at Gondokoro, and finally informed him that the only way in which he could procure meat would be by undertaking a large-scale razzia. Placed in his predecessors' predicament Baker, after further prolonged but fruitless negotiations, gave due warning and at the end of May seized a portion of Alloron's herd. The action confirmed the uneasiness of the Africans at the presence of this unprecedented force. The Belinian Bari, although enemies of the trading companies and rivals of Alloron, combined with the latter in nightly attempts to recapture the cattle and to share in the plunder of Baker's riches, while towards the end of July they were even joined in these operations by their traditional enemies the Lokoya.[1]

---

[1] *Ismailia*, vol. i, pp. 220–83. J.B. MS. 15/IV/71 to 10/VI/71. In *Ismailia* Baker attributes these difficulties with the Bari to the nefarious influence of Muḥammad abū Suʿūd, a member of the wealthy Aqqād family, who, having inherited the control of their Sudan business in 1870, bitterly resented the intrusion of the Government into his domain. Abū Suʿūd arrived with eight boats from Khartoum, however, only after hostilities had already started, and although his friendly reception by Alloron seemed to convince Baker that the latter had acted at his instigation, their relationship was in fact by no means cordial: on 10 July Julian Baker noted in his diary that abū Suʿūd's people were attacked by

Baker's subsequent actions were by no means calculated to bridge this gulf. Cut off from Khartoum his men were 'entirely dependent' upon such stocks of corn as they could grow for themselves, and soon after the arrival at Gondokoro Baker was 'driving all hands forward in the work of cultivation'.[1] The soldiers, however, worked 'shamefully' and of the corn that was sown over half was destroyed either by small birds by day or by the Bari during the night, so that on 26 August 1871 it became evident that the corn supplies would be exhausted after two or three weeks.[2] Before dawn on the 30th, Baker led out a force of 600 men on a massed raid to Belinian where there was 'an immense quantity of corn all over the country'. The force set fire to the neighbouring villages and encamped near the hill, where Baker and his nephew decided 'to buy corn from the natives if we can make terms with them, or take it from them if we cannot'. After prolonged negotiations a local chief suggested a combined raid against his enemy, who owned a great quantity of corn and cattle, and Baker agreed only to find that his ally deserted him at the last moment. 'All the villages for about three miles along the mountain' were therefore destroyed and the leaders returned to Gondokoro rejoicing in the fact that 'we shall now be able, knowing the country, to catch the cattle at any time', but without having solved the problem of corn supplies.[3]

The discontent of the soldiers came to a head on 13 December when their commander Muḥammad Ra'ūf[4] insisted that the lack of provisions made a return to Khartoum inevitable. Threatened with total failure, Baker led a foraging force of three hundred men to the south. After a distance of only twelve miles they reached a well-populated area with abundant corn. Failing to persuade the

the 'abids'. In the later stages of the expedition abū Su'ūd's overt opposition became one of the principal difficulties encountered, so in retrospect it may have seemed justifiable, and it was certainly convenient, to use him as a scape-goat for the distressing gulf formed between the Bari and the Government. The more plausible explanation is to be found in the fact that the Bari's reaction to the expedition was conditioned by their previous experience of extraneous forces, aggravated by Baker's subsequent bellicosity.

[1] B.MSS. Lady Baker to Edith, 19/V/71.
[2] J.B. MS. 26/VIII/71. *Ismailia*, vol. i, pp. 319–22.
[3] J.B. MS. 30/VIII/71 to 24/IX/71.
[4] Muḥammad Ra'ūf, c. 1832–1888. Later Governor of Harar 1875–1878, he succeeded Gordon as Governor-General of the Sudan 1880–1882.

Bari to exchange corn for trade goods or cattle, Baker seized the supplies and for the next month detachments of troops scoured the country, despatching large quantities of corn by boat to Gondokoro. At the same time about 800 ill and dispirited soldiers with 300 'Dependents' were returned to Khartoum, and Baker, with a force of 500 able men and ample provisions for over a year, was able to attempt the rest of his programme. It is, however, by no means surprising that his sojourn among the Bari is remembered by them in a series of lampoons the bitterness of which is almost impossible to translate.[1]

The transport of the steamer over the 120 miles separating Gondokoro from the navigable Albert Nile south of the Fola Rapids was the next essential step. It would throw Lake Albert open 'to the improving influences of navigation',[2] and would firmly establish Egyptian power in the Equatorial kingdom of Bunyoro. Originally Baker had hoped that the sections of the steamer would be transported by camels and donkeys but the condition of the White Nile prevented their shipment to Gondokoro. He was therefore dependent on obtaining the services of about two thousand Bari porters and he hoped that Bedden, an apparently friendly chief to the south of Rejaf, would supply him with them. Payment was to be made in cattle and the manner in which these were procured is another striking example of the extent to which Baker had failed to free himself from the methods of his predecessors. 'The Sheik came today, with about 25 abids, in order to help us to take cattle. We want about 3,000 head to give to the natives for carrying our baggage up the country, and now that we have no horses, we could not manage to catch cattle without their assistance.'[3] Razzias brought in over 2500 head and with these, together with 212 soldiers and the sections of the steamer, Baker sailed down to the cataracts south of Rejaf, leaving a strong force to defend Gondokoro. Bedden however, whether from distrust of Baker or, as Baker suggests, because he hoped to obtain the cattle more easily by plunder, refused to co-operate and attacked the camp by night. His action destroyed all hope of

[1] A. C. Beaton, 'Chapter in Bari History', *S.N.R.* 1934, p. 190. On his arrival at Gondokoro, Gordon wrote to his sister: 'They have been badly treated and it is extraordinary the intense hatred there is of Baker.' G. MSS. G. to A. 4/V/74.

[2] The phrase is Speke's, p. 472.

[3] J.B. MS. 20/XII/71.

being able to transport the steamer immediately and Baker decided to push on south with his troops alone. 'There seems,'
wrote Julian Baker, ' to be no end to the difficulties in this beastly
country.'[1]

The difficulties, occasioned by the obstruction of the White
Nile and the failure to establish peaceful relations with the Bari,
had indeed reduced 'the greatest expedition of modern times' to
a mere shadow of its former self. Yet if Baker found himself in a
predicament, so also did Abū Su'ūd,[2] al-'Aqqād's representative.
During the months which the expedition had been forced to spend
at Taufikia Baker had revisited Khartoum and while there had
learnt for the first time of the contract by which the firm of al-
'Aqqād paid the Government £3000 p.a. for the sole trading rights
south of Gondokoro. Baker insisted that this arrangement, which
not only recognised a formidable *imperium in imperio* but also
deprived the Khedive of the sole commodity which could immediately contribute to the expedition's expenses, should be abolished;
and it was agreed that Abū Su'ūd, provided that he gave two-thirds
of his profits to the Government, would be free to trade until
9 April 1872 on which date Baker would enforce a Government
monopoly.[3] Abū Su'ūd, as has been seen, reached Gondokoro in
June 1871 obviously hostile to the expedition and faced with the
necessity of rapidly withdrawing his large stocks of ivory from all
his scattered stations. Having contacted his stations among the
Makaraka he left for the south at a time when it seemed that Baker,
entangled with the Bari, might be unable to follow him. Paying a
rapid visit to his station at Foweira on the Victoria Nile and to the
court of Bunyoro, Abū Su'ūd decided to make no attempt to
evacuate but to remain in the south, gambling on the possibility
that if Baker failed to advance southwards he would be able to
continue his trading undisturbed. It was therefore a considerable
disappointment when on 6 March 1872 he saw Baker arriving at
Fatiko determined to establish Egyptian authority.

Fatiko was one of four stations among the Acholi which were
garrisoned by several hundred Danaqla settlers. Some of these
men had already spent ten years in the country and had been
forced to adopt a standard of living lower in many respects than

---

[1] J.B. MS. 5/II/72.
[2] See above, p. 96, n.1.
[3] *Ismailia*, vol. i, pp. 155–60.

that existing in the Equatorial Kingdoms. Far from being in a position to supply the Africans with European or Egyptian trade-goods, many of the Danaqla were dressed in skins or bark-cloth purchased from Bunyoro, and the surrounding Acholi were beginning to form part of Mutesa's commercial empire, obtaining their scanty supply of brass from Buganda. Armed force was almost the only asset of the Danaqla, and the succession rivalries in Bun-yoro following the death of Kamrasi two years previously had given plenty of scope for its exercise; while to the west across the Albert Nile or to the south-east among the Lango and other tribes, their armed expeditions were extending the area of raiding for ivory, cattle and incidentally slaves.[1] Although all the stations were under the nominal control of al-'Aqqād's firm, many of the Arabs had entered the country in de Bono's service and bitter rivalry, sometimes reinforced by the tribal divisions of their homeland, persisted between their respective vakils. They were, therefore, by no means a well-disciplined force immediately capable of active and united opposition to Baker. Yet while their loyalty to Abū Su'ūd was unenthusiastic they strongly resented the intrusion of the Government's expedition which challenged their dominion, and they formed one of the hardest problems which faced Baker and his successors in Equatoria and the Bahr el Ghazal. Their presence materially weakened the Government's control of the area, and even when they were enrolled as official garrisons they continued to live more as independent settlers than as disciplined agents of the administration.

Confronted with the covert and potentially formidable opposition of Abū Su'ūd and these Danaqla, it was fortunate for Baker that the Acholi clans near Fatiko were prepared to co-operate with him. In these clans living in a loose alliance with the neighbouring stations a new class of men, the interpreters, was rapidly emerging as an important group in the community. A few were the sons of chiefs, combining traditional status with a new-found importance; others had casually managed to pick up Arabic, like Wani of Labore, a former pupil of the mission at Gondokoro, who had returned to his village and had made it an important resting-place on the route between Gondokoro and Fatiko. All of them were the indispensable intermediaries between African tribal communities and the Arab intruders with whom it was politic to form a loose,

[1] *Ismailia*, vol. ii, pp. 84–119.

and if possible distant, alliance against rival tribes.[1] At Fatiko, on his previous exploration, Baker had befriended two such men who now exerted themselves on his behalf. The local villages welcomed the possibility of more considerate allies and a fairly wide range of peaceful contacts was established. Baker was able, therefore, to obtain two hundred reliable porters, and, having agreed to allow Abū Su'ūd to wait in the country until porters from the Makaraka arrived, he marched southwards, leaving almost half his force to guard a recently constructed magazine holding most of his ammunition. Apparently he anticipated little difficulty in Bunyoro.

Marching through a desolate, partially swampy wilderness, he reached Abū Su'ūd's southernmost station at Foweira on the Victoria Nile. After considerable discussion the garrison, faced with the alternative of immediate evacuation to Khartoum, reluctantly agreed to enter Government service, and Baker, having inspected their valuable collection of ivory which was now Government property, prepared to visit Bunyoro.[2] Presents were despatched to Kabarega, Kamrasi's successor, porters were secured with great difficulty, and eventually on 25 April 1872 they arrived at Masindi, where Kabarega then had his capital. Baker's hopes were concentrated on Bunyoro as through lack of time he had reluctantly renounced his plan of visiting Buganda. These hopes were based on the belief, which he shared with Speke, that Kabarega would welcome the opening of trade and on the fact that during his previous visit he had successfully protected Kamrasi against an attack by de Bono's soldiers. He hoped in particular to enlist Kabarega's aid in opening up the river route to Lake Albert and in launching the steamer.

Baker soon discovered, however, that Kabarega was interested solely in the possibility of an alliance against his rival, Rionga. In agreeing to this alliance[3] he was again forced to accept the methods of his trading predecessors and renounce the aloof rôle befitting his civilizing mission. But even this agreement to fight

[1] On the stations themselves there were of course also numerous interpreters—youths or women who had been captured and now enjoyed an established position amongst their captors—but these had severed their links with the tribal communities and their influence was therefore of a totally different nature to the tribal interpreters.

[2] J.B. MS. 2—11/IV/72.

[3] J.B. MS. 28/IV/72 and 12/V/72 reveal that Baker was more deeply committed to offensive action against Rionga than he cares to admit in *Ismailia* vol. ii, pp. 221–2, 370.

Rionga failed to allay Kabarega's distrust of his intentions. The situation steadily deteriorated and Baker with his small force found himself surrounded by a hostile and powerful population. The climax came when Kabarega, following an attempt on the part of Julian Baker to conduct military manoeuvres in Masindi, nearly succeeded in poisoning the entire expedition. Setting fire to Masindi, Baker conducted a fighting retreat and against great odds succeeded in reaching Fatiko on 2 August 1872 with remarkably few losses. Immediately on his arrival he was greeted with an armed rebellion of Abū Su'ūd's irregulars who were suppressed only after a pitched battle in which 141 of them were killed.[1]

Entrenched at Fatiko Baker attempted to salvage something from the wreck of his grand design. The veteran vakil, Wad al-Mak,[2] although a ringleader in the rebellion against Baker, was pardoned and enrolled in Government service together with about 300 other Arabs, who chose this course rather than the alternative of flight to Khartoum in company with Abū Su'ūd.[3] Detachments of this motley band were ordered to conquer Bunyoro for Rionga with whom an alliance had been made during the retreat from Masindi. A strong fort was built at Fatiko, and the surrounding Acholi agreed to supply the garrison with corn. Meanwhile messengers arrived from Mutesa requesting Baker to visit Buganda or at least to send a representative. Some of these messengers gave Baker the impression that they considered Lake Tanganyika to be merely a continuation of Lake Albert, thus vastly extending the possible limits of Ismā'īl's empire once a steamer should be launched on the Albert Nile.[4]

From these facts and fancies and from his successful survival through so many difficulties and dangers, Baker, on his return to Gondokoro, was able to distil a jubilant and enthusiastic account of his expedition. 'All obstacles have been surmounted. All enemies have been subdued—and the slavers who had the audacity

---

[1] S. W. Baker, 'Experience in Savage Warfare', *J. Roy. United Service Inst.*, 1873 and *Ismailia*, vol. ii, pp. 200–97.

[2] See above, p. 57.

[3] Later Baker wrote to his successor, 'I think you will find Wat-el-Mek and Suleiman useful, at the same time they are great ruffians, and you must keep a tight hand over them lest they relapse into their old habits of kidnapping girls.' G. MSS. Baker to Gordon, 8/VII/74.

[4] This impression was due to the use of the name 'Mwita Nzige' for Lake Edward as well as Lake Albert.

to attack the troops have been crushed. The slave trade of the White
Nile has been suppressed—and the country annexed, so that Egypt
extends to the equator.'[1] Lady Baker added that 'after great
difficulties and trials we have conquered and established a good
Government throughout the country'.[2] A report in similar vein
was submitted to Ismā'īl, who, according to Baker was 'very hot
about his new territory',[3] and Baker's triumphant saga made a
deep impression in England.[4] The reality was not nearly so impressive. Bunyoro and Buganda were far from being annexed to
Egypt, and in the area under nominal control few fundamental
changes had been achieved. Baker later admitted to his successor
that at Fatiko it was 'simply impossible' to procure sheep or cattle
'either by taxation, or by purchase', and that the Acholi 'were still
in hopes that the old custom might be renewed when ivory would
be purchased in exchange for cattle' taken in razzias from the
neighbouring Lango—a custom which was in fact revived as soon as
Baker left the country.[5] At Gondokoro, although Alloron had
become an ally of the Government, amongst the rest of the Bari
cattle razzias continued uninterruptedly. Baker himself, during
his time at Fatiko, ordered Wad al-Mak 'to go on to Ismailia
(Gondokoro) order Raouf Bey to make constant razzias, and come
back at once with the post and the captured cattle'.[6]

Virtually all that Baker had accomplished was to effect the transfer of nominal sovereignty from Abū Su'ūd to the Government.
Control over the scattered stations remained extremely slight; the
few neighbouring village communities, isolated from the rest of
their tribes and to some extent integrated with the traders'
stations, accepted the new alliance, but beyond them hostile and
violent relationships continued unchanged. It was calculated that
over £1 million had been spent on the expedition,[7] and Baker

---

[1] B. MSS. S.W.B. to John Baker, 20/V/73.
[2] B. MSS. Lady Baker to Edith, 29/VI/73.
[3] Ibid., S.W.B. to John Baker, 3/IX/73 and F.O. 84/1371. Vivian to Granville,
6/IX/73 enclosing copy of a part of Baker's report.
[4] See below, Chapter VI.
[5] G. MSS. Baker to Gordon, 27/X/74 & 8/VII/75.
[6] J.B. MS. 14/XI/72. Wad al-Mak returned with the report that 'after several razzias in which they took about 3,000 cattle besides sheep and goats Raouf
Bey refused to give him any cattle to bring here telling him he must take cattle
on the road,' ibid., 8/III/73. On Baker's arrival at Gondokoro several razzias
were undertaken against Belinian, ibid. 18 & 20/IV/73.
[7] O.S. Ad. Reg. 34/111 Hansal to Ritter von Cischini, 28/XII/73.

himself received over £40,000 which was almost certainly a far greater net profit than that gained by any of the European merchants who had preceded him.[1] Against this enormous expense could be set only the considerable hoards of ivory confiscated from Abū Su'ūd, that at Fatiko being estimated by Baker at 1500 kantars worth at Cairo possibly £50,000,[2] and the fact that the steamers and supplies taken by Baker to Gondokoro continued to form a large part of the material basis of the administration throughout the remaining years of Egyptian rule in Equatoria. This discrepancy between expenditure and returns, between hopes and achievements, between reports and reality, was due partly to the obstruction of the White Nile, partly to the unenthusiastic co-operation of many of his subordinates, and partly to his own impatience and ready recourse to force. But added to this was the fact that with the Bari, with Abū Su'ūd's irregulars, and with Kabarega, Baker was confronted with situations in which the creation of a 'legitimate commerce' and the foundation of a powerful and widely recognized administration involved problems of a far more complex nature than his previous analysis had led him to believe. These problems remained to greet his successor.

3. Gordon's administration, 1873–1876

Before he was appointed by Ismā'īl to be Governor-General of 'Equatoria', Gordon had had no connections with Africa. The incredible campaigns by which, as a young captain in the Royal Engineers on loan to the Emperor of China, he defeated the Taiping rebellion in 1864 and at the same time became a national figure, had been followed by a period of almost complete obscurity at Gravesend, where he constructed forts for the War Office and deepened his highly unconventional evangelical mysticism. From there he was despatched as a Colonel to an almost equally unimportant post on a Danube International Commission, and it was at Constantinople in 1872 that Nubar Pasha, one of Ismā'īl's leading statesmen, asked him if he could recommend an Engineer Officer to succeed Baker. This overture was followed shortly after Baker's return to Cairo with a firm offer which Gordon accepted by 5 September

[1] B. MSS. S.W.B. to John Baker, 29/V/73.
[2] Ibid.

1873.[1] For diplomatic reasons Ismā'īl was ready to appoint a British subject to succeed Baker,[2] and he congratulated himself on obtaining someone with Gordon's reputation and capabilities, while since Gordon's ignorance of the Sudan and tropical Africa was equalled by most of his contemporaries this did not seem to be a serious handicap.

Gordon's attitude to his task differed considerably from that of his predecessor. Unlike Baker he nourished no comprehensive plans for development, but brought with him a pacific pragmatism and a deep reluctance to use force. Whereas Baker had proudly informed the Khedive that the latter could confidently expect his empire to expand like the British in India, Gordon the introvert found himself wondering what was the ultimate use of India to the British, and his detachment enabled him eventually to perceive more clearly the real nature of the social processes taking place in the area under his command.[3] This insight developed only in the disillusion induced by the disappointments of experience, and at first he eagerly accepted the chance 'to fight the slave trade' and to find the active service that the Army denied him. He revealed to a friend his attitude and his limited objectives in the following terms:

> An operation had to be formed viz. the connection of two southern Egyptian posts with the northern posts. I considered that with God's will, I could accomplish this with less pain to the natives than Arabs would, and therefore took this place. But beyond being civilized in my operations and making allowance for these virgin tribes, this is no mission of humanity.[4]

[1] Douin, vol. III (iiia), p. 3. This volume by Douin is almost certainly as complete an account of Gordon's years in Equatoria as will ever be written. Of the other multitudinous books B. M. Allen, *Gordon and the Sudan*, 1931, and H. E. Wortham, *Gordon an Intimate Portrait*, 1933, are among the most useful, while Lytton Strachey despite the tendentious falsifications is still not without interest. See also M. F. Shukry, *Equatoria under Egyptian Rule. The unpublished correspondence of Colonel C. G. Gordon with Ismail Khedive of Egypt and the Sudan during the years* 1874–6. With introduction and notes, Cairo, 1953.

[2] 'His Highness', wrote the British Consul-General reporting Ismā'īl's wish to appoint Gordon, 'hopes H.M.G. will see in this proof of his determination to organise the Government of the Country thoroughly and to suppress the slave trade; and that they will give their consent and assist in securing Gordon's services', F.O. 84/1371 Vivian to Granville, 30/VIII/73.

[3] F.O. 84/1371. Copy of Baker's report, enclosed in Vivian to Granville 16/X/73; G. MSS. G. to Augusta.

[4] W. MSS. Gordon to Waller, 29/1/75.

It was, however, an undertaking of considerable significance at a time when European interest in the Nile Valley and East Africa was beginning quickly to increase. The opening of the Suez Canal in 1869 enormously enhanced the strategic importance of North-East Africa, and at the same time British public concern over the Arab slave trade led in 1871 to a Parliamentary Select Committee on the East African slave trade and a consequent policy of active intervention at Zanzibar.[1] The White Nile was still the principal and obvious route into the fertile interior of equatorial Africa, and Baker's expedition aroused great interest in the United Kingdom where it was seen as an example and a challenge.[2] But for the moment, with her early start, Egypt retained the initiative and the future colonization of eastern equatorial Africa was still largely dependent on Gordon's attempt to consolidate and expand her power.

Gordon did not encounter the physical obstacle which had so greatly frustrated Baker's plans. Shortly before his arrival at Khartoum on 13 March 1874, the news was received that the sudd barrier on the White Nile had been removed after months of labour on the part of hundreds of soldiers, at one time working under the personal direction of Ismā'īl Aiyūb, the new Governor-General. It was an achievement which, as Gordon reported to Nubar Pasha, 'has, in fact, restored these provinces to His Highness',[3] and it enabled him to make a lightning visit to Gondokoro. There he discovered a collection of straw huts housing a garrison whose authority was confined to the radius of half a mile, beyond which it was quite impossible to venture unarmed. In the ten months since Baker's departure no improvements had been attempted, and, although Gordon found Ra'ūf and his 300 troops in good order, it was significant that their principal request was for a large increase of forces. His first impressions were those of almost complete disillusionment: government, security and revenue were non-existent, and the only Egyptian possessions in his provinces were the 'forts' at Gondokoro and Fatiko. As he returned to Khartoum, he wrote of 'such misery in these parts—poor creatures nearly

[1] See below, chapter VI.
[2] Ibid.
[3] *Provinces of the Equator. Summary of letters and reports of H.E. the Governor General, Part I, Year 1874*, publications of the Egyptian General Staff, Cairo, 1877, p. 5. Gordon to Nubar Pasha, s.d. Subsequently referred to as *Provinces of the Equator*.

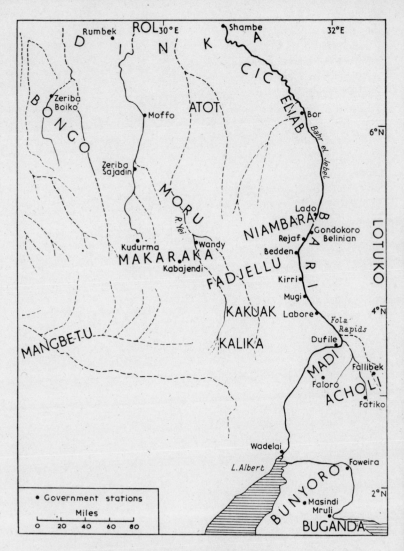

Map 6. THE PROVINCE OF EQUATORIA 1869–1889

(from Petermann's Mitteilungen 1880 Tafel 4)

skeletons . . . it would be an improvement to transport the whole lot and make them work in a more hospitable clime'.[1]

He hurried to Berber to quicken the arrival of the European members of his staff together with reinforcements, had a skirmish at Khartoum with the Governor-General over finance and their relative spheres of command, and, spending ten weeks establishing a station at the mouth of the Sobat, he did not return to Gondokoro until September. The delay was justified by the necessity of eradicating the slave-trading on the Bahr el Zeraf, and by the opportunity which it afforded for him to become mentally and physically acclimatized to his new surroundings. As a result of his experience here he suspected, even before reading Schweinfurth's book, that the overland route from the Bahr el Ghazal was of far greater importance to the slave trader than the river route, and he soon realized that the slave trade was a minor factor in Equatoria.[2]

Yet, however justifiable, the delay was unfortunate as it prevented Gordon from pressing on with his primary objective of opening up Lake Albert and the route to Buganda. Baker had briefed him on the importance of launching a steamer on Lake Albert as an essential means of introducing a legitimate trade, and Ismā'īl stressed the necessity of secure communications with Mutesa which would capture for Egypt the ivory trade 'at present almost entirely directed through Zanzibar'.[3] Gordon hastened, therefore, to turn to the task of transporting the steamer to the Albert Nile. By the end of September, Kemp his chief engineer, together with 500 Makaraka porters was despatched with some sections of the steamer and was ordered to found a station at Dufile, a village on the west bank above the Fola Rapids.[4] In a few weeks Kemp returned successfully, but Gordon was unwilling to undertake a rapid advance on the Equatorial Kingdoms without first securing his lines of communication. Movement between Gondokoro and Fatiko was dependent on the chance arrival of a caravan from the Acholi station or the equally uncertain expedient of obtaining porters from the Bari or the trading stations among the Makaraka;

---

[1] W. MSS. Gordon to Waller, 10/IV/74; G. B. Hill (ed.), *Colonel Gordon in Central Africa, 1874–1879*, p. 15. This is a collection of extracts of the voluminous correspondence carried on between Gordon and his sister, Augusta; the originals are in G. MSS.

[2] W. MSS. Gordon to Waller, 18/V/74.

[3] G. MSS. Ismā'īl to Gordon, 4/II/75. See also Baker to Gordon, 27/X/74.

[4] Douin, vol. III (iiia), p. 81.

until small groups of eight or ten men could move freely along this central highway there was no likelihood of extending Egyptian rule to the equator. In addition to this, no one had ever accomplished a complete survey of the river between Gondokoro and Dufile, and Gordon hoped that navigation might be possible at least between the cataracts thus obviating the necessity for 'enormous marauding caravans' to traverse the country.[1] He decided therefore to form a line of stations along the river and later to attempt to transport the heavier parts of the steamer by sailing boat through the cataracts.

The operation involved a closer contact with the Bari. At Gondokoro the alliance with Alloron, commenced by Ra'ūf while Baker was in the south, had become cemented to such a degree that the chief was in the habit of making daily visits to the camp. He had persuaded as many as twenty other headmen to make their submission, and he proved a reliable source of information regarding the intentions of the formidable Lokoya tribe. This was however but a minute achievement. It was still extremely difficult to obtain any services from the Bari in the immediate neighbourhood and those at Belinian remained aloof.[2] Anxious to spread more widely the net of control and to secure a somewhat less swampy and malarious situation for his principal base, Gordon established two stations on the west bank: Lado, a few miles north of Gondokoro, destined to become the Provincial headquarters and in the 20th century to give its name to the whole area under Belgian control, was laid out on the pattern of an Indian cantonment, with short yet broad and straight streets and shady trees; and to the south, below the conical volcanic hill of Rejaf a cluster of mud and straw huts, impregnably defended by a ditch and a cannon, proclaimed the intrusion of the imperial factor. At first it proved to be a firm yet equitable intrusion. A headman who persisted in raiding the cattle of a friendly tribe found himself exiled to Khartoum for a few months. Then, as Gordon proceeded to found stations further to the south, force in the shape of a cattle razzia was used to convince Bedden, Baker's protagonist, and a few other headmen of the need to submit; but mercy, which was demonstrated in the return of some cows, in the gift of a few presents and in a chance personal encounter between Gordon and Bedden,

[1] G. MSS. Gordon to Augusta, 7/V/75.
[2] G. MSS. Gessi to Gordon, 21 and 25/IX/74.

succeeded in removing bitterness and in establishing at least a
basis for future confidence.[1]

By July 1875 it was possible for an individual to travel alone to
Bedden or Kirri;[2] the marauding caravans, with their escorts and
pilfering, were no longer necessary; the news was spreading
amongst 'virgin tribes' that the intruders were not to be feared;
the Bari could obtain recompense for injuries; and even the
soldiers saw 'the great advantage' of no longer having to fear
'every bit of high grass'.[3] Gordon started to introduce a copper
currency and, although his hope that this innovation would destroy
'the feudal system of chiefs' by letting 'their subjects see that they
can stand on their own feet' displays an inadequate understanding
of Bari society, some measure of his far-reaching success in momentarily creating a completely fresh pattern of relationships can be
gained from the fact that he started to obtain ivory by this means.[4]
The policy of a patient and gradual extension of sovereignty, of
justice and confidence preceding taxation,[5] was beginning to yield
its dividends, but Gordon was not ubiquitous and the advance to
the south could be delayed no longer.

This advance was a time of strain and disappointment. After
a satisfactory reconnaissance of the river as far as Kirri, Gordon
was told by a veteran Dongolawi that during a high Nile previous
travellers had succeeded in taking small boats through the cataracts
of Bedden and of Gougi.[6] This was encouraging news yet it was a
far harder task to edge the heavily laden 40 ton nuggers[7] through
the rapids with the aid of obstreperous Bari on the end of improvised
and constantly breaking ropes, supervised by none too capable or
enthusiastic Arab soldiers; and it was only at the cost of mental
and physical exhaustion and the loss of a few boats that Gordon
managed to get the convoy of nuggers and a screw-steamer through
to Labore by the beginning of October. Little more than twenty
miles of uncharted waters separated him from Dufile and the

[1] Douin, vol. III (iiia), pp. 105–217.
[2] See map no. 6.
[3] G. B. Hill, pp. 85–90.
[4] Ibid. pp. 49–51. Linant was also instructed to introduce a copper currency during his visit to the southern stations; Douin, vol. III (iiia), p. 160.
[5] In a letter to Kharif Pasha Gordon urged the necessity for patience; Douin, vol. III (iiia), p. 194.
[6] Douin, vol. III (iiia), p. 192.
[7] Large broad-beamed boat used on the Upper Nile.

navigable Albert Nile, and with a small body of men Gordon
pressed forward to survey the final obstacle in the river. The Fola
Rapids had been seen by no previous European travellers, and
from the conflicting local reports Gordon had been led to hope
that they would prove no more formidable than the Bedden or
Gougi rapids; but on 17 October, standing on a precipitous
rocky bank he looked down on a two-mile stretch where
the massive river, suddenly contracted into two channels of
fifteen and twenty yards wide, 'boiled down, twisting into all
sorts of eddies', cascading over a slope of one-in-six. The
dream of a navigable, if difficult, highway stretching from
the Mediterranean to Lake Albert had vanished. At the same
time almost as bitter a disappointment was provided by the
attitude of the tribes.

As he moved southwards from Kirri, Gordon had encountered
'shy and unknown tribes'—the southernmost sections of the Bari—
and on 10 August, after he had lost a nuggar while negotiating the
Gougi rapids, these Bari, although supplied with numerous
presents, seeing his difficulties ceased to help him and became
openly hostile. After a few tense days in which Gordon had
decided to undertake razzias against them, they became apparently
compliant as resistance was impossible since they were hemmed in
between the river and mountains inhabited by rival tribes only
eight miles to the west. 'So we are all now friends again, and they
will not have the cow-tax levied on them. I am very glad of it, for
it was merely ignorance that actuated them.'[1] Yet Gordon was
wrong in thinking that their hostility was based on mere ignorance
rather than the bitter lessons of past experience. On the east bank
opposite stretched the lands of the Moogie section of the Bari;
it was an area through which the traders' caravans had plundered
their way to the south, and although Baker had found some of
their headmen co-operative as his expedition struggled southwards,
his men while bringing reinforcements to Fatiko had 'shamefully
attacked and burnt numerous villages simply because some of his
carriers ran away'. The Moogie, however, had managed to kill
twenty-eight soldiers and two interpreters, and, embittered by the
Government's attack yet elated by the casualties they inflicted in
return, they had subsequently harrassed the caravans passing

1 G. MSS. Gordon to Augusta, 10–14/VIII/75.

through their territory, and they had infected their neighbours on the west bank with this hostile attitude.[1]

A few days after their apparent submission to Gordon open hostility broke out afresh, and for more than a week there was fighting on both banks. It culminated in a catastrophe on 4 August, when a detachment of over forty men was completely defeated by the Moogie and all save four were killed, including their leader Linant de Bellefonds, the younger son of the distinguished French engineer and explorer,[2] who had recently returned from a visit to Buganda. It was a serious set-back, devastating to the morale of the soldiers, and had the river not prevented the Moogie from following up their success, Gordon considered that his whole force would have been destroyed.[3] Confronted with this legacy of bitterness, Gordon was forced to use the methods of his predecessors. With the arrival of reinforcements from Makaraka and Fatiko, repeated 'taxations' of the recalcitrant tribes took place; on the west bank Gordon succeeded in establishing some degree of order, but on the east the Moogie remained hostile, though more cautious.[4]

As Gordon advanced yet further southwards to complete the line of stations to Dufile he found himself faced with the hopeless problem of finding provisions. He was far from his base, with the months slipping by; patience became impracticable, he was driven to accept the razzia system. From Labore on 24 September he wrote:

> Here is a stretch of conscience: when we got here, the natives who were friendly could not sell or would not sell us Dhorra. There was a *rather* hostile (not very hostile) sheik near us and so I sent and took the Dhorra from him. This is fearful work for me, but what can I do. I must either throw up the whole matter and come down or else do this.[5]

These difficulties persisted. Threats of seizing corn and removing villages were needed to procure porters,[6] raids continued to be

---

[1] G. MSS. Baker to Gordon, 29/VIII/74. Long reported that on his way to Buganda in April 1874 there were 3–4000 hostile Moogie on his flanks; Chaillé-Long, op. cit., p. 40. Linant also experienced their hostility; Douin, vol. III (iiia), p. 161.

[2] See above, p. 8.

[3] G. MSS. Gordon to Augusta, 29/VIII/75 and G. B. Hill, pp. 106–12.

[4] Douin, vol. III (iiia), p. 264.

[5] G. MSS. Gordon to Augusta, 24/IX/75 (his italics).

[6] Ibid. 3/I/76, 23/II/76.

carried out on chiefs who neglected conciliatory efforts and refused to co-operate, and on occasions these raids were undertaken not primarily for security reasons: 'Yesterday forced by the want of cows, I had to make a razzia on a tribe near here and took 140 cows. They were certainly *semi*-hostile, but it is no excuse'.[1] He finally came to regard Labore and Kirri as 'main stations' since 'they possess passages across the river and enable raids to be made on the East bank where a vast extent of country exists' belonging to the unsubdued Moogie.[2] The chain of stations was successfully forged but he had failed to solve the more fundamental problem of creating fresh and peaceful relationships between the invaders and the indigenous people.

In the light of the successive disappointments caused by the Fola Rapids, the imbedded hostility of the southern Bari sections and the difficulties of procuring supplies by commercial intercourse, Gordon gained a deeper insight into the activity in which he found himself engaged; and with his habit of introversion and contemplation he clearly realized that the problems would not be solved in terms of western civilization. His failure, like that of Baker and that of his successors, to establish a widely recognized system of 'justice', legalized taxation and an ordered economic development was fundamentally due to the fact that despite the restless activity of these Europeans they were ultimately little more than spectators of a social process over which they exerted but little influence.

> As far as Dufile and I may say Magungo the roads are safe, and I can do nothing more, for I cannot govern not knowing the language, and even if I did, I could not expect to change the habits of the officers etc. or of the natives. I feel it would be better for them to work out the problem of how to live together by themselves. I look upon any improvement in either as being quite hopeless, and at any rate, I do not see how in any way, I can better either parties by a longer stay.[3]

The slow-moving, often indolent and sometimes inefficient inmates of the stations were, as a permanent factor, of far greater potential significance than the hustling, competent, energetic Europeans. As he described to a friend the process by which around

[1] Ibid. 2/II/76, 2/IV/76 (his italics).
[2] Ibid. 16/IV/76.
[3] Ibid. 10/IV/76.

the stations there grew up 'a semi-native semi-arab by contact population of lads and women' who came to work for the soldiers but, finding the station 'much more amusing than their native houses', refused to be repatriated,[1] as he realized that 'the natives who may be called slaves come and go with respect to their masters as they like' and even felt that they were 'a trifle too independent' since they demanded to be enrolled as soldiers declining his offer of equal pay if they would act as porters,[2] as he encountered an example of a whole village, many of whose inhabitants were Arabic speaking, moving into the neighbourhood of a station,[3] and as he watched the inevitable string of Acholi, Bari, or Madi wives everywhere accompanying the soldiers, he came to the firm belief that 'no nation could uproot Egypt from these lands even if they possessed them. Arabic must be the language of these countries'.[4]

It was natural that a European would have little influence over this process of biological adaptation, of acculturation by intimate contact, and his intervention in the internal affairs of these station communities was very restricted; but it was frustrating to discover that, besides this limitation, he had no widespread control over the looser contacts which the stations continued to form with the surrounding tribal societies. This lack of control was due partly to technological restrictions, partly to the attitude of his officials, and partly to his dependence on the Danaqla settlers. Firearms, together with cannons, rockets and the use of river transport were sufficient to give the Egyptian forces a substantial technical supremacy over the surrounding African communities, although the massacre of Linant's detachment demonstrated how precarious this could be in certain circumstances. But the technological advances which in the next fifty years were to revolutionize the problems of communication and control had yet to be made, and contemporaries accepted Livingstone's opinion that the problem of introducing Western civilization could be solved only by the aid and example of scattered European settlements.

Gordon was forced therefore to rely on his subordinates to a very large extent; and, since those of his European staff who were not incapacitated through illness were fully engaged on missions to

---

[1] W. MSS. Gordon to Waller, 29/I/75.
[2] A.S.S. MSS. Gordon to the Secretary, 9/III/75.
[3] G. MSS. Gordon to Augusta, 23/II/76.
[4] Ibid. 22/X/75.

Buganda, on provincial affairs at Khartoum, or later on an
exploration of Lake Albert, this meant in effect a reliance upon his
Egyptian and Sudanese officials. Some of these were experienced
army officers who had rendered distinguished services with an
expeditionary force sent by Ismā'īl to aid the French in Mexico,
and one of them, Nūr Bey, earned Gordon's unstinted praise.[1]
Others, however, were political exiles; most of the officers loathed
the virtual banishment which their appointment entailed; and with
their completely different cultural background few had any
sympathy with the concept of fostering economic development or
of establishing a system of justice over the pagan tribes beyond the
immediate bounds of the station communities. The governor of
Dufile was dismissed for ill treating two interpreters, which,
Gordon wrote, 'undoes all my work for weeks, for these interpreters have great influence in persuading or disuading the natives
from carrying'.[2] Even a 'good officer with no evil intention'
attempted to obtain ivory by force, and although they possessed
plentiful supplies of copper and other trading goods they made no
effort to start commercial intercourse.[3] The officers in charge of
outlying stations would 'never write what we would call reports'.[4]
Even close at hand there was the constant danger of disobedience
so that 'the whole affair' was 'like walking on rotten ice', and in
despair Gordon concluded that the soldiers 'are about as likely to
civilise these parts as they are to civilise the moon'.[5]

In addition to these disadvantages Gordon was deeply dependent
on the Danaqla. Thoroughly acclimatized, these northern Arabs
alone had an intimate knowledge of the area and its peoples, and
with his complete ignorance of the country Gordon relied on their
experience and co-operation to a much greater extent than Baker.
He had in fact, despite Baker's annoyance, taken Abū Su'ūd into
his service, and had gleaned a great deal of useful information before
dismissing him in November 1874 when it was clear that he was
more of a liability than an asset;[6] while although in January 1875

[1] G. B. Hill, p. 119.
[2] G. MSS. Gordon to Augusta, 3/XI/75. A few days later at Labore he discovered that 'natives had left the neighbourhood through the Mudir bullying
them. Sent off Mudir;' ibid., 20/XI/75.
[3] Douin, vol. III (iiia), p. 241.
[4] G. MSS. Gordon to Augusta, 10/IV/76.
[5] G. B. Hill, p. 123, and p. 139.
[6] Douin, vol. III (iiia), pp. 69–89.

he was furious when he learnt indirectly that Wad al-Mak had recently hung a chief for not supplying him with porters, by September he had forgiven the murderer since he found him 'so very useful'.[1]

Vast areas remained virtually under Danaqla rule. At the important river stations of Shambe[2] and Bor only a token force of ten or twenty regular soldiers supported the activities of several hundred Danaqla who ranged over the rich hinterlands of the Rohl and the Lotuko. On the one occasion when the fertile area of the Makaraka with its thriving and unruly settlements was visited by a European official, he had shots fired through his tent during the night, discovered 3–400 young girls in one zeriba, and recorded that the 600 porters engaged to carry ivory to Lado 'made a fight with the Yambari (Nyangbara) a condition of their service'.[3] At the end of November 1874 Gordon reported that in six of the eleven government stations stretching from the Sobat to Foweira the regular troops were heavily out-numbered by Danaqla;[4] and although, faced with numerous reports of their lawlessness, he was convinced as early as October of the necessity 'of clearing this country of Dongolese', he never succeeded in accomplishing this task. Instead, despite their ingrained independence, they were inevitably accepted as allies, and, virtually unsupervised in many districts, they continued to 'trade' and rule by their former violent methods.[5]

These reflections and disappointments increased Gordon's impatience to open a route to the Equatorial Lakes and so to be able to return rapidly with a clear conscience from a task which was becoming increasingly uncongenial. His efforts to ameliorate the lot of the Bari, Makaraka, Madi, and Acholi, although an essential preliminary to a permanent Egyptian annexation of Equatoria,

[1] He added 'it is very bad I own, but he is an old black and knows the country perfectly' G. MSS. Gordon to Augusta, 8/IX/75, and G. B. Hill, p. 67.

[2] Ghaba Sciambil, De Malzac's former station.

[3] C. Chaillé-Long, Central Africa ... expeditions to the Lake Victoria and the Makraka Niam-Niam, 1876, pp. 257–70. E. Marno, Reise in der Egyptischen Aequatorial-Provinz und in Kordofan, Vienna, 1878, pp. 68–147. A few months later, when confronted with reports of disorders among the Makaraka, Gordon despairingly confessed that with the troops at his disposal it was quite impossible to interfere or risk a war with 'the fierce and warlike Niam-Niam', G. MSS. Gordon to Augusta, 7/IX/75.

[4] Provinces of the Equator, p. 32. Gordon to Nubar Pasha, Nov. '74.

[5] Ibid., p. 27. Gordon to Nubar Pasha 18/X/74.

represented but a minor portion of the great design. The gal-
vanizing impulse behind Ismā'īl's intervention in the basin of the
Upper Nile had been the explorers' accounts of the Equatorial
Kingdoms; it was their trade which was to justify the enormous
expenditure; it was their power and position which was to give
Egypt a permanent ascendancy in Central Africa; and, although
the full implications of this were not at that date realized, it was
their occupation which was to secure for Egypt the headwaters of
the Nile. 'The lawlessness of certain Bari tribes ... utterly
demoralized by the ivory traders' had from the first appeared
merely as a hindrance to the attainment of these ultimate objectives,
and by the beginning of 1876, with the completion of the chain of
stations from Lado to Dufile, this obstacle had been overcome to
a sufficient extent to enable Gordon to concentrate his whole
attention on the Equatorial Kingdoms.

Baker, it will be remembered, before he left Fatiko, had despatched a force of Danaqla and a few regular soldiers to assist
Rionga in the conquest of Bunyoro. The first reports showed an
apparently satisfactory advance on Masindi, but the defence in
depth, which was maintained by this comparatively well-organized
state, easily absorbed the impact of this attack, and when Gordon
arrived at Gondokoro in 1874 it was reported that Kabarega was
fully reinstated in power. He decided therefore to take no immediate
action against Bunyoro, especially as on his arrival at Gondokoro
he was greeted by emissaries from Mutesa. It seemed an admirable
opportunity to open negotiations which would lead, by peaceful
methods if possible, to an eventual recognition of Egyptian
sovereignty over Buganda. Gordon immediately entrusted
Chaillé-Long, an American officer on his staff, with the task of
accompanying the emissaries on their return journey, and confidently awaited the unfolding of future developments.[1]

In Mutesa, however, he was confronted with an African ruler
who combined the inherited political wisdom of an ancient and
firmly established dynasty with a remarkably acute appreciation
of the role which diplomacy and evasion could play in the task of
protecting the independence of his country. This appreciation was
partly derived from the stimulus of contact with Arab traders from
Zanzibar, who had been arriving in Buganda intermittently since
c. 1840 and whose presence materially contributed to Mutesa's

---

[1] Douin, vol. III (iiia), pp. 26–29.

successful opposition to the Egyptian advances. Numerically weak, yet commercially strong, these traders constituted no threat to the independence of Buganda but were content to gain their profits by supplying the rulers with firearms and trade goods in return for ivory and slaves. With these allies Buganda rapidly increased its power while Bunyoro, less favourably placed to profit by these opportunities, dissipated its strength under the impact of 'Aqqād's and de Bono's companies and Baker's invasion. Warned by his neighbour's fate Mutesa gave a hostile reception to some of 'Aqqād's emissaries, attempted to enter into an alliance with the Sultan of Zanzibar, and during Baker's conflict with Kabarega mobilized a powerful army. The apparently friendly envoys sent to meet Gordon on his arrival were therefore little more than spies despatched to report on the movements and strength of this alien intruder.[1]

Precautions, and this initial advantage as compared with Bunyoro, would have been of little value, however, had Gordon ever been in a position to support his demands by overwhelming force. Instead he always found himself at a disadvantage. Chaillé-Long, his first envoy, accompanied only by two Sudanese sergeants, was ill for the greater part of his stay at Rubaga, Mutesa's capital, and barely escaped with his life on the return journey.[2] Linant de Bellefonds, despatched shortly after Chaillé-Long's return, arrived with a small force at Rubaga in April 1875 only to discover that the explorer Stanley had arrived from Zanzibar five days previously on the journey which was to take him to the mouth of the Congo. Mutesa, astutely enlisting Stanley as an ally, was able to prevaricate before Linant's request for a treaty recognising Egyptian sovereignty, and the latter returned to Gordon carrying only an appeal by Stanley addressed to the British public for Christian missionaries.[3] The answer to this appeal was later to strengthen Mutesa against the Egyptian advance by bringing diplomatic intervention in his favour and it led eventually to the British occupation of Buganda,[4] but these results lay in the future, and for the remainder

---

[1] Sir J. M. Gray, 'Mutesa of Buganda', *Uganda J.*, 1934. Gordon himself later realized this fact; 'Mutesa sends a lot of men down and they eat the Dura which is scarce; in fact he sends down to hear the news and get presents', G. MSS. Gordon to Augusta, 21/I/75.

[2] Chaillé-Long's itinerary and report were published in *Provinces of the Equator*, pp. 37–80. See also Douin, vol. III (iiia), p. 89. ff.

[3] Douin, vol. III (iiia), pp. 156–87.   [4] See below, Chapter VI.

of Gordon's rule in Equatoria the outcome of the struggle for
ascendancy over the sources of the Nile depended solely on the
relative local strength of Egypt and Buganda.

In January 1876 Gordon, determined as has been seen to complete his task, paid a rapid visit to Foweira and, continuing
southwards, reinstated Rionga at Mrouli. Still uncertain of
Mutesa's attitude, Gordon entrusted Nūr Bey with the task of
negotiating an agreement whereby Egyptian troops would occupy
two posts on the Victoria Nile and Lake Victoria, while he returned
to Dufile to collect reinforcements and to hasten the exploration of
Lake Albert. The next news received from Buganda was brought
in a letter from Nūr Bey jubilantly announcing that, at Mutesa's
request, he had established his force at the capital, Rubaga. This
astounding turn of events seemed to have solved at one step the
whole intractable problem of a peaceful extension of Egyptian
sovereignty, and Gordon triumphantly informed the Khedive of the
annexation of Buganda. It was only when he reached Foweira
again in August that this satisfaction was shattered. News from
Rubaga revealed that far from annexing the country, Nūr Bey
had been duped into a position where his force, severed from all
supplies and surrounded by a dense population, had been rendered
completely impotent and dependent for its survival on the good
will of Mutesa. With the restricted resources remaining to him, it
was impossible for Gordon to attempt an immediate trial of force
with Mutesa, so, making arrangements for a withdrawal to Mrouli,
he turned northwards and reached Lado on 11 October.[1]

At the time this withdrawal seemed to be merely a temporary
set-back. Gordon had written earlier suggesting that a young
American officer should succeed him, but he was still uncertain
whether he himself would return or not. In either case he felt that
a further two years would suffice to launch steamers on the Victoria
Nile and Lake Victoria, to arrive at some definitive understanding
with Mutesa, to complete the exploration of the area and thus to
establish Egyptian rule permanently over the sources of the Nile.[2]
In the three years of his tenure of office, save for a brief period at
Lado and Rejaf, very little progress had been accomplished
towards solving the vast and complex problem of introducing
legitimate commerce. But he hoped that within two years the pro-

---

[1] Douin, vol. III (iiia), pp. 267–338.
[2] G. MSS. Gordon to Augusta, 20/VIII/76.

cess of pacification would be sufficiently advanced to permit
private traders to undertake commercial activities under a powerful
and adequate supervision,[1] while although the exploration of Lake
Albert, undertaken by his adjutant Gessi in an open steel lifeboat,
had reduced the immense stretch of water envisaged by Baker to
its relatively small proportions, its navigation nevertheless opened
up considerable commercial possibilities. The initial capital outlay
had represented an enormous burden which Egypt could ill afford,
but under Gordon's control the revenue of the area began to overtake the costs of administration.[2] On Gordon's return it seemed
therefore that Baker's and his combined efforts had laid the
foundations of an alien imperial hegemony in the heart of tropical
Africa, and their example, unique at that moment, had a considerable impact upon European contemporaries.[3] Egypt, however,
had missed her opportunity. The failure in these early years to
conquer the Equatorial Kingdoms and to consolidate her initial
advance was to prove decisive. Stanley's arrival in Buganda was
representative of the increasing European interest in the interior
of East Africa and in the Lacustrine Kingdoms in particular,[4]
while in the succeeding years the problems arising in other areas
of Ismā'īl's empire prevented any significant and permanent
development of the Egyptian foundations in Equatoria. To these
problems we must now turn our attention.

[1] He suggested that approaches should be made to Aqqād and to Zanzibar
traders in Buganda, Douin, vol. III (iiia), pp. 296, 330.
[2] Ibid. pp. 256–9.
[3] See below, Chapter VI.
[4] Oliver, p. 35; and see below, p. 178.

IV

ORDEAL AND SURVIVAL

1. The threat from the slave traders, 1869–1879

ALTHOUGH the creation of an equatorial empire, incorporating the Lacustrine kingdoms, was perhaps the most ambitious and significant project to be launched by Ismāʿīl, it was but one of his many undertakings which in the decade following 1869 imperiously demanded attention and expenditure. The appointment of Werner Munzinger, a capable Swiss administrator and explorer, to be Governor of Massawa in 1871 inaugurated a policy of aggression in north-east Africa, ending in a war with Abyssinia in which two disastrous defeats were inflicted on large Egyptian armies of 2,500 and 12,000 men in 1875 and 1876. Equally unsuccessful was an attempt to establish a foothold at the mouth of the River Juba on the east coast of Africa,[1] and although the occupation of Somaliland led to the capture of the famous city of Harrar in 1875 it brought no tangible benefits to compensate for the steady wastage of Egypt's limited resources.[2] Between 1863 and 1876 Ismāʿīl recklessly added an average of £7,000,000 a year to the public debt of Egypt which grew from £3,293,000 to £94,000,000, and for this 'large amount of indebtedness there was absolutely nothing to show but the Suez Canal' on which £16,000,000 of the total had been spent.[3] By 1875 money could be raised only at ruinous rates of interest and on 8 April 1876 Ismāʿīl was forced to suspend payment of his treasury bills. A Commission of the Public Debt was established and Commissioners were appointed by the European Powers led by Britain and France.[4] Retrenchments were carried out ruthlessly, the railway to the Sudan was abandoned, and the period of Egyptian expansion and independence was drawing to a close.

The first serious challenge to the stability of Egyptian rule in the Sudan came from the west of the Nile valley, from the vast sprawl of zeriba settlements in the Bahr el Ghazal, with their tentacles

---

[1] See below, p. 179–80. [2] Douin, vol. III (iii), pp. 583–629.
[3] Cave's report, quoted in Cromer, *Modern Egypt*, 1908, vol. i, pp. 11–12.
[4] Cromer, vol. i, pp. 12–15.

penetrating deeply into the fertile basins of the Wele and Ubanghi, and with their caravan communications stretching through Darfur and Kordofan, along which, secure from Government monopoly and intervention, the slaves and ivory could reach their markets. It was a challenge which stemmed and drew its strength from the established exploitation of the area, and, as in Equatoria, the Egyptian administration never found itself able to transcend the problems posed by the developments of the previous decades. After a struggle of increasing gravity the immediate challenge to Egyptian rule was successfully surmounted in 1879, but only a brief respite was allowed before it reappeared and merged into the Mahdist movement finally helping to destroy the foundations of Egyptian rule in the Sudan.

The struggle started at the end of 1869 when Muḥammad al-Hilālī arrived in the Bahr el Ghazal to bring the country under Egyptian administration. Claiming to have left Morocco twenty years previously in order to undertake a Pilgrimage to Mecca, and asserting that he had obtained an intimate knowledge of Dar Fertit and even a right of ownership over the copper mines of Hofrat en Nahas, Hilālī had arrived in Khartoum accompanied by 200 partisans and had suggested to Ja'far Pasha, the Governor-General, that he should be entrusted with the conquest of this area. Having recently purchased Poncet's zeribas on the river Rohl,[1] and feeling that Darfur had no plausible rights over the area, Ja'far Pasha was inclined to support him, and, with Ismā'īl's guarded assent, he supplied him with some regular troops and some irregulars, under the command of Kuchūk 'Alī, a veteran Turkish trader who owned a zeriba in the area.[2] Soon after their arrival in the Bahr el Ghazal, Kuchūk 'Alī died, and Hilālī was left to deal with the traders and especially Zubair, who was naturally unwilling to relinquish his supremacy in the area.[3] After a period of tense intrigue, hostilities broke out, Hilālī was killed in 1872 and Zubair's prestige was correspondingly enhanced. The following year he took the offensive against the Rizeiqat Arabs, who had threatened his communications with Kordofan, and after a brief campaign he decisively defeated them. Confronted with this *fait accompli* Ismā'īl was forced to come to terms with Zubair. At the

---

[1] See above, p. 82.
[2] Ja'far Pasha to Ismā'īl, 29/1/69, quoted in Douin, vol. III (i), pp. 451–53.
[3] See above, p. 69.

end of 1873 it was agreed to recognise him as Governor with the
rank of Bey, and to supply him with a small garrison of regular
troops in return for a tribute in ivory worth £15,000 p.a. As with
Muḥammad Khair and the Shilluk, the profits of violence had
obtained imperial sanction,[1] but with his resources already strained
by his other commitments Ismāʻīl had no alternative to this brazenly
opportunist arrangement.[2]

Zubair's next step further revealed his power and increased the
Government's dilemma. During his campaign against the Rizeiqat
some of the latter had escaped to Darfur, and, receiving no satisfaction from the Sultan, Zubair embarked on the conquest of this
ancient, independent kingdom. Marshalling his already powerful
resources, and conscripting reinforcements from each zeriba,[3]
Zubair was able to lead forth an army of 7,000 men. After a series of
hard-fought battles culminating in the death of the Sultan, he
entered el Fasher on 3 November 1874. Ismāʻīl had long contem-
plated the conquest of Darfur: its wealth and fame excited his
ambition, while its convenience as a place of refuge and its
strategical position dominating the caravan routes to the Bahr el
Ghazal rendered its independence a threat to his authority.[4] But
Zubair's advance manifestly constituted an even greater danger,
and, when the news of his early successes reached Cairo, Ismāʻīl
despatched the Governor-General in an attempt to forestall him
in the occupation of el Fasher. He arrived, however, shortly after
the capital had been occupied and the subsequent treatment of
Zubair is a story of subterfuge and deceit. Since Zubair's power
was needed to complete the conquest he was at first given to understand that Darfur would be placed under his command, but having
pacified the country he found himself in August 1875 ordered to

[1] See above, p. 77.
[2] Douin, vol. III (ii), pp. 150–70.
[3] Gessi to Gordon, July 1874, in C. Zaghi, *Gordon, Gessi e la Riconquista del Sudan*, Florence, 1947, p. 94. (This book is a valuable collection of un-published documents relating to Gessi, and includes his complete correspondence with Gordon. It is henceforth referred to as *Riconquista*). A year later Gordon reported that Zubair was troubling Makaraka for reinforcements and that 'My 2nd. in command in the Mudirat of the Rohl has deserted to Sebehr Pasha and taken with him 6000 cows from my Province', G. MSS. Gordon to Augusta, 18/VII/75.
[4] An independent witness agreed with the necessity of the conquest: 'Neither a regular system of taxation nor the suppression of the slave trade in the Upper Nile countries is possible until Egypt shall have made good its footing in Darfoor'. Schweinfurth, vol. i, p. 383.

return to the confines of the Bahr el Ghazal with no compensation
for the services he had rendered. Unwilling apparently to attempt
an immediate trial of strength, he decided to make a personal appeal
to the Khedive and, somewhat reassured by specious promises, he
arrived at Cairo in June 1876 only to find himself retained in hon-
ourable but impotent captivity.[1]

The difficulties for the Government, however, did not diminish.
By 1877 Darfur was in revolt, the isolated Egyptian garrisons in
the area were in danger, and Zubair's son, Sulaimān, with zeriba
leaders and over 3,000 men was at Shaka preparing to aid the
rebellion. Such was the situation which confronted Gordon on his
appointment as Governor-General of the Sudan after his return
from Equatoria. Although by a series of rapid camel rides he
relieved the beleagured garrisons, and although in the course of a
hurried visit to Sulaimān's headquarters he persuaded three of the
astonished leaders to join the Government's service and induced
Sulaimān to return with the remainder to their zeribas, the
experience revealed to him the difficulty of suppressing the
extensive slave trade and the strength of the challenge from the
Bahr el Ghazal traders.[2] For six months, however, he was intermittently absent on urgent visits to the Abyssinian frontier, to
Cairo, and to Harrar, so that he was unable to take any remedial
measure before he learnt that Sulaimān had again risen in open
rebellion, and that the challenge had entered its most critical
stage.

The persistent ferocity of the rebellion had several causes.
There was a justifiably bitter resentment of Zubair's treatment by
the Government;[3] there was a jealous envy of Idrīs Bey, appointed
by Gordon to be Mudir of the Bahr el Ghazal, which was increased
by the fact that Idrīs was a Dongolawi and so the traditional rival
of the Ja'liyin who formed the majority of Sulaimān's supporters;[4]
there was a mounting intolerance, reinforced by religious fanaticism, of the semi-westernised, semi-materialistic exacting Egyptian

---

[1] Douin, vol. III (iii), pp. 480–504.

[2] 'The population of the Nile,' he wrote, 'had emigrated into the Bahr Gazelle
regions to escape from Government exactions', and their slave troops were 'the
terror of central Africa.' (G. B. Hill, pp. 281–3.)

[3] Gordon accused Zubair of inciting Sulaimān to rebel, and there is little
doubt that ammunition was smuggled through to the rebels; see Gordon to
Allen, 9/IV/80, B.M. Add. MSS. 47609.

[4] R. C. Slatin, *Fire and Sword in the Sudan*, 1896, pp. 12–15.

administration with its use of European officials;[1] and, above all, there was the traders' belief that their ascendancy in the Bahr el Ghazal was being threatened from all sides. The rebels' exploitation of the wealth and human resources of the area gave this challenge a menacing strength. In the early summer of 1878 Sulaimān seized Idrīs' station with its valuable supplies of arms and ammunition and proclaimed his intention of conquering the southern provinces and of marching on Khartoum. With a private army of 6,400 slave troops drawn from his thirty-one zeribas, and about 9,000 Jellaba and other troops ready to support him; with Darfur, once again in revolt, and actively aiding him with recruits; and with the vast vested interest in the slave trade, including many adherents in Kordofan and 'half the population of Khartoum' anxious that he should succeed, this was no idle threat.[2]

Gordon entrusted Gessi with the task of defeating this challenge. An impulsive, vivacious Italian, who had fought under Garibaldi, a highly entertaining companion with 'an inexhaustible fund of quaint humour',[3] Romolo Gessi had met Gordon in the Crimea and Rumania, and accompanied him to Equatoria where he had undertaken several important assignments. He left Khartoum with 40 regular soldiers in July 1878, and, collecting reinforcements from the garrisons of Fashoda and Lado, he marched inland from Shambe reaching Rumbek in early September. Delayed by the rainy season and the necessity of waiting for further reinforcements from the Makaraka garrisons, it was not until December that he reached Wau where with the aid of congreve rockets he routed the rebel garrison. This success, together with the defection of Abū Amūri, a veteran trader with considerable influence who brought with him several hundred armed men, seriously weakened Sulaimān's prestige. Other traders withdrew their support, hundreds of slave troops deserted him, and local chiefs were encouraged to hunt down the scattered Arab traders.[4] Gessi advanced to Dem Idrīs some miles to the west of Dem Zubair, where,

[1] Gessi reported that the rebel's war cry was 'This is our land—we know no Effendina here', G. B. Hill, p. 372. A German traveller who visited Zubair's zeribas shortly before the outbreak of the rebellion, also encountered considerable difficulties caused by religious fanaticism ('F. Bohndorff's Reise nach Dor Abu Dinga', *Das Ausland*, 1884).

[2] Zaghi, *Riconquista*, pp. 224, 280, 281; G. B. Hill, p. 340.

[3] C. T. Wilson & R. W. Felkin, *Uganda and the Egyptian Sudan*, 1882, vol. ii, p. 153.

[4] B.M. Add. MSS. 40665. Gordon to Standen, 23/XII/78.

with a force still greatly inferior to that of Sulaimān, he dug himself in. For the next four months a ghastly war of attrition took place. He withstood numerous desperate and exhaustive attacks and surrounding villages were ravaged, until in May he was finally able to take the offensive and Dem Zubair was captured. Sulaimān escaped to the north, but, finally surrounded, he surrendered on 18 July 1879 and was shot together with his associates.[1]

2. Gessi in the Bahr el Ghazal, 1879–1881

The campaign had defeated the immediate challenge, but fresh difficulties had further complicated the situation in the Bahr el Ghazal. The zeriba district had the 'aspect of a country destroyed by fire'; granaries were empty and harvests ruined; 'thousands and thousands of natives' had fled for refuge to the Azande or to the inaccessible swamps of the Dinka; many of the armed slave troops had scattered through the country establishing themselves as petty tyrants or, escaping to the north with Sulaimān, had fallen into the hands of the Arab frontier tribes, such as the Rizeiqat and Habbaniya, thus formidably increasing the strength of these virtually independent tribes; and, apart from this destruction and upheaval, about four thousand Arabs, whose attitude towards the area differed but little from that of Sulaimān and his associates, had come over to Gessi at various stages of the campaign and now hoped to continue their activities as before.[2]

The difficulties of establishing effective control over so large an area and of shaping the ingrained patterns of contact into new modes of productive and mutually beneficial development were so great that Gordon seriously doubted the wisdom of attempting such a task. The disillusionment induced by his experience in Equatoria, where the problem was however far simpler as the immigration of Arabs had been restricted to the river route and consequently was far easier to control, deepened during his years as Governor-General into a pessimism embracing the whole process of penetration into Central Africa from the Sudan. This was

[1] C. Zaghi, *Vita di Romolo Gessi*, Milan, 1939. This contains a very full account of the campaign.

[2] After the capture of Dem Zubair Gessi reported that he could not immediately pursue Sulaimān as 'ma présence est ici nécessaire pour protéger les natifs contre mes propres arabes', (Gessi to Gordon, 6/V/79, in Zaghi, *Riconquista* p. 354. See also, Gessi to Camperio, 17/XII/79, ibid., p. 428, and Gessi to Ra'ūf, 13/II/81.

mainly due to the fact that upon him fell the principal responsibility for implementing an anti-slavery convention signed by Ismā'īl with Great Britain in 1877,[1] which pledged Egypt to abolish slave trading within seven years, and his energies as Governor-General became increasingly devoted to the sole end of destroying the slave trade.[2]

It was a problem incapable of solution with the means at his disposal. Although direct imports down the Nile Valley into Egypt had been considerably lessened by restrictive measures, the slave trade from north-east Africa across the Red Sea into Arabia seems to have increased in the seventies, and by 1876 it was thought that as many as 30,000 slaves *p.a.* were involved. Some were kept for domestic service and work in plantations in Yemen and the Hejaz, others were sent to the Persian Gulf where there was an increased demand as the result of the preventative measures being taken at Zanzibar and the east coast,[3] many were sold to pilgrims at Jeddah, and the most valuable—eunuchs and Galla women from Abyssinia—were still shipped to Egypt and through the Suez Canal to Turkey.[4] The merchants of Jeddah had their agents in the inland markets of Berber, Shendi, Khartoum, Sennar, Gallabat, Kassala and el Obeid where the slaves were collected from the Jellaba and wealthier merchants and taken by unfrequented routes to the coast ready to be shipped across in fast-sailing dhows. A similar network existed from the Somali coast with its tentacles stretching deep into the Galla country of southern Abyssinia, and Egypt attempted to police a thousand-mile coast-line from Berbera to Kosseir with one gunboat in 'a very inefficient state' and three small steamers.[5]

Gordon had long realised that the overland route from the Bahr el Ghazal was one of the focal points of this traffic and in an attempt to bring aid to Gessi he made a second visit to the area south of Darfur and Kordofan. He found himself confronted afresh with proofs of the extent of the trade. From June 1878 to March 1879,

[1] See below, p. 181–2.
[2] Shukry, p. 295.
[3] See below, p. 180.
[4] F.O. 84/1450 Memorandum by A. B. Wylde, 25/XI/76.
[5] F.O. 84/1472 Vivian to Derby, 26/V/77 enclosing reports of Commander Morice Bey R.N. to Kharīf Pasha, 9/III/77, 18/III/77, 4/IV/77. Other numerous reports substantiated the picture painted by Wylde and Morice, e.g. F.O. 141/108 Derby to Vivian, enclosing report from H.M.S. Vulture 2/VI/77.

63 caravans containing 2000 slaves were captured, and he thought that 80 per cent of the caravans escaped without detection.[1] His anger vented itself against the Jellaba: 'some hundred' were cleared out of Shaka, 470 dealers were driven out of Taweisha, at Kalaka 1,000 slaves were liberated, and throughout the area these intinerant traders were hounded to the north, separated from their families, and robbed of their goods by the Baqqara Arabs acting with Gordon's encouragement.[2] In the wake of these severe measures a wave of bitter discontent spread over the principal markets and riverain areas of the Sudan which later was swept into the rising tide of Mahdism;[3] but this severity, however necessary, did not solve the problem and Gordon wearily began to believe that the only remedy was to abandon the Bahr el Ghazal and to enforce a strict blockade on the whole area, leaving the Arabs and their servants to perish through lack of supplies and reinforcements. 'As for the future of these lands' he wrote to Gessi in March 1879, 'I hope to see you and talk over it. I am dead against any occupation of these countries. I want no ivory, I only want the people to be quiet'.[4]

His pessimism had led him into a wholly negative attitude. He had come to regard the problem of this slave trade as one to be solved solely by the constraint of overriding power; he had lost all faith in the constructive work of administration, which alone could attempt to find a permanent solution. Gessi, however, retained a positive approach to the problem, and throughout the campaign against Sulaimān he was composing plans for the future development of the area. He agreed with Gordon's policy of evicting the Jellaba, and proposed to extend it to the 750 whom he estimated to be in the Bahr el Ghazal, thus severing the overland route. Concomitantly he hoped to render the administration and the zeribas less dependent on Arab settlers by extensively using the bazingers or former slave troops in their stead, and trusted that, after the eviction of the Jellaba and the consequent disappearance of an accessible market for slaves, many of the Danaqla and

[1] G. B. Hill, pp. 346–9. Gordon estimated that during 1875–9 some 80–100,000 slaves were exported from the Bahr el Ghazal area (ibid. p. 369).

[2] Ibid., pp. 348, 358, 369.

[3] Slatin, p. 21; and see below, pp. 152–3.

[4] Gordon to Gessi, 31/III/79, in Zaghi, *Riconquista*, p. 322. See also Gordon to Baker 1/IX/78 in Murray & White, p. 243.

Ja'liyin settlers would voluntarily return to their riverain home-
lands in the north.[1] Into this vacuum he planned to introduce
legitimate commerce.

Although Gessi confidently anticipated that the export of ivory
would fully cover not only the cost of the campaign against Sulaimān but also the administrative expenses for the immediate future,
he realised that the supplies would be exhausted eventually and
that an alternative export would be needed. There were strong
reasons to believe that cotton could supply this. As a tree it grew
naturally in the region, and with the abundant labour forces of the
zeribas he thought it would be relatively easy to effect a rapid
expansion of its cultivation even to an estimated yield of 50,000
kantars. The Government by purchasing it at 2 thalers[2] per kantar
and selling it for 10 at Khartoum would make a substantial profit,
while by introducing a widespread use of money its growth would
promote an economic development which, unlike the restricted
sale of ivory, would benefit the cultivators as well as their chiefs.[3]
With these arguments Gessi was able to convince Gordon on
meeting him in June 1879 that the permanent occupation and development of the Bahr el Ghazal presented the sole feasible solution
to the problem of the slave trade, and he was accordingly given
full authority to initiate this policy.[4]

In the fifteen months before his departure in September 1880
Gessi vindicated to a surprising extent his faith in the economic
possibilities of the area. During this brief period he despatched
3,000 kantars of ivory worth about £90,000 at Khartoum which
amply covered all his expenses, and large supplies were still
stored in the zeribas or being collected from the interior.[5] In
addition to this tangible result, he made significant progress in the
development of other possibilities. A small amount of cotton was

[1] Gessi to Gordon, 2/XI/78, 21/XII/78, 29/I/79, in Zaghi, *Riconquista*,
pp. 240-94.

[2] 1 Maria Theresa Thaler = 20 Piastres = 4 shillings.

[3] Gessi to Gordon, 2/XI/78 in Zaghi, *Riconquista*, p. 242. It is interesting to
note that six years later a missionary in Nyasaland made the same point: 'Ivory
only enriches the chiefs and some vagabond native hunters and makes all of them
tyrants. Agriculture and industry will benefit the many' (W. MSS. Misc. Fort
to Waller, 13/II/84).

[4] On the meeting at Taweisha see Zaghi, *Riconquista*, pp. 395-6.

[5] Casati to Camperio, Sept. 1880, in Zaghi, *Riconquista*, p. 480. See also p. 475.
Gessi considered that the war against Sulaimān had only cost the Government
c. £800, and to offset this he had captured c. £8,000 in cash at Dem Zubair
(Wilson and Felkin, vol. ii, p. 202).

sown very successfully; 1,000 kantars of rubber, 1,000 kantars of tamarinds and a large supply of honey were sent to Khartoum; it was demonstrated that palm-oil, rice, sugar, and timber, which had previously been imported from Trieste to Khartoum, could be produced; copper from the mines of Hofrat en Nahas supplied the needs of the province, and since the iron ores previously worked by the Bongo and Luo were pronounced to be as good as those of Styria, Gessi hoped to establish some forges with equipment from Khartoum.[1]

The major obstacle to the rapid development of these resources was their inaccessibility. After the weary voyage up the river to Meshra er Req, which was sometimes prolonged or even rendered impossible by the accumulation of a barrier of swampy vegetation, there stretched a hundred miles of inhospitable country, impassable in the wet period, before the fertile zeriba belt was reached. Gessi, like his trading predecessors, found it impossible to enrol the Dinka as porters[2] so the burden continued to fall on the tribes surrounding the zeribas;[3] but, besides being unpopular, porterage was inefficient and extravagantly wasteful of potential agricultural labourers, so there was every incentive to find an alternative. Very occasionally, during the season of high water, the traders had previously succeeded in taking boats up the river Jur to Wau. Gessi therefore energetically commenced the construction of small 50 ton boats which were loaded with ivory and other goods and sent down from Wau to Khartoum to be sold at a considerable profit.[4] The navigation of the river Jur remained however a laborious and dangerous undertaking,[5] and Gessi had scarcely begun to face this problem of communications before he was recalled.

The other major obstacle often encountered in under-developed countries—an inadequate labour supply—did not, however, confront him. The Kreish, Ndogo, Bongo, Luo, and other tribes surrounding the zeribas were adaptable agriculturists, whose tribal structure and independence had been weakened under the impact

[1] Gessi to Chief of Staff, 15/V/80, and to Camperio, 8/I/80, in Zaghi, *Riconquista*, pp. 472–5, 465.

[2] W. Junker, *Travels in Africa*, 3 vols., 1890–2, vol. i, p. 63.

[3] Gessi to Gordon, 19/VI/79, in Zaghi *Riconquista*, p. 389.

[4] Gessi to Gordon, 12/IX/79, in ibid., pp. 426, 592.

[5] J. Emily, *Mission Marchand*, 1913, prints a vivid photograph of a convoy of boats struggling through a minute channel of free water surrounded and completely dwarfed by the vast expanse of papyrus swamp.

of the trading communities. Many therefore were willing to follow
the example of the Golo chief Kayonga and his people, who
enthusiastically collected rubber and cultivated cotton.[1] In
addition to these tribal sections, there were the numerous slaves
abandoned by the Arabs. At Dem Bekir, for example, Gessi found
four hundred slaves whom he organized into 'agricultural colonies'.[2]
Amongst all these people a desire for cotton clothing was apparently
a sufficient incentive for labour, and Gessi established eight looms
worked by young African apprentices who produced excellent
cloth of the 'damur' quality.[3] In these ways Africans would be
introduced to a higher standard of living which would reduce the
stigma of inferiority when compared with their Arab neighbours.
The most significant administrative innovation in this process of
raising the status of the Africans was the primary school established
at Dem Zubair. It was attended by the sons of chiefs and 'bazinger'
soldiers, and Gessi hoped 'in a few years to be able to draw the
clerks from the indigenous populations'.[4]

These projects were merely in their infancy, but they gave
reason to believe that, with determination and capital investment,
economic development was possible. This would prove profitable
to the administration and to private enterprise,[5] and at the same
time would bring to the local Africans an enormous advance when
compared with the miserable situation to which they had previously
been reduced.[6] Yet although the solution of these economic
problems was a vital part of Gessi's task, it was only one aspect
of the situation which confronted him, and in the extension of
confidence and control over the vast area committed to his charge
he was considerably less successful.

[1] Wilson and Felkin, vol. ii, p. 189.
[2] Gessi to Ra'ūf, 13/II/81, in Zaghi Riconquista, p. 534.
[3] Ibid., p. 542.
[4] Casati to Camperio, September 1880 in Zaghi, Riconquista, p. 478 and Gessi
to Ra'ūf, 13/II/81 ibid., p. 541.
[5] In March 1880 Gessi informed a representative of commercial interests in
Milan that large profits were awaiting private enterprise and that the government
monopoly was confined to the ivory trade. ibid., p. 465.
[6] Beyond this, somewhat naturally at this early stage, Gessi did not look;
but some of the issues inherent in a policy of vigorous economic development
were already beginning to reveal themselves. Junker, for example, strenuously
advocated forced labour (vol. ii, p. 97) and Casati while demanding many increased facilities for private enterprise stressed the 'semi-selvaggio' nature of
African society. One feels that he would perhaps have sympathised with Leopold's Congo policy (Mus. Af. It. MSS. Casati to Camperio, 30/VIII/83).

He established substantial improvements only in the north-
eastern district of the zeriba belt, stretching from Dem Zubair
to Rumbek. From this district he succeeded in evicting the Jellaba.
By executing some Danaqla who had murdered their slaves, he
attempted to convince those Arabs who were allowed to remain
in the area that he had 'brought the natives into an exceptional
protection'.[1] Many of the tribal sections which had fled from the
vicinity of the zeribas during the campaign returned. The north-
western sections of the Dinka living between Meshra er Req and
the Bahr el Arab, who had retreated into their swamps and even
taken refuge with their rivals the Nuer, were beginning to reoccupy
their land after an absence of five years. Gessi claimed to have given
assistance to 40,000 of their families,[2] and it is significant that
as late as 1897 the members of Marchand's expedition were
welcomed by the Dinka as soon as they proclaimed themselves to
be the 'sons of Gessi'.[3] To the north, however, beyond the zeriba
district, the Jellaba evicted by Gessi had found refuge in the
market-centres of southern Darfur, and, despite the Government
garrisons placed by Gessi at Hofrat en Nahas, Shaka, Kalaka and
other key positions, they continued to carry out incursions into
the Bahr el Ghazal. In February 1880 Gessi reported four attempts
to break into his area, and these culminated eventually in a mass
razzia. Five hundred Jellaba, five hundred bazingers, and four
hundred horsemen raided the newly returned Dinka and were
repulsed with difficulty only after they had captured cattle and
slaves.[4] Simultaneously to the south-east the Atot Dinka were in
revolt, severing the route between Rumbek and Shambe, with the
result that a large punitive expedition, or cattle raid, was needed to
suppress them.[5] Both incidents revealed the limits of Gessi's
fragile success, and to the west, among the Azande, the slenderness
of his control was even more apparent.

With their considerable supplies of ivory and their command
of the routes into the unexploited areas to the south, with their
turbulent dynasties extending their power over a vast region, and
with their social organization, their intelligence, and their unusually

[1] Zaghi, *Riconquista*, p. 420.
[2] Ibid., Gessi to Ra'ūf, 13/II/81, p. 546.
[3] Emily, p. 55.
[4] Ibid., Gessi to Gordon, 24/II/80, 28/XI/79, pp. 436, 459. Gessi to Ra'ūf,
13/II/81, p. 547.
[5] Ibid. p. 546.

rapid response and adaptation to extraneous influences, the Azande and their numerous subject-peoples were the key to the attempt to solve the problem of the slave trade by establishing an ordered economic development in its stead. Events in the seventies before Gessi's arrival had, however, made this a difficult undertaking. In 1869, at the time of Schweinfurth's visit to the Bahr el Ghazal, the traders' expeditions impinged on a line of Zande and Mangbetu rulers, stretching from Munza in the south-east to Mopoi in the north-west.[1] Some, like Ndoruma, were triumphantly hostile; others were willing to trade; all had managed to preserve their independence and confronted the intruders with an assured equality. Their supplies of ivory, bartered for copper, beads or even firearms, were however dwindling, and their attempt to prevent the traders reaching fresh areas, together with the brutal behaviour of the latter, made a trial of strength inevitable. The subsequent crisis revealed the fatal weakness of their position: in every case the traders found it was only too easy to exploit dynastic rivalries.

In the north, having defeated in 1872 al-Hilālī's attempt to oust him from his supremacy in the region,[2] Zubair turned his forces against Mopoi and his nephew Tikima, whose alliance he had been anxious to obtain in the earlier days. Weakened by mutual jealousy and hatred, both chiefs were defeated. In his memoirs Zubair asserts that they united against him,[3] but the structure of Zande society and Junker's account of conditions in the area a decade later makes it far more probable that Zande tradition is correct in ascribing their downfall to dynastic intrigue.[4] Mopoi with a broken remnant of his people withdrew into the interior. Tikima's relatives, captured, armed, and trained by the Arabs, returned to their people as the powerful intermediaries of the Arabs, but they had lost their independence and the traditional basis of their authority was completely destroyed. The traders established zeribas in their territory and dynastic rivalries were further exploited in the search for ivory and slaves. As in the case of Surur[5] their subjugation was never so complete as that of the Bongo and other smaller tribes in the original zeriba area; but

[1] See above, pp. 63, 68.
[2] See above, p. 121.
[3] Jackson, pp. 52–55.
[4] Hutereau, pp. 199–200.
[5] See above, p. 63.

after Zubair's victory many of the northern Azande found themselves compelled to act as porters and an increasing number of
their women were exported as slaves, while their leaders were
debased to the position of 'yeomen', if not of serfs, in the alien
hierarchy which was rapidly extending its power, and which by
1876 was already entrenched on the left bank of the Mbomu
river.[1]

In the far south a similar process took place. Even at the time of
Schweinfurth's visit to the Mangbetu it was possible to discern
that Munza's security was threatened both by his attempt to assert
a trading monopoly and by the hatred of his Mangbetu neighbours.[2] By 1873 these dangers materialized and Nyangara, a jealous
relative, persuaded the Arabs to attack Munza. Tangasi the capital
was burnt, Munza was killed, and the independence and strength
of the Mangbetu disappeared in the succeeding anarchy.[3] It was
only in the centre of Zande territory, at the sources of the rivers
Sue and Werre, that Ndoruma and Mbio succeeded by their fierce
hostility in preserving their power; yet, jealous of each other, their
position was insecure and they were merely the final, beleagured
outpost of Zande independence north of the river Wele. Elsewhere
by the time of Gessi's arrival the pattern of oppressive and destructive exploitation was becoming firmly established.

To a certain extent Gessi realized the vital importance of preventing this destruction and of conserving and harnessing the
wealth and power of the Azande;[4] but, distracted by the immediate
necessities of defending his northern frontier against the Jellaba
and of attending to the affairs of the zeriba belt, he was unable to
give much attention to their problems. In the greater part of this
vast area effective power over the Azande remained in the hands
of the traders and their agents. After Sulaimān's defeat the traders
were entrusted with the task of procuring ivory for the Government, but their methods of obtaining it remained unchanged. In
the south-east 'Abd Allāhi, the nephew of 'Abd al-Ṣamad,

[1] Junker, vol. ii, p. 123. Besides his own observations Junker became friends
with Zemio, Tikima's son, and from him gained an insight into the process here
described. Another traveller in the area reported that in 1876 Pirintzi, 'com-
pagnon de Ziber-Pacha', was at war with the Abu Dinga beyond the Mbomu
(P. Potagos, Dix années de voyages, 1885, p. 293).
[2] See above, p. 64.
[3] Hutereau, pp. 287–302; Doᶙin, vol. III (iiia), pp. 150–2.
[4] E.g. Gessi's report to Cairo, 15/V/80, in Zaghi, Riconquista, pp. 470–6.

exploited the rivalries of Wando's sons north of the Wele, and Munza's former capital was garrisoned by 'a rabble of Nubians . . . many of whom had fought under Soliman and had then escaped to these parts'.[1] In the south-west 'Alī Kobbo, a Nubian formerly in the service of the loyal trader Abū Amūri, was 'absolute ruler of thousands of natives' and obtained ivory, goats, and slaves from the lands south of the Wele. To the north-west of the Mbomu, Rabīh Zubair, one of Sulaimān's commanders who had succeeded in escaping to the west, was able to establish his power in Dar Banda before embarking on a series of conquests which carried him eventually to Lake Chad and to his final defeat by French forces in 1900.[2] Jellaba still succeeded in penetrating to these areas[3] and slaves continued to be exported surreptitiously via Darfur.[4]

It was only in a few limited cases that Gessi was able to attempt to introduce a fresh pattern of relationships. Tikima's son, Zemio, and his brother Zassa, who had been trained as subordinate vassals by the traders, were reinstated and entrusted with the command of Government expeditions. When the intransigent Ndoruma gave his allegiance to Gessi he was confirmed in his position, and he was ordered to retain the 800 odd rifles he had formerly captured from the traders in order to protect himself against the possible incursions of the Jellaba.[5] These were, however, only the first steps towards regaining the confidence of the Azande. Mbio remained hostile and the value of Gessi's reforms was greatly diminished by the fact that Zemio and Zassa utilized their new commands to overthrow and oppress other smaller chieftains.[6]

Gessi had captured the citadel of the slave trade, but it continued to trickle through its outposts. He had cleared the Jellaba from the centre of the stage, but they bided their time in the wings. He had brought opportunity and hope to some people, but many remained outside the radius of his influence. He had demonstrated the fruitful possibilities of economic development, but the problem

[1] Junker, vol. ii, pp. 160, 257–60, 275.
[2] Zaghi, Riconquista, p. 259.
[3] Gessi himself discovered nineteen whom Rifā'ī Aghā, one of his most trusted lieutenants, was hiding in his zeriba. (Gessi to Gordon 14/IX/79, ibid., p. 428.)
[4] Junker, vol. iii, pp. 205, 213.
[5] Gessi to Gordon, 8/V/80, in Zaghi, Riconquista, p. 468.
[6] 'They plotted the overthrow of independent chiefs, and after procuring the ivory required by the government they also looked after their own interests. . . . Zassa was quite alive to the value of captured slaves.' Junker, vol. ii, pp. 151, 361.

of communications remained. Almost single-handed, and with the scantiest of materials his was a remarkable achievement; but it was already evident that the task required several administrators and abundant resources. In the brief period of 15 months following Sulaimān's death he had started to lay the foundations for recovery, but, wishing to confer personally with Ra'ūf Pasha, who had succeeded Gordon as Governor-General in 1880, he left the Bahr el Ghazal and, emaciated by a horrible journey through the sudd, he died on 30 April 1881. His successor, Lupton, was soon confronted with an even greater ordeal.

3. Emin in Equatoria, 1877–1881

This challenge of the Bahr el Ghazal slave trade and Sulaimān's insurrection, together with Ismā'īl's other commitments, were the fundamental reasons why the Egyptian advance in Equatoria was finally abandoned. In February 1877, however, at the time of his appointment as Governor-General of the Sudan and before he became engulfed in these problems, Gordon still envisaged consolidation and expansion in the south. In a conversation with Vivian, the British Consul-General at Cairo, he made it clear that he 'doubted if Egypt, after all her sacrifices, could stop short of Lake Victoria', and stated that he was instructed to place a steamer on the lake as soon as possible. The fact, however, that, during his leave in England, he had come into contact with a small group of humanitarians, who were planning to introduce legitimate commerce into Buganda from the east coast of Africa,[1] increased his readiness to respect the independence of Mutesa. He told Vivian therefore that he thought Egypt might well be prepared to proclaim the neutrality of Lake Victoria once she reached it and to recognize Mutesa, provided guarantees were given that the latter would act as 'a friendly ruler'.[2]

To prepare the way for this final advance Gordon decided to send yet another emissary to Mutesa, and chose for this task a certain Emin Effendi. A Silesian Jew born in 1840, Eduard Schnitzer had studied medicine in Germany and served as a medical officer in the Ottoman service for nine years in Albania and Asia Minor,

[1] See below, pp. 183–4.
[2] F.O. 84/1472 Vivian to Derby, 9/IV/77, enclosing memo. of conversation with Gordon. Vivian added: 'From conversations that I have had with Cherif Pasha, I gather that the Khedive entirely endorses these views'.

before he arrived in Khartoum in 1875. Proclaiming himself to be a
Turk with the name of Emin, he had been appointed the following
year to be Chief Medical Officer in the Equatorial province, where
he successfully undertook a mission to Mutesa during Nūr Bey's
'occupation' of Rubaga.[1] Summoned to Khartoum in May 1877,
he was asked to embark on a second journey to Mutesa 'in order
to arrive at a final settlement with him',[2] and was authorized to
visit Kabarega and even Rumanika of Karagwe if possible. Short-
sighted, small and cultured, vacillating when confronted with the
need for action, and completely enthralled with the opportunities
for botanical, zoological and geographical research afforded by his
journey, Emin, with his tolerance, generosity and easy friendliness,
though not the man to command a decisive imperial offensive,
was well qualified for his role as mediator. Unarmed, and accompanied only by a few servants, he succeeded in gaining Kabarega's
confidence to such an extent that this hitherto intransigent enemy
willingly agreed to send envoys to Khartoum, and although he
spent a rather frustrating three months at Rubaga, Mutesa also
seemed willing to send envoys.[3]

Kabarega's envoys were welcomed at Khartoum but it was
already evident that these openings would not be followed up.
Prout, the American who succeeded Gordon in Equatoria, quickly
returned in ill health to Khartoum, and Mason, another American,
also returned in August 1877 after thoroughly exploring Lake
Albert in Baker's steamer which had finally been launched on the
Albert Nile.[4] With their departure and with Emin absent on his
mission, there was no one to implement a coherent policy of expansion, and a few months later Gordon began to realize that
Egypt did not possess sufficient resources for such a policy. Early
in 1878 he was invited by Ismā'īl to serve on a Commission of
Inquiry into the financial situation of Egypt, and although he soon
relinquished the task, he caught a glimpse of Ismā'īl's insecurity
and of the complete bankruptcy and disaster which was so soon to
overtake him. During a hurried visit to Harrar he wrote a letter
to Julian Baker which reveals his reactions to this discovery:

[1] G. Schweitzer, *The Life and Work of Emin Pasha*, 2 vols. 1898. Chapters
I–V.
[2] Emin, *Die Tagebücher*, 4 vols. Braunschweig, 1917–1927, vol. i, 11/V/77.
Mutesa was apparently to be asked to agree to an Egyptian occupation of
Urondogani, ibid., 23/IX/77.
[3] Ibid. 13/IX/77—21/V/78.   [4] *Bull. Soc. Khéd. Géog.* 1878, p. 5 et seq.

I have not the very slightest hope of doing anything permanent out here. Absolute as he, (Ismā'īl) is, he is impotent out of Cairo. Things cannot go on long there, as they are now. H.H. has been more absolute, than any potentate in the world. All other potentates have had to surrender their prerogatives, and so must he. My visit to Cairo opened my eyes to his great weakness. He has no one to guide him in any way, his ministers are only his servants. He is a wonderful man but the weight is too much for him and there must come a collapse . . . not one of the places Zeyla, Tajurah, Berberah or Harar anything like pay their expenses, neither does Darfur. The most sensible thing would be to evacuate all of them. This is sad after the expenditure of so much money and so many lives. Darfur must have cost, at least the death of 30,000! . . . Under a Foreign master at Cairo and with a subvention of 80,000 Pounds, and 20 officers, I could manage this country, but I think I would vacate a lot of it; query what will be the ultimate use of the Equator province?[1]

Sulaimān's insurrection and his experiences with the slave trade deepened this pessimism, and by the end of October 1878, after a review of the financial situation in the Sudan which revealed an annual deficit of nearly £100,000, Gordon decided to evacuate all the stations on the Victoria Nile and to retain only those flanking the river to Lake Albert.[2]

His determination to withdraw was strengthened by reports which revealed the flagrant abuse of power indulged in by many of the officials in these distant provinces. During his journey up the Nile to launch his campaign against Sulaimān, Gessi discovered at Kaka, Fashoda, and Shambe several hundred slaves who were being exported on Government steamers by Ibrāhīm Fawzī, the successor of Prout and Mason as Governor of Equatoria.[3] Gordon recalled Fawzī and appointed Emin to the post,[4] but a letter from the new Governor confirmed the serious state of affairs. Bakhīt Bey, placed in charge of the zeribas among the Makaraka by Gordon three years previously, openly ignored orders to aid Gessi and attempted to smuggle over forty slaves past Lado;[5] the officials

[1] B. MSS. Gordon to Julian Baker, 17/IV/78—9/V/78.
[2] Gordon to Baker, 29/X/78, in Murray and White.
[3] Zaghi, *Riconquista*, pp. 214–15. See also Emin, *Tagebücher*, vol. i, 14/V/78.
[4] Junker, vol. i, p. 513.
[5] There was however good reason for his reluctance to aid Gessi, as in the previous year he had taken a large expedition into the Bahr el Ghazal on Fawzī's orders but had suffered many casualties through a lack of provisions (Junker, vol. i, pp. 392 seq.).

among the Lotuko took 'a crowd of slaves' to Bor, many of whom died or 'disappeared' before Emin could release them; desertions, thefts, raids, disobedience, and stations in decay, convinced Emin that there reigned 'everywhere here a spirit of opposition' which caused him 'very considerable concern'.[1]

Emin inherited a disordered province of declining importance. The Egyptian thrust into equatorial Africa had lost its force and a tenuous straggle of small isolated stations was all that remained of this imperial intrusion. As custodian of this remnant Emin was not called to command a highly significant enterprise formed with the vision of a pioneer like Baker. Instead he was entrusted with the unenviable task of attempting to control the development of the station communities and to ameliorate their often harsh and dreary contacts with the neighbouring African tribes. Gordon had glimpsed the difficulties and frustrations attendant on such a task, and, disillusioned, had sought to escape from it;[2] in many ways, however, Emin was peculiarly suited for it. His patience, frugality, and fluent adaptability enabled him not only to accept this role but even to be reasonably content with it. Throughout his time in the Sudan he observed the practice of Islam and, marrying a Galla woman, his sole surviving connection with Europe was the scientific and geographical periodicals to which he contributed his scrupulously exact observations. He was a man far better attuned than most Europeans to work under a Middle Eastern government in Africa.

Like Gessi, he fully realized the vital necessity for economic development to enable the peoples of his province to meet the challenge of the alien forces penetrating into their traditional way of life. 'A new era', he told Gordon, 'will begin for this country when people will work instead of taking things easily, will labour instead of enriching themselves at the expense of their neighbours. For this reason I would like for this country fertile seeds, and, I hardly dare to say so, some Chinese.'[3] The seeds were to broaden the economy of the area, and to render it less dependent on the export of ivory which only too often was 'stigmatised with blood'. He was already experimenting with rice which he had introduced from Uganda; he was anticipating favourable yields from maize,

---

[1] C.M.S. MSS. Emin to Gordon, 27/X/78.
[2] See above, pp. 112–15.
[3] C.M.S. MSS. Emin to Gordon, 27/X/78.

coffee, cotton and sugar; and although the local tribesmen were suspicious of these agricultural innovations, he found them 'most willing to collect indiarubber if a small reward is promised them' and reported that 'whole forests' of this valuable product covered the tops of hills and the banks of rivers.[1] The Chinese were to remedy a more serious defect. Economic development and effective administrative control were hampered by the appalling difficulties of communication. Roads were still completely non-existent.[2] Throughout the province streams were liable to rise in a few hours and turn into raging torrents which it was impossible to cross for days and, in some cases, even for months.[3] Camels, donkeys, and the elephants imported by Gordon from India, sickened and died, so that porters remained the sole means of transport. 'Under present conditions no real progress can be made, or at least it must be so slow that decades will hardly suffice to set upon a solid basis the work which has hitherto been done with so much trouble.' Only Chinese labourers, Emin thought, could establish good communications and open up the country.[4]

Even more serious than this lack of roads within the province was the fact that for long periods Lado again became virtually isolated from Khartoum. Soon after Emin was appointed Governor the river became blocked with the sudd which had so impeded Baker, and it was not until April 1880 that a steamer managed to get through. This isolation was a crushing handicap during Emin's first eighteen months in power[5] and was an additional reason why

[1] Report on the Equatorial Province, written by Emin c. 1883 and printed in Schweitzer, vol. i, pp. 81–89.

[2] In contrast to Buganda, whose highways impressed travellers coming from the north.

[3] An officer for example had to wait 19 days to cross the small River Bibia, and in 1878 the River Asua severed all communication with the south for several months (C.M.S. MSS. Emin to Gordon, 27/X/78, and Emin, *Tagebücher*, vol. ii, 2/VIII/83).

[4] Emin to Schweinfurth, May 1881, in *Emin Pasha in Central Africa*, 1888, p. 417. Emin continues: 'Will you support me in this matter if I apply officially to the Government? Will you convince the Belgians that a few hundred Chinese established in any suitable place—under the direction of *practical* Europeans— would form a better nucleus for the civilisation of Africa than any number of Indian elephants and ironclad steamers? . . . Would not the introduction of Chinese settle the slave trade once and for all?' The idea was not so fantastic as it might seem: the Uganda Railway was, after all, built mainly by Indian labour.

[5] At one stage Emin was even ordered to abandon the River and retire on Makaraka (Emin, *Tagebücher*, vol. ii, 11/III/80).

it would have been quite impossible to attempt an advance to the
Lakes. Later, the isolation was due not so much to the physical
obstacles but to the declining resources of the Government, so
that during the six years preceding the fall of Khartoum there
were only nine arrivals of steamers, and three of these brought
no merchandise at all.[1] Commerce was crippled by this paucity of
imports, and of the small trickle of goods which did reach the
province only a minute proportion was given to the Africans in
exchange for their products, almost all of it being absorbed by the
station communities.[2] Nor was this deficiency made good by
private enterprise, for with a government monopoly over ivory
there was no return cargo sufficiently valuable to justify the
hazards which confronted private individuals. The trading community of Lado was confined to an Egyptian, a Copt, and a Greek.
Their capital in 'cotton, alcohol and utensils' scarcely amounted
to 1500 Thalers,[3] and these small traders had a bad reputation, at
least with missionaries:

> Along the Nile are Greek traders, equally bad with the Arabs (in
> Uganda). These men are now fixed at Fashoda and are extending
> their business in the Equatorial Provinces. Met with several. They
> trade in *raki* chiefly, and are introducing the 'drink' trade, besides
> dealing in everything pandering to the worst vices of mankind. They
> will soon be at the gates of Uganda and if such men take the place of
> the Arabs, the end will be worse than the beginning.[4]

Since the peoples of Equatoria were thus denied the benefits,
and were protected from the dangers, of large-scale economic
development, their contact with the outside world was restricted
to the hybrid communities of the scattered government stations;
and it was with these communities that Emin was chiefly concerned.
He took a far greater part than Gordon in the process of acculturation: at Lado, which by 1881 had developed into a fair-sized
'town' of 2,000 'tokuls',[5] he founded a mosque, a Koranic school,

[1] Schweitzer, vol. i, p. 142.
[2] 'Of all imports probably less than 10% in beads, cloth and copper went to
the native chiefs in payment of the ivory supplied by them. . . . Commodities
are never imported from Khartoum in sufficient quantities to develop a normal
traffic with the natives and thus the best intentions of Emin Bey and others were
entirely defeated.' Junker, vol. ii, p. 28.
[3] Junker, vol. i, p. 497; Vita Hassan, *Die Wahrheit über Emin Pascha*, Berlin,
1893, vol. ii, p. 34.
[4] C.M.S. MSS. Nyanza 1879. Pearson to Wright, 29/I/79.
[5] Vita Hassan, vol. i, p. 13. A 'tokul' is a round mud hut.

and a hospital which he ran practically single-handed.[1] Nevertheless his position was essentially that of an extraneous 'technical expert', whose function in this evolving society was to be a symbol representing the alien and hardly understood, yet revered, authority of Khartoum and Cairo; standing above, judging and repressing the internecine feuds of the stations. By discountenancing robbery, corruption and the slave trade, his influence over these communities, slight as it was, mitigated the harshness of their impact on the surrounding tribal societies, and at least prevented an intensification of the abuses fostered by his predecessor. It was in this negative, indirect way, by filling this almost inconspicuous role, that he made his greatest contribution to the history of the peoples of the southern Sudan.

The slightness of his control and influence over the stations was paralleled by the faintness of their impact on the surrounding tribes. Both these facts were mirrored in his diary and especially in the records of the tours of inspection which he periodically undertook. On these tours he travelled from station to station, staying a few days to inspect their accounts, to initiate small agricultural improvements or to install a loom for the manufacture of 'damur' cloth, and to attempt to regulate their internal affairs. Even these visits, however, were very few and far between, and, apart from the riverain posts linking Lado and Dufile, the stations were not visited more than once or twice throughout the whole of the five years preceding the onset of the menace from the Mahdiya. Apart from these tours his contact with the outlying stations was limited to the despatch of scanty supplies, to the removal or promotion of some official, and to the occasional arrival of an ivory caravan bringing news perhaps of a successful razzia. His personal contact with the tribes of his province was even more restricted. On his tours he usually followed the beaten track between the stations, and his remoteness from tribal problems in contrast to later administrators in Africa is probably best illustrated by the fact that throughout these years he only once records that he was asked to arbitrate in a dispute on tribal boundaries.[2]

Emin could therefore attempt to exert only a superficial control over developments in the vast area committed to his charge, and

[1] P. V. Zucchinetti, 'Mes Voyages au Bahr-el-Gabel.' *Bull. Soc. Khéd. Géog.*, 1881.
[2] Emin to Hansal, 23/V/81, in *Emin Pasha in Central Africa*, p. 297.

variations in the influence exerted by the stations were largely
dependent on factors beyond his control. All the stations were
remarkably self-contained, but the distinction persisted between
those to the east, reached from the Bahr el Jebel, and those to the
west, which flanked the route leading inland from Shambe and
southwards to the Mangbetu, and which were more intimately
linked with previous developments in the Bahr el Ghazal and the
more intensive Arab settlement of the area.[1]

In the eastern part, from the Lado—Dufile line stretching east-
wards to the Lotuko and the Acholi, the independent Danaqla
traders had never been firmly established and their power had been
partially broken and harnessed by Baker and Gordon. Their
dependence on the Bahr el Jebel for all communication with the
outside world also made the export of slaves too expensive and
dangerous to be worthwhile, provided that a responsible European
was in control at Lado. In this area therefore the impact of the
alien communities on tribal society was less disruptive and the
clash of interests was easier to harmonize than in the west. The
dragomen, or 'detribalized' African interpreters, remained the
link between the Danaqla or official garrisons and the tribal
sections in their immediate neighbourhood; and in co-operation
with these interpreters the chiefs of these sections found their
power enhanced by their connection with the stations. The links
formed between the inmates of the station and its neighbouring
African village or tribal section were often remarkably strong: in
1878 when Emin visited Fabbo on his way to Fatiko, the principal
station among the Acholi, he confessed that he was 'somewhat
surprised that here as in Faloro the people wanted to have the
Danaqla back again',[2] and in 1881, during a tour of the Lotuko
and northern Acholi areas, he continually remarked on the good
relations existing between the stations and their immediate
neighbours.[3] On his tours of inspection Emin encountered several
of these semi-Arabized chiefs. Agouk, for example, the local
Acholi chief near Fadibek, 'a former flourishing station given up
on Gordon's orders', seemed to Emin 'a thorough Dongolaui in
appearance and manners, dresses exactly as they do, sits on an
Anqareb (wooden bedstead) and regales his guests with coffee'.

[1] See map no. 6.
[2] Emin, *Tagebücher*, vol. ii, 29/XII/78.
[3] Ibid., 21/III/81.

This Acholi chief repeatedly asked for the re-establishment of the station and even brought ivory to Fatiko as a present, while beyond Fadibek Emin reported that 'at every hamlet we passed the chief came to greet us generally dressed in a long coloured shirt and a tarbush'.[1]

Thus in the immediate vicinity of the stations the local tribesmen were beginning to participate peaceably in the foundations of a new way of life. It has been suggested that there are three broad stages in the assimilation of Islam by a pagan people. In the first place certain elements of material culture—dress, ornaments etc.—are adopted. Closely linked with this is the first infiltration of Islamic religious practices, which are easily absorbed into pagan traditional patterns since the pagan's belief in Dynamism makes him ready to experiment with new techniques: the amulets of the Fakir mingle with the charms of the witch doctors. Finally there comes a loss of faith in the traditional religious sanctions and a genuine belief in the efficacy of those of Islam. There are of course infinite degrees of belief and practice which are gradually reached in this final stage, and it would be false to suggest that these stages represent exact and rigid divisions; but it seems that the acceptance of, or entrance upon, this final stage is marked primarily by the use of a sacred prayer-place, by the observance of the Islamic Feasts and the Fast of Ramadan and by the orientation of graves towards Mecca, accompanied by a progressive renunciation of practices which are condemned by Islam.[2]

The evidence is insufficient to be able to suggest with any degree of confidence the extent to which Islam was penetrating into the tribal societies surrounding the stations in Equatoria. It has already been seen, however, that elements of material culture were being accepted quite freely, and the fact that at Lado 'all the chiefs of the neighbourhood' were present at the Feast of 'Id al-Ṣaghīr in 1881[3] indicates that in some places possibly a genuine belief was taking root. Nor is this wholly contradicted by Emin's remark that 'during more than twenty years rule, Islam has scarcely made ten proselytes in the whole of our provinces—a greater proof of administrative failure could hardly be furnished'; for, although

[1] Ibid., 17–20/X/80; *Emin Pasha in Central Africa*, p. 272. The significance of this change is enhanced when it is remembered that the Acholi shared the common Nilotic scorn for clothing of any kind.

[2] J. S. Trimingham, *Islam in Ethiopia*, 1952, pp. 271–4.

[3] Emin, *Tagebücher*, vol. ii, 27/VIII/81.

this comment throws a flood of light on his conception of the task facing an administrator placed in his position, the fact that it was written in despair, after a disheartening tour of the Rohl district, makes it probable that he here underestimates the spread of Islam, and it is of course difficult to know exactly what he meant by the word 'proselyte'.[1] His remark does, however, demonstrate how restricted was the influence of the station communities over even their nearest neighbours.

In these lands east of the Bahr el Jebel, beyond the immediate bounds of the few tribal villages and chiefs intimately connected with the stations, the impact of the alien intruders was still slighter. When it is remembered, however, that Emin was only given a brief respite of five years before he was forced to struggle desperately against the challenge of the Mahdiya, that he inherited a province inperfectly pacified by Gordon and thoroughly disordered by the 'interregnum' which preceded his appointment, that after 1881 he was prevented from revisiting these eastern lands, and that throughout this area the segmentary nature of the tribal societies rendered the constructive or extensive use of any indigenous authority virtually impossible, it is remarkable that he succeeded in expanding the area of influence and confidence.

In some places this expansion was a slow and patient process. Tribal sections, previously hostile to the Government, gradually came to recognise the importance of accepting the protection of the imperial power, and to a certain extent they began to acknowledge its authority. Alloron, the Bari headman at Gondokoro who had been the ally of the traders and who after resisting Baker had finally co-operated with Ra'ūf and Gordon, was an important figure in this process. Although the foundation of Lado had greatly diminished the importance of Gondokoro, Emin continued to maintain a small garrison there partly for the sake of the lemon trees originally planted by the Austrian missionaries, and principally as an indispensable base for convoys journeying to the important centres amongst the Lotuko. Alloron's loyalty was an advantage to this garrision, and by his example and influence he succeeded in persuading Befo, Chief of Belinian and a bitter opponent of Baker, to accept Government protection. Partly as a result of this alliance, Rugong, the son and successor of Legghe who as chief of the Lokoya had for so long defied the traders from

[1] Emin to Schweinfurth (no date) in *Emin Pasha in Central Africa*, p. 414.

his mountain stronghold, submitted and, although his area was 'still virtually independent', Emin considered that it could be crossed 'almost without an escort'.[1] Other Bari, Lotuko and Pajulu headmen, encouraged sometimes by a small gift of cloth or cognac and needing protection against hostile neighbours, attached themselves to the Government, supplied porters, and agreed to pay a grain tax,[2] while during his tours of inspection Emin was sometimes visited by neighbouring independent headmen with gifts or the request for the construction of a station in their neighbourhood.[3] Yet this promising extension of peaceful influence was still in its weakest infancy, and oppression had left a bitter undercurrent of hostility. The rumours of the Mahdi's challenge to the Government were soon to reveal the fragility of these alliances, and Alloron himself became a leader of the intrigues against Emin.[4]

Elsewhere, and especially on the frontiers of these lands east of the Bahr el Jebel, the expansion of alien influence followed an older pattern. From Fadjulli, a station amongst the eastern Acholi, expeditions were penetrating the lands to the east and by 1881 they had come into contact with the Lango and the Turkana.[5] From Tarrangole amongst the Lotuko, they were reaching forth to Irenga and were hoping soon to be in contact with the Galla and the kingdom of Kaffa. These untouched tribes were willing to barter ivory for beads and Emin wrote optimistically that 'only beads, copper and cloth are needed to enable us to push forward further and further'.[6] But the supplies of these trade goods were inadequate, the difficulties of fostering legitimate commerce continued to be great, and the evidence suggests that in these frontier districts, remote from Emin's control, the official and irregular garrisons found it easier to employ the violent methods of their trading predecessors. From Dufile to Wadelai it was impossible to travel by land because of Madi hostility;[7] beyond

[1] Ibid., pp. 218–20; Emin, *Tagebücher*, vol. ii, 25/I/79, 18/III/80 and 28/III/81—3/IV/81.
[2] Emin, *Tagebücher*, vol. ii, 9–11/X/82, 16/IX/81. The area surrounding Fatiko supplied the stations from Dufile to Mruli with grain, which was so plentiful that an observer reported that the tax was paid 'with ease and even without murmuring', Wilson and Felkin, vol. ii, p. 68.
[3] *Emin Pasha in Central Africa*, p. 231.
[4] See below, p. 160.   [5] Ibid., p. 250.
[6] Emin, *Tagebücher*, vol. ii, 4/V/81, 12/V/81, 22/VIII/82. Letter from Lupton, 27/IV/81.
[7] Ibid., 29/I/80; *Emin Pasha in Central Africa*, p. 152.

Wadelai, to the west of Lake Albert, razzias were often undertaken;[1] the garrison on the Victoria Nile, re-established by Emin
in 1880 after Gordon had ceased to be Governor-General, continued to exploit the rivalry between Rionga and Kaberega;[2] in
1882, during Emin's temporary absence in Khartoum, a large and
unsuccessful razzia was undertaken against the Lango;[3] and some
measure of the failure of the Egyptians to establish a legitimate
trade can be glimpsed from the fact that the Acholi continued to
supply Mutesa, via Rionga, with ivory in exchange for brass[4] and that
even the Lotuko imported brass-coils from Zanzibar via Buganda.[5]

Thus beyond the immediate vicinity and intimate impact of the
station communities, and apart from a significant but restricted
and fragile growth of protective alliances carefully fostered by
Emin, the contact between the intruders and the tribal societies
seems to have followed the customary patterns of violence. Many
tribes remained hostile and fresh tribes became alienated; but large
tracts of untouched land afforded an easily accessible asylum, and
Emin, by his tours of inspection and by his control over the
riverain stations from Lado to Dufile, at least prevented widespread
destruction and enslavement in these eastern districts.

It was, however, the districts to the west of the Bahr el Jebel
that increasingly demanded his attention, and at the same time
presented a far harder problem of control. As it became obvious
that Egyptian domination over the Lacustrine kingdoms was no
longer an immediate possibility, Emin's interest began to be focussed on the fertile Mangbetu area, and the extension of Egyptian
rule in the upper basin of the Wele became his primary objective.
To achieve this he hoped to pioneer a route from Wadelai westwards
through unexplored country to the upper tributaries of the Wele.
This would have opened up fresh tribes, would have considerably
lessened the need for long convoys of porters to transport the ivory of
the Mangbetu along the routes northwards to Lado and Shambe, and
if successful would have formed a spring-board for a drive southwards towards the River Congo.[6] Yet before he could devote

[1] Emin, *Tagebücher*, vol. ii, 12/XII/79.
[2] Ibid. 9/XI/80, 5/X/82. Examining the records of the Mruli garrison Emin
discovered that 1,000 oxen had been eaten in 7 months, ibid. 18/I/80.
[3] Ibid. 13–16/VII/82.
[4] Ibid. 28/X/80; *Emin Pasha in Central Africa*, p. 278.
[5] Emin, *Tagebücher*, vol. ii, 5/IV/81.
[6] Ibid., Emin to Prof. Behm, 24/III/80, and 20/X/82; *Emin Pasha in Central
Africa*, pp. 144, 258–9.

himself to this project he found himself compelled to grapple with the situation in the districts of Makaraka and Rohl.

From the very beginning of his time as Governor, Emin realised that the presence of numerous Danaqla in the lands to the west of the Bahr el Jebel constituted a serious obstacle to any attempt to control developments in that area. 'I believe', he wrote to Gordon, 'that under a rational system Makaraka and Rohl will be a paradise: it is essential however to eject the Danagla'.[1] He did not, however, realise at first the difficulties of this undertaking. It will be remembered how Chaillé-Long,[2] entrusted by Gordon with the task of establishing official garrisons among the Makaraka, had been confronted with the opposition of the Danaqla zeriba settlers, and although an official, Baḵẖīt Bey, was subsequently appointed to the command of the district he seems merely to have adopted their oppressive methods.[3]

Yet in Makaraka district this oppression, though firmly established was neither indiscriminate nor unrelieved. With the Makaraka themselves a *modus vivendi* was achieved, and the courage, ability, intelligence and industry of these isolated Zande invaders was harnessed by the Danaqla. In 1877 it was estimated that about 1,500 adult male Makaraka ruled over about 11,000 people of subject races, who formed a sub-stratum of agricultural labourers, porters, and 'tax-payers'.[4] The Danaqlas' relations with the Makaraka and their subject peoples were carried on chiefly through Ringio, an Azande of aristocratic birth who had been to Khartoum in Petherick's service. 'Thoroughly imbued with the manners and customs' of the Danaqla, Ringio commanded 'considerable influence with his fellow-countrymen'; after the establishment of official garrisons at Wandi and the other principal stations he became 'a true servant of the government', and accompanied Emin on his tours of inspection.[5] It was he who raised

[1] He continued: 'Pour Makaraka je garantis si Votre Excellence me laisse libre-main, toujours y compris l'éloignement des Danagla!' C.M.S. MSS. Emin to Gordon, 27/X/78.   [2] See above, p. 115.

[3] 'Quant à la province de Makraka tant le gouverneur Atrouche bey, que le commandant des troupes, le lieutenant-colonel Behit bey, s'occupaient exclusivement de l'ésclavage'. Gessi to Ra'ūf, 13/II/81, in Zaghi, *Riconquista*, p. 524.

[4] Junker, vol. i, p. 482. The estimate for the Makaraka was based on a census of all the chief's bondsmen. Extensive plantations surrounded the principal stations and the 'continuous procession of fields and villages' reminded Emin of the fertile settlements in Buganda (Emin, *Tagebücher*, vol. ii, 8/VIII/80).

[5] Junker, vol. i, p. 304, vol. ii, p. 452. cp. also, Emin *Tagebücher*, vol. ii, 26–30/X/82.

a levy of men to transport the steamer sections to the Albert Nile,[1] and, although the 'genuine Niam-Niam' or Azande would never serve as carriers, many of them with his encouragement enrolled as volunteer soldiers. Nearly all the soldiers at Lado were from the Makaraka district,[2] and it became a fairly common occurrence for a caravan of several hundred persons from Makaraka district to travel to Lado in order to exchange corn for cloth and spirits with the station's inhabitants.[3] After a lengthy visit to the area Junker considered that the Danaqla and official garrisons, by imposing peace and preventing any further disruptive Zande expansion, had 'created the conditions in Makaraka which made the advance of civilization possible'.[4]

Yet it was only a possibility, and this integration of the Makaraka with the Danaqla did but cloak and mitigate the oppression and destruction. Ringio told Junker that the continual demands and levies of the intruders created 'considerable disaffection' even within this integration,[5] and beyond its bounds the chaos continued unchecked. In November 1877 Junker accompanied an expedition of 1,000 men which struck southwards deep into the lands of the Kalika, a Madi sub-tribe, in search of ivory. An alliance was formed with some chiefs and for days the neighbourhood was laid waste. Hundreds of oxen and women were taken; and wherever possible they were later exchanged for ivory by the Danaqla and the regular troops.[6] The motive and the methods of their activity continued unchanged, and when five years later Emin visited these southern tribes he found many of them completely destitute of cattle.[7]

In the district of Rohl conditions were even more serious. Potentially it was the most important and richest district of the province. Situated on the strategic highway between Shambe on the Bahr el Jebel and the ivory lands of Mangbetu and the south, it included the grass plains inhabited by the powerful and cattle-rich Agar, Gok, and Cic Dinka tribes and the fertile agricultural lands of the eastern Bongo, Madi, and Mittu tribal groups. The

---

[1] G. Casati, *Ten Years in Equatoria*, 2 vols., 1891, vol. i, p. 253.
[2] Wilson and Felkin, vol. ii, p. 104.
[3] Junker, vol. i, p. 241–2. Emin, *Tagebücher*, vol. ii, 1–2/VIII/80, 7–10/V/83.
[4] Junker, vol. i, p. 498.
[5] Ibid., p. 494.
[6] Ibid., pp. 449–71.
[7] *Emin Pasha in Central Africa*, p. 365.

zeribas, founded originally by de Malzac, the Poncets, and Petherick, and subsequently owned or hired from the Government by Ghattās and ʿAbd al-Ṣamad, had passed under the nominal administration of the Government, and in 1874 Gordon established a station at Shambe. Despite these changes the Danaqla settlers continued to undertake raids for ivory, cattle and slaves,[1] and although the mudir of the district, Yūsuf al-Shallālī, supported Gessi in the campaign against Sulaimān, he actively took part in the slave trade sending several batches of slaves to Khartoum on his own account,[2] while like his trading predecessors he made a profit of 200 per cent on cotton-goods sold to the Danaqla. After Sulaimān's defeat many Jellaba found refuge in the Rohl zeribas. They reinforced the Danaqla irregulars and remained completely outside the orbit of Gessi's effective control, so that in 1881 when the district was placed under Emin, he found himself confronted with disorder on a formidable scale.

On the arrival in Lado in September 1881 of a deputation of Agar chiefs with complaints against some Danaqla who had seized their children, Emin decided to undertake a tour of inspection. Both at Rumbek and Ajak he discovered more than a thousand slaves many of them having recently been brought from south of the Wele; at Bufi a local official had collected over 100 slaves, and in the same place over 400 slaves were reclaimed as relatives by Africans from the surrounding tribes; at Biti, another zeriba settlement, he captured a Fakir from Bornu who had collected 26 slaves 'by going from village to village among the Mangbettu' and had already been imprisoned for slave-trading during Gordon's administration.[3] Throughout the area he found hundreds of Danaqla with their numerous dependents living at the expense of the surrounding tribes; and in one village he found a Danaqla living 'like a sultan', whose corn magazine, despite the fact that the harvest had yet to be gathered in, would have supplied Lado station for 6–7 months.[4]

This pressure was principally borne by the scattered and sedentary agricultural tribes. Some sections suffered almost

---

[1] Junker (vol. i, pp. 422–8) describes how in some districts 'cattle-raising has almost disappeared', and how several small tribes 'being preyed on from all sides' had fled to find refuge with the Zande chiefs Mbio and Ansea. 'Everywhere', he continues, there were 'traces of pillage and extermination'.

[2] Zaghi, *Riconquista*, pp. 327, 457.

[3] Emin, *Tagebücher*, vol. ii, 5/IX/81—12/XI/81.   [4] Ibid. 21/XI/81.

complete annihilation and disintegration: one Madi chief, an agent of the Danaqla, had gained authority over about 5,000 men from other tribes.[1] The fierce nomadic Dinka tribes were better equipped to preserve their independence, and at Rumbek, even after twenty years of settlement, it was still impossible to obtain porters from the neighbouring Agar. But many of their women and children were carried off,[2] and, although they still possessed vast herds of cattle,[3] the inroads caused by the recurrent razzias had forced the Agar to reduce their bride-price from 50–60 cows to 8 or 10.[4]

In the midst of this oppression it is a striking witness both to their own independence and to Emin's symbolic prestige that the deputation of Agar chiefs should have travelled the long distance to Lado to seek his assistance. This prestige was Emin's sole support. At the large settlement of Ajak, where the Arabs were reputed to be contemplating armed opposition, his small escort of ten soldiers formed 'a comical contrast' to the two hundred Danaqla drawn up as a 'guard of honour';[5] but here as elsewhere he proceeded to emancipate those slaves who were able to request his aid, and stringent regulations were issued concerning the future taxation of Danaqla settlers and the registration of all slaves. Situated as he was, however, with no-one on whom he could rely to exercise supervision over this turbulent area, Emin could achieve no permanent improvement. His visit resulted in a large-scale emigration of many of the Danaqla,[6] but the abuses continued, and he was soon to be faced with a mass rebellion on the part of the Dinka.

In February 1882, soon after he had returned from this tour, Emin left by steamer to pay a visit to Khartoum. He hoped to persuade the Governor-General to grant him a greater degree of autonomy for, unlike Baker and Gordon who had been directly responsible to the Khedive, Emin was subject to the Governor-General's control, and he felt himself shackled by the fact that his

[1] Wilson and Felkin, vol. ii, p. 129.
[2] In Ajak Emin restored about 400 slaves who had been recruited from the Agar, 'Kitj' and Atwot. Emin, *Tagebücher*, vol. ii, 11/XI/81.
[3] In two Agar districts alone there were 5–6,000 head of cattle.
[4] Ibid., 27/IX/81.
[5] *Emin Pasha in Central Africa*, p. 331.
[6] 400 accompanied him to Khartoum while others went to the Bahr el Ghazal. Ibid., p. 413.

decisions were sometimes easily overruled or modified by appeal to Khartoum. In 1881 his plans to erect military stations to safeguard the route to Mangbetu had been countermanded. He had also had to withdraw an expeditionary force he had sent to Mangbetu as it had aroused the opposition of the Danaqla and he feared lest Khartoum would be sympathetic to their complaints.[1] Yet despite serious frustrations and continued disorder in many districts, as Emin left Lado in 1882 the internal difficulties of the province seemed by no means to be insurmountable. Although as yet no broad economic development had been initiated, during 1881, the first full year in which he had been connected by steamers with Khartoum, he had been able to obtain for the Government a surplus of £5–6,000 thus proving that the province was self-supporting and that its development would be a worthwhile undertaking.[2]

Although violence, destruction and bitter hostility often prevailed in the large areas which remained beyond the range of his effective control, the Egyptian province of Equatoria was still the sole attempt to establish a wide framework of law and order in the depths of tropical Africa. Around the station communities a new way of life, based ultimately on the wider horizons of a universal religion, was struggling into existence. The resources for a vast Egyptian expansion were manifestly non-existent; but, although the activities of Stanley on the Congo, of the African Lakes Company on Lake Nyasa, and of missionaries in Buganda and on Lake Tanganyika, were directing European attention elsewhere,[3] the Nile remained a major highway into the heart of Africa. Emin must have felt that there was every reason to hope that the foundations laid in Equatoria and the Bahr el Ghazal had not been constructed in vain. It was only when he reached the River Sobat that he heard of the success of the Mahdi.

[1] Ibid., p. 420–1. Emin to Schweinfurth, 31/I/82.
[2] Ibid., p. 420. Emin to Schweinfurth, 25/XII/81. He hoped to alleviate the transport problem by using a light steamer to link up with an overland route to the Sobat, thus by-passing the ever-recurring 'sudd' barriers on the main river.
[3] See below, pp. 178–9.

V

THE DESTRUCTION

THE final collapse of Egyptian rule in Equatoria and the Bahr
el Ghazal was due to events in Egypt and the northern
Sudan, which engulfed in complete destruction this fragile
structure of authority. The many crippling commitments incurred
by Ismāʻīl proved to be suicidal; his numerous enterprises became
mutually destructive. The attempt to expand simultaneously in
Darfur, Abyssinia, the Somali Coast and Equatoria involved him
in retreat, retrenchment, and failure in all these fields, while for
Egypt itself the financial burden was disastrous. The losing struggle
to avoid bankruptcy ended in July 1879 with Ismāʻīl's deposition,
but the system of Dual Control by which France and Britain, the
principal creditor countries, appointed two Controllers to advise
Tawfīq, his successor, proved unable to establish stability. In 1881
the Egyptian sections of the Army, led by an Egyptian officer
Aḥmad ʻUrābī, mutinied against the Turkish officers and Government, and Tawfīq was shorn of all real authority. In January 1882
Britain and France presented a joint-note proclaiming support for
Tawfīq, which immediately intensified Egyptian civil and military
opposition to all forms of foreign interference. Hostility to Europeans rapidly developed and in June fifty Europeans were killed in
Alexandria. A month later the British fleet bombarded Alexandria,
an army was landed, and with the defeat of ʻUrābī's force on 13
September 1882 the British occupation of Egypt was effected.[1]
The immediate concern of the British was to curtail all commitments and to avoid any expensive entanglements, but this might
possibly have led to a careful consolidation[2] in the Sudan had it
not been for the intervention of the Mahdiya.

The first serious challenge to Egyptian rule had drawn its
strength from the threatened vested interests of the Bahr el Ghazal
traders, and Sulaimān's defeat, it will be remembered, had left a
legacy of bitter hatred.[3] The trade of the leading merchants at

---

[1] Cromer, vol. i, pp. 149–331.
[2] E.g. Dufferin's opinions quoted by Shibeika, pp. 56–58.
[3] See above, pp. 124–7.

El Obeid and other centres had been disrupted; the Jellaba, or petty itinerant traders, had been stripped of all their possessions and forced to return to their overcrowded, heavily-taxed homes; the Danaqla and Ja'liyin settlers had been ousted from their comfortable zeribas; the restless nomadic Baqqara tribes, who had been the allies of Zubair, resented the attempt of the Government to circumscribe their freedom and tax their cattle: all these awaited an opportunity to return to their old activities and if necessary to rid themselves from the shackles of Egyptian rule. And this was but one of the sources of mounting discontent in the northern Sudan. The burden of oppressive taxation, inequitably collected by an alien soldiery, had steadily increased until large areas were simply uncultivated and the inhabitants had disappeared into more inaccessible regions; throughout the Sudan there were few who were actively disposed to support this incompetent, though often well-intentioned, Government. The Mahdi's passionate proclamation of a return to the pristine springs of religious simplicity revealed in glaring contrast the corruption and materialism of the 'Turks'. It welded together the various and incoherent sources of discontent and succeeded in temporarily transcending the barriers of tribal jealousies. And the peoples of the southern Sudan were gradually drawn into the vortex of these events.

Born in 1844 the son of a Dongolawi boat-builder who claimed to be a descendant of the Prophet, Muḥammad Aḥmad studied at a Koranic school in the Gezira and at a mosque near Berber. From there he joined an ascetic Sufi fraternity and established a lodge south of Khartoum on Aba Island in the White Nile, where his family joined him in their boat-building activities. His determined piety and rigorous asceticism led him to criticize his Shaikh or leader whereupon he was excommunicated from the fraternity. Forced to think and act as an individual, Muḥammad, surrounded by religious and secular abuses, became convinced that he was the long expected Mahdi who would reform Islam and would establish justice and equity upon the earth. He began to write letters to religious leaders confiding to them his mission, and he toured Kordofan Province receiving promises of support. The Governor-General investigated these activities through the local Kadi (religious judge) and then sent a peaceful mission to Aba Island under Abū Su'ūd, the former antagonist of Baker.[1] Muḥammad

[1] See above, pp. 96, 99, 114.

Aḥmad, however, rejected this overture and Abū Suʿūd was next ordered to effect his capture with two companies of regular soldiers from Khartoum. Muḥammad could rely only on some three hundred ill-armed followers—men for the most part attracted by his sanctity and his call to a 'jihād' or holy war. On 12 August 1881 their fierce enthusiasm routed the incompetently led soldiers: the Mahdiya had begun. After this skirmish the Mahdi withdrew with his small group of followers from his exposed position on Aba Island into the inaccessible stronghold of Jebel Gedir in the Nuba Mountains. Here he was joined by many of the Jellaba whom Gessi and Gordon had evicted from the Bahr el Ghazal and Shaka, and by many refugees who had fled from the harsh taxation in Kordofan. It was also the country of the Baqqara, with whom the Mahdi established close contact. His most trusted and powerful disciple and successor, ʿAbd Allāhī, came from the Taʿaisha Baqqara, and the Baqqara as a whole formed his cavalry corps and fighting strength in these early years. Government officials, however, completely underestimated the new religious cohesion which sublimated tribal differences and they were confident that the movement could easily be suppressed.[1]

The nearest garrison to Jebel Gedir was at Fashoda, a hundred miles away, and the local Mudir, seeking the glory of suppressing the rising, prepared to take independent action. Since 1870, when Baker had witnessed the disorder and disruption of Shilluk society caused by the incursions of the garrison at Fashoda,[2] distressingly little progress had been achieved. In 1875, exasperated by the Mudir's oppression, the Shilluk attacked Kaka, killed the Mudir when he went to its relief, and were prevented from capturing Fashoda only by the arrival of reinforcements from Khartoum.[3] Six years later the Austrian Consular Agent reported that hundreds of Jellaba regularly travelled to Fashoda to purchase crowds of slaves, who were captured and sold by the government forces in order to cover the tax of £12,500 which they were ordered to send annually to Khartoum.[4] Some sections of the Shilluk, however, under the leadership of their reth Kaiku had accepted the presence of the garrisons and were willing to co-operate in an attack on the

[1] Shibeika, pp. 20–30; P. M. Holt, The Mahdist State in the Sudan, 1958, pp. 37–48.
[2] See above, p. 92.
[3] Zaghi, Riconquista, p. 130, Vakil to Gordon, 18/X/75.
[4] O.S. Ad. Reg. F.34/281. Hansal to Schaeffer, 7/V/81.

Mahdi, so in December 1881 the Mudir was able to lead out a force of 400 soldiers and 1,000 Shilluk spearmen; but, taken by surprise, the expedition was almost completely annihilated with practically no loss to the Mahdi's forces.[1]

The defeat had widespread repercussions. For the garrisons among the Shilluk the death of their ally, Kaiku, was considered 'an irreparable loss', and when Emin on his way to Khartoum passed through Fashoda at the end of February 1882 he discovered that a mass rising of the Shilluk was feared.[2] More important still was the fact that it greatly increased the prestige of the Mahdi and compelled the authorities at Khartoum to take active measures. A force of 4,000 men was extracted from garrisons throughout the Sudan and under the command of Yūsuf al-Shallālī, who had served as Gessi's second-in-command, it was launched into the Nuba Mountains. Carelessness, low morale and incompetency were again contrasted with the fervour of the Mahdi's followers and on 30 May 1882 the army was completely defeated.[3] The Egyptian Government, caught in the crisis which was leading to the British occupation, could do nothing immediately to remedy the dangerous situation in the Sudan. The Mahdi was able to sweep into Kordofan capturing El Obeid in January 1883, and simultaneously, as a side issue, to carry the war into Darfur and the Bahr el Ghazal.

Gessi had left the Bahr el Ghazal in September 1880 and his successor, Frank Lupton, a young English merchant seaman who in 1878 had been sent by Gordon to take command of the Lotuko district under Emin,[4] did not arrive there until the end of 1881. Although the evidence is scanty there can be little doubt that during this interregnum the promising yet precarious projects initiated by Gessi had been neglected by the subordinate officials, while the Arab settlers and traders had taken the opportunity to consolidate their position and recommence their trade.[5] Lupton had no real opportunity to assert control over the province and he remained 'a mere figure-head'.[6] Effective power stayed in the

[1] Shibeika, p. 31; Holt, p. 48.
[2] A.S.S. MSS. Schweinfurth to Allen, 15/I/82; Emin, *Tagebücher*, vol. ii, 28/II/82.
[3] Shibeika, pp. 37-40; Holt, pp. 49-50.
[4] Hill, *Biographical Dictionary*.
[5] Junker, vol. iii, pp. 133-218.
[6] Emin to Schweinfurth, 3/III/83, in *Emin Pasha in Central Africa*, p. 430.

hands of Zemio the Arabized Zande chief, of traders like
'Uthman Badawi 'and 'Abd Allāhi 'Abd al-Ṣamad, or of the
scattered subordinate officials whose sympathies lay chiefly with
the dispossessed Danaqla settlers. The opening months of 1882
were occupied with a bitter campaign against Mbio, the last
independent Zande ruler north of the Wele, who was finally
defeated and taken as a captive to Wau.[1] In August however the
first warning of the Mahdi's intervention arrived with the rebellion of Chief Jango of Telqauna.

Telqauna, a small, isolated plateau strategically placed south-
east of Hofrat en Nahas and about a hundred miles north of Dem
Zubair, had been one of the first outposts of the overland Arab
traders who had settled there before Ḥabashī and Petherick had
started to explore the Bahr el Ghazal,[2] and in the time of Heuglin
and Schweinfurth it had been 'a well-known market' for ivory and
slaves and contained 'numerous settlements of immigrant Niam
Niam'.[3] Chief Jango, the head of this motley yet influential
community, had been one of the first to rise against Sulaimān:
supplied with ammunition by Gessi, he had so menaced Sulaimān's
lines of communication that the latter had been compelled to
despatch a large force in a vain endeavour to suppress him.[4] In
June 1879 he had welcomed Gessi on a visit to Telqauna but
subsequently he was robbed by an Arab official, and although
Gessi granted him redress this incident may well have unsettled
his allegiance.[5] But the decisive factor leading to his rebellion was
undoubtedly the influence of the Mahdi which reached him through
Madibbū, chief of the Rizeiqat Baqqara tribe.

From the first the Mahdi, as has been seen, was in close contact
with the Baqqara tribes of western Kordofan. Madibbū, who had
come into conflict with Gessi and the administration in Darfur,[6]
visited Jebel Gedir, was present at the complete defeat of Yūsuf
al-Shallālī in June 1882, and returned with captured ammunition,
horses, and slaves, together with a holy standard and numerous

---

[1] Junker, vol. iii, pp. 139, 302, 319. Emin, *Tagebücher*, vol. ii, 1/XI/82.
See also Evans-Pritchard, *Zaïre*, 1956, pp. 687–701.

[2] See above, p. 66.

[3] Inscriptions on the maps in Heuglin, op. cit., and Schweinfurth, op. cit.
Niam-Niam = Azande.

[4] Zaghi, *Riconquista*, p. 365.

[5] Ibid., pp. 383–4, 536.

[6] Zaghi, *Riconquista*, p. 437; Slatin, p. 149.

proclamations from the Mahdi.[1] Emissaries were sent out and on 18 August 1882 Jango responded by killing some Bashi-Buzuks[2] and seizing their property. Lupton promptly despatched a force against him, but Jango succeeded in escaping and joined Madibbū who was besieging Shaka. Towards the end of the year he returned with reinforcements but was defeated with the loss of 600 men.[3]

While occupied with these dangers, Lupton found himself gradually drawn into a full-scale war with the Dinka. As might be expected with this vast, loose group of powerful, independent tribal sections, the struggle started sporadically in a series of scattered incidents. It developed, however, on a wide front, and, although the evidence is slight, there is reason to believe that the influence of emissaries from the Mahdi was reflected in the emergence of Dinka prophets, who succeeded in transcending traditional loyalties and in combining temporarily the various Dinka sections in united action against the occupiers of the zeriba belt.[4]

The Dinka hatred of the alien intruders was the product of prolonged oppression: the habit of cattle raiding while passing through the 'corridor' leading from Meshra er Rek to their zeribas had been established by the traders;[5] during the campaign against Sulaimān some Dinka sections had suffered considerably, and although Gessi attempted to rehabilitate them it will be remembered that this was only partially successful,[6] while in the eastern reaches, in the district of Rohl, their demand for redress rapidly hardened into a determination to exterminate their oppressors. When Lupton was moving against Jango in August 1882 he learnt that a party of 75 of his bazingers—or locally recruited troops—had been massacred while taking ivory to Meshra er Rek, and retaliatory raids were immediately undertaken.[7] In July far away to the east, at Shambe of the Bahr el Jebel, Emin, returning from Khartoum, discovered that the station's commander with the greater part of the garrison had been destroyed

---

[1] Slatin, pp. 156–7.
[2] Turkish term for irregular soldiers, in service of the Government.
[3] Wingate, pp. 28–29.
[4] See below, pp. 158, 161.
[5] See above, p. 61.
[6] See above, p. 131.
[7] Wingate, p. 29.

by the local Dinka while taking part in a cattle razzia against them.[1] These scattered incidents intensified, and by December 1882 Lupton was forced to recall all his forces from the west and south in an attempt to suppress this trouble. In the following months outlying stations amongst the Dinka were overrun, and he was completely cut off from his port at Meshra er Rek. In July 1883 the garrison of Rumbek while conducting an unauthorized razzia was annihilated by the Agar Dinka, the ancient zeriba was captured, another government force was destroyed, and throughout the northern Rohl district the Dinka were in revolt. Then in September Rifā'ī Aghā, Lupton's able and loyal lieutenant, was killed together with 400 men by the Dinka.[2]

Through Lupton's letters one catches glimpses of the new forces at work in Dinka society. He found himself confronted simultaneously by a combination of different Dinka tribes who were making 'good use of captured firearms'; even the Nuer aided them; and the leader of this united opposition in the northern area was a certain Mayendut, 'the great vakil of Mr. Ahmet the Mahdi', who had a 'green flag that was sent by the Mahdi to be carried before the men who fight for him'.[3] Two years later another Dinka prophet arose to unite the tribes and to threaten Emin at Lado,[4] and it has been suggested that the Nuer prophets, who in the 20th century opposed the British, also possibly drew some of their inspiration from the Mahdiya;[5] but this contact with the north must have been slight and unorganized. Divisions amongst Lupton's opponents soon appeared, some of the Rizeiqat started to raid the Dinka for slaves, and by November 1883 their chief Madibbū was fighting the Dinka rather than the Government.[6]

Aided by these divisions, by a strong expedition from Lado which recovered Rumbek, and by supplies of corn and men from the Zande chief Zemio, Lupton was able to survive. He re-established contact with Meshra er Rek where there was a steamer from Khartoum, he defeated and killed Jango, and by the end of

---

[1] Emin, *Tagebücher*, vol. ii, 5/VII/82.

[2] Lupton to Junker, 6/XII/82, 3/IV/83, 19/VII/83, 10/VIII/83, 23/IX/83, in Buchta, *Der Sudan unter Agyptischer Herrschaft*, Leipzig, 1888; Emin, *Tagebücher*, vol. ii, 4–5/VIII/83.

[3] Lupton to Malcolm Lupton, 6/XI/83, in *P.R. Geog. Soc.* 1884, p. 250.; Lupton to Junker, 11/IV/83, 5/V/83 in Buchta, p. 148.

[4] See below, p. 161.

[5] E. E. Evans-Pritchard, *The Nuer*, 1940, p. 187.

[6] Lupton to Junker, 26/XI/83, in Buchta, op. cit.

1883 he was feeling fairly hopeful. By themselves the difficulties with the Dinka seemed by no means insurmountable, and although he realized that nearly all the Arab traders and settlers in the area were zealous followers of the Mahdi he was confident that he could survive the internal challenge.[1]

The end came quickly with a fresh intervention from the north. After the Mahdi's capture of El Obeid in January 1883 it became evident that Khartoum and the whole Sudan was threatened by the rising. Despite the upheaval following the British occupation of Egypt a large army was collected and despatched to Khartoum under the command of a retired British officer, General Hicks. In the scrub desert between the White Nile and El Obeid the expedition of 10,000 men became paralysed by thirst, discipline disappeared, and finally the whole expedition was annihilated by the Mahdists on 5 November 1883. The desperate gamble had failed: only Khartoum and a few garrisons remained, and the fall of Darfur was inevitable.[2] In January 1884 news of this disaster reached Lupton, and Karam Allāh, a Dongolawi who had previously traded in the Bahr el Ghazal, arrived with 5–8,000 men to take possession of the Bahr el Ghazal for the Mahdi. Deserted by his officials and soldiers, Lupton was forced to surrender. On 28 April 1884 he sent his last message to Emin: 'It is all up with me here. Everyone has joined the Mahdi, and his army takes charge of the mudirieh the day after tomorrow. . . . Look out you. Some 8,000 to 10,000 men are coming to you well armed'.[3]

Hitherto Equatoria had lain beyond the radius of the Mahdi's influence. After his return to Lado from his visit to Khartoum in 1882 Emin was indeed beset with many troubles but these arose from the internal problems of his province. The difficulty of exercising any effective control over officials or Danaqla was demonstrated by the flagrant insubordination of Bahkīt Bey, the Mudir of Makaraka district, who marched on Lado and was defeated with difficulty.[4] In 1883 an inspection tour of the Mangbetu area revealed the devastation and anarchy which the Danaqla and sporadic official expeditions had brought to this formerly prosperous land; but here, as in the Rohl district, Emin could achieve little by

[1] Lupton to Junker, 13/VII/83, and to Emin early 1884, in Buchta, pp. 148, 155; Vita Hassan, vol. i, p. 106.
[2] Shibeika, pp. 77–106.
[3] Wingate, pp. 136–7; Holt, pp. 70–72.
[4] Emin, *Tagebücher*, vol. ii, 8/XI/82–13/XII/82.

his visit, and he longed for 'an intelligent European' who could supervise the affairs of this distant frontier.[1] And during these dreary months of stagnation in which he waited impatiently for supplies from Khartoum, Emin lost the loyalty of the two most influential chiefs in the province. Alloron of Gondokoro, stirred apparently by the successful rising of the Dinka, was reported to have invited the chiefs of Belinian and the Lokoya to attack Lado, and Emin authorized his assassination; while Ringio of Makaraka was destroyed by Ibrāhīm Aghā, the successor of Bakhīt Bey.[2] Yet despite these disturbances and the complete lack of positive progress, the position still seemed thoroughly secure. In 1883 there was a clear profit of £12,000, and in 1884 Emin was planning further expeditions to the Congo. On 11 May he wrote to a friend in the ivory trade: 'The trumpet blast of war having now, so to speak, died away in the distance, I have returned with renewed energy to the labour of cabbage planting, "beatus ille qui procul negotiis!" '[3]

With the arrival of Lupton's final message in May 1884, this sense of stability immediately disappeared. At a panic-stricken meeting in Lado it was decided to despatch a delegation to Karam Allāh and to withdraw all the outlying garrisons. Many of these garrisons, however, ignored his orders and waited with some of the Danaqla settlers to see the turn of events. In June, Ibrāhīm Aghā, the Mudir of Makaraka district, deserted to the Mahdists with considerable quantities of government stores.[4] No longer a symbol of an unquestioned authority emanating from Khartoum, Emin, hesitant and bewildered, was quite incapable of grappling with the situation. It was characteristic both of his anomalous position, surrounded as he was by untrustworthy officials in the midst of potentially hostile Africans, and of his own timidity, that, when he heard that the Makaraka chiefs were of their own accord pursuing Ibrāhīm Aghā, he felt that 'naturally' he could have 'no official knowledge of all this'.[5]

[1] Ibid., 1/VII/82.

[2] On Alloron see Emin, *Tagebücher*, vol. iii, 1/XII/83, 19/V/84; Junker, vol. iii, p. 378; Vita Hassan, vol. i, p. 111. On Ringio see Junker, vol. iii, p. 334; Emin found him troublesome, but suggests he was killed in a razzia. (*Tagebücher*, vol. ii, 21/VII/83 and 6/VIII/83).

[3] Emin to Harders, 11/V/84, in Schweitzer, vol. i, p. 157.

[4] Emin, *Tagebücher*, 21/VI/84, 9/VII/84.

[5] Emin MSS. Emin to Junker, 25/VI/84.

He escaped fortuitously. Karam Allāh's advance into Equatoria was delayed by a formidable revolt of the Bazinger troops in the Bahr el Ghazal, and, when he did advance, reports of his harshness strengthened the resistance of the official garrisons in Equatoria. In March 1885, however, after a bitter struggle he captured Amadi, a key station on the River Yei in the Rohl district, and the way lay open to Lado. Emin, having fortified the capital, hurriedly participated in a chaotic evacuation of non-belligerents towards the south, and there can be no doubt that Karam Allāh would have conquered the Province had he not suddenly halted his advance and precipitately retired towards the north-west. His army was needed to suppress trouble in Darfur and to reinforce the main Mahdist army, so he returned with many slaves and the southern Sudan remained free from any further overland invasions.[1]

Emin and Equatoria had escaped, but little of the structure of Egyptian authority survived. The fertile areas of Makaraka and Mangbetu were abandoned, and, while Karam Allāh had been beseiging Amadi, news reached Lado that the garrison at the river-station of Bor was beseiged by Nuer and Dinka tribes. United under the leadership of a prophet called Donlutj, the beseigers 'behaved like Dervishes and wore rosaries'.[2] Karam Allāh had also sent emissaries amongst the Bari, who were embittered by the cattle raids which the garrisons continued to undertake, and the assault on the 'Turks' gradually transcended traditional rivalries. The garrison at Bor was exterminated, and towards the end of 1885 both Lado and Rejaf were fiercely attacked by the local Bari led by Befo, chief of Belinian, who was assisted by Dinka, Aliab, and Mandari elements. Further south the Acholi too were in revolt. The officials at Lado were able to survive these attacks and they captured one of the most famous of the Dinka prophets, but the garrisons were henceforth confined to the narrow river strip linking Lado and Dufile and to the few isolated stations at Wadelai and on the west bank of Lake Albert.[3]

Emin's control over even this slender remnant steadily decreased. The fact that as a passive and impotent spectator he had been content to observe Karam Allāh's progress into Equatoria from afar, had been partly the cause of his salvation—for a man with

---

[1] Ibid., Emin to Junker, 14/V/85. Slatin, pp. 411-12.
[2] Emin, *Tagebücher*, vol. iii, 26/XII/84.
[3] Ibid., 14/X/85 to 16/II/86; Emin MSS. Emin to Junker, 16/X/85, 23/XI/85.

the temperament of Gordon and Baker would almost certainly have attempted to engage the enemy at Amadi and would probably have been overwhelmed in the attempt; it had, however, hardly increased his prestige amongst his subordinates, and at the crucial council when it was decided whether to retreat to the south or not, Emin had withdrawn from the deliberations and had left his Egyptian and Sudanese officials to argue out the issue. In the absence of firm leadership personal jealousies and intrigues abounded, and Emin at Wadelai was unable to exert any effective influence over his subordinates.

Above all there lurked the problem of their future. In January 1885 Khartoum had fallen to the Mahdi and there was no further hope of Egyptian aid from the north. Faced with the possibility of an imminent return of the Mahdists, and surrounded by increasingly hostile tribes, it was imperative to establish contact with the outside world. The only possible route lay southwards through the Lacustrine Kingdoms to Zanzibar. Aided by his former friendship with Kabarega of Bunyoro, Emin was able in January 1886 to send messages to the coast with the German traveller Junker who had been exploring the River Wele and had joined Emin in Lado. It was May 1887, however, before he received news that the explorer Stanley was leading an expedition to his relief,[1] and it was April 1888 before Stanley succeeded in contacting him on the shore of Lake Albert.[2] The relief expedition moreover was seriously weakened by its weary struggle through the dense equatorial forests and Stanley had to return almost immediately to bring up the rearguard which he had left on the Congo. It was decided therefore that Mounteney-Jephson, one of his officers, should remain with Emin and that together they should prepare for Stanley's return and a subsequent march to the coast with all those of Emin's people who wished to leave Equatoria.

The Sudanese officials and soldiers were, however, by no means anxious to abandon their relatively comfortable stations and to embark on a hazardous and arduous evacuation which, if successful, would only lead to an unknown and insecure future. Emin himself was reluctant to abandon his Province, but, hesitant, vacillating,

[1] See below, p. 202.
[2] H. M. Stanley, *In Darkest Africa*, 1890, vol. i; Schweitzer, vol. i, pp. 266–81.

and deterred by Stanley's unmitigated brusqueness, he could not bring himself to discuss with the latter any possible alternative. The bankruptcy of his authority was soon apparent. Jephson and he attempted to prepare for Stanley's return, but the suspicion and opposition amongst the officials and soldiers increased until in August 1888 an open mutiny broke out and both Europeans were imprisoned at Dufile. This impasse was resolved only by a fresh intervention of the Mahdists. After the death of the Mahdi in June 1885 the Khalifā, 'Abd Allāhī, continued his policy of an offensive *jihād*. Campaigns on the Abyssinian and Egyptian frontiers claimed most of his attention, but in June 1888 he also sent a force of 1,500 men by steamers up the White Nile, which arrived in October at Lado and marched southwards determined to exterminate the final remnant of Egyptian power. After severe fighting at Dufile, however, the Mahdists withdrew again to the north, where they remained entrenched at Rejaf, content to use it as a base for slave and ivory raids until they were finally dislodged by Belgian forces advancing from the Congo in 1897. Meanwhile, during this confusion, Emin and Jephson succeeded in sailing southwards to keep their rendezvous with Stanley at Lake Albert, and on 10 April 1889, after a final vain attempt to persuade the Sudanese mutineers to return with them, Emin abandoned Equatoria and marched to the coast with Stanley's expedition.[1]

It was the end of an era, the final moment of a failure. The merchants, in their contact with tribes utterly unprepared for their arrival, had abandoned commerce and taken readily to plunder. The mission, conquered by the climate and the situation of conflict, had withdrawn. Baker's hopes of initiating a beneficient imperial rule over central Africa, of effecting 'a vast improvement among the tribes by the suppression of the Slave Trade and by the introduction of agricultural and commercial enterprise', had from the first encountered the realities and vested interests of the ivory trade, with its established pattern of violence. Subsequently Egypt had been unable to sustain the effort on the scale envisaged by Baker, so that the achievements of Gessi and Emin had lagged far behind even their more modest objectives. Nevertheless, the Egyptian experiment in the southern Sudan had retained its unique position in the colonization of Africa until the intervention

[1] A. J. M. Jephson, *Emin Pasha and the Rebellion at the Equator*, 1890; Wingate, pp. 459–65; Holt, pp. 197–8.

of the Mahdiya destroyed all hope of building on these foundations. Threatened and isolated by the invasion of the Bahr el Ghazal and the capture of Khartoum, Egyptian authority had slowly disintegrated until it was impossible to salvage anything creative. There remained merely the memory of disruption. Contact with the outside world had involved the peoples of the southern Sudan, with but few exceptions, in increased suffering and hardship. A minute minority had entered, or had been forced into, a new way of life with wider horizons; but the majority had remained understandably suspicious and hostile. Where the impact of the intruders had not been utterly destructive, it had been merely superficial. In most cases only a bitter legacy of hatred survived; but already yet another intrusion was developing.

VI

BRITISH INTERESTS AND THE
SOUTHERN SUDAN

1. The slave trade and the highway

WITHIN a decade of Emin's evacuation of Equatoria the attempt to bring the people of the southern Sudan into contact with the outside world started anew. By the twentieth century, however, Britain controlled the process, and at the same time the southern Sudan from being in the forefront of African history became once again one of the most remote parts of tropical Africa. In order to understand this change it is necessary to leave the direct consideration of developments in the area itself, and to examine their significance as reflected in the growth of British interests.

Before the return of Speke and Grant in 1863 there was little active British interest in the southern Sudan. Although in the early 1850's the Savoyard trader, Brun Rollet, complained that British commerce was invading the Sudan 'comme le sable du désert',[1] this penetration was the work of powerful British mercantile firms established in Alexandria and Cairo and the ivory trade on the White Nile was but one of their many interests. These firms had played an important part in the agitation for the removal of the government monopoly,[2] but beyond supplying a few individual European merchants with credit[3] they did not actively participate in the White Nile trade, and by 1863 the fortunes and importance of even the local European merchants based on Khartoum were greatly in decline.[4] Nor was there much official interest in the area. The appointment of Petherick as an honorary Vice-Consul at Khartoum in 1850 was merely a by-product of the monopoly controversy.[5] The post was created on the initiative of the British

---

[1] Brun Rollet, p. 316.
[2] See above, p. 22.
[3] E.g. Vaudey, see above p. 31.
[4] See above, p. 72.
[5] See above, p. 30.

Consul-General in Egypt, and was little more than a private arrangement between Cairo and Khartoum, while in 1859 Petherick's request for full Consular powers was approved without difficulty as it cost the Foreign Office practically nothing and was supported by the Consul-General in Cairo.[1]

The slave trade was the only other issue which attracted British official interest. The great popular Abolitionist crusade had focused British attention on the Atlantic slave trade throughout the first half of the nineteenth century, but by 1863, with the abolition of slavery in America, the Atlantic slave trade had almost ceased and the British public was gradually becoming aware of the evils and extent of the Arab slave trade. In East Africa Zanzibar was the central point of this trade: here Indian traders financed and stocked the Arab caravans which were beginning to penetrate even beyond the Great Lakes into the Congo basin in search of ivory and slaves, and here was the great slave market which swelled the Sultan's revenues. British action against this trade was still confined in 1863 to attempts by Treaty with the Sultan of Zanzibar to restrict[2] and to forbid[3] all export of slaves beyond his African dominions, and the few available British cruisers could catch only a small proportion of the several thousand slaves which continued to be exported annually to the Persian Gulf. Livingstone's Zambezi expedition in 1857 to 1863 and the experiences of the Universities' Mission to Central Africa in Nyasaland were beginning to expose to the British public the havoc which this trade was causing in the interior, but knowledge was still scanty and plans to combat its influence were as yet unformed.[4]

British concern also over the slave trade in the Sudan and the Red Sea was slight and spasmodic before 1860. The report of an official visit to Egypt in 1838 by John Bowring, an intimate friend of Bentham and later a Governor of Hong Kong, revealed the extent of the slave trade in north-east Africa. Bowring provided Buxton with much information and a memorial was presented to Muḥammad ʿAlī,[5] but with the major British effort directed on the Atlantic there was no continuing interest. In 1860, however,

---

[1] F.O. 78/2253 Memo by Petherick, 26/III/1868. His request for fuller power, 17/VIII/1859, is in F.O. 78/1465.
[2] In 1822.
[3] In 1845.
[4] Coupland, pp. 134–152; Oliver, pp. 3–4.
[5] F.O. 78/381. Bowring's report, March 1839.

the reports of the Austrian missionaries and Consul at Khartoum on the state of violence on the White Nile[1] were forwarded to the Foreign Office by the British Consul-General in Cairo, and Petherick was instructed by the Foreign Secretary, Lord John Russell, to 'use his utmost influence to stop these Razzias'.[2] Petherick subsequently reported that 'the slave trade has been energetically pursued . . . and is ostensibly increasing' and he gave details of de Bono's and Muḥammad Khair's activities,[3] but it still seemed a relatively minor affair and there was little that the Foreign Office could do about it.

Speke's return, however, enormously enhanced the importance of the White Nile. His description of the fertile and populous Lacustrine kingdoms of Buganda, Bunyoro, and Karagwe showed that these were the key-points of indigenous power in East Africa and the chief hope of establishing a legitimate commerce in the interior which might defeat the Zanzibar slave trade. The White Nile was suddenly seen to be the 'natural' and most practicable means of access to this area, and Murchison's suggestion[4] that the British Government should encourage Ismā'īl to extend Egyptian sovereignty over the upper reaches of the river forced the Foreign Office to define its attitude to the southern Sudan.

Russell referred the project to Colquhoun, the British Consul-General, who on Speke's arrival in Egypt in 1863 was prepared to urge the Viceroy to establish Egyptian authority at 'various stations beginning at Gondokoro'. Even then, however, he doubted whether this would effectively stop the slave trade if domestic slavery remained an established institution in Egypt and Turkey.[5] Various facts combined to strengthen these doubts. Reports from the Consuls at Jeddah and Smyrna revealed an extensive slave trade carried on by steamers in the Red Sea belonging to the Egyptian Government,[6] and in March 1865 Petherick arrived in Cairo to present a long memorandum on the injustices inflicted by the Governor-General in the Sudan, in an alleged attempt to drive European traders from the country and to establish an Egyptian

[1] See above, p. 75.
[2] F.O. 84/1120 Russell to Petherick, 31/XII/60.
[3] F.O. 84/1144. Petherick to Russell, 25/XI/62.
[4] See above, p. 81.
[5] F.O. 84/1204. Colquhoun to Russell 17 August 1863.
[6] E.g. Calvert to Reade, 30 November 1864, and Bulwer to Russell, 6 January 1865, F.O. 84/1246.

monopoly. His complaints, wrote Colquhoun, were confirmed 'by one who has no interest in the country to bias her—Miss Tinné'.[1] Colquhoun therefore reported firmly and decisively against Speke's proposal:

> Supposing the Egyptian Government were allowed to establish its authority at Gondokoro ... that frontier then would be close to the territories of the Equatorial Kings mentioned by Captain Speke. Is the present Egyptian Government calculated to follow out honestly and beneficially to its neighbours a fair system of commerce and civilization? I doubt it, except it were held in check by the presence of Agents of the principal European Governments who would always have to contend against the trading propensities of its present ruler.[2]

This distrust of an extension of Egyptian power into Equatorial Africa remained a factor of cardinal importance in the British attitude. In part it was linked with the earlier struggle against monopoly which had originally led to Petherick's appointment, but there can be little doubt that the predominant consideration was the fear that Egypt, however good the intentions of its ruler might seem to some observers, would prove an inadequate ally in the struggle against the slave trade.

The other factor which is evident during this early period, and which continued to dominate policy at the Foreign Office, was a cautious economy, based on a desire to avoid any entanglement which might entail expenditure difficult to justify in the House of Commons. Petherick's departure left the Khartoum Consulate vacant, but Baker's reports and the publication of his book in 1865 kept alive public interest,[3] and the attention of the Foreign Office was again directed to the area by Robert Arthington, perhaps the most important Protestant missionary strategist in the nineteenth century. A millionaire, who lived in solitary penury devoting his time to amassing information on Africa, Arthington recognized the supreme importance of inland waterways for the rapid evangelization in which he was chiefly interested, and later he purchased steamers for several missionary Societies for use on the Congo

[1] On Alexandrine Tinné, see above, p. 71.

[2] F.O. 78/2253, Colquhoun to Russell, 6 April 1865 enclosing Petherick to Colquhoun, 17 March 1865.

[3] Gladstone wrote enthusiastically to Murchison suggesting a public testimonial. 'Baker has done us very great honour in a distant and barbarous land ... and he has achieved his work without costing the state a shilling'. Murray and White, p. 124. Baker was knighted.

and African Lakes.[1] As early as 1866 he was interested in these possibilities, and like Speke he then envisaged an approach through the southern Sudan. In January 1866, forwarding to the Foreign Office reports from missionaries attached to the Pilgrim Mission of Basle[2] with details of atrocities in the White Nile communicated to them at Khartoum by Piaggia,[3] he commented: 'this abominable system of most wicked cruelties hinders us from planting mission stations promptly along the Upper Nile and sweeping with the Gospel . . . around Victoria Nyanza, through the interesting Kingdom of Rumaniki (sic) in Karagwe, even forward to the East Coast'.[4]

Spurred on by this communication Clarendon, Russell's successor at the Foreign Office, asked Stanton, the new Consul-General at Cairo, to report how 'we might best put a stop to the horrible state of things which undoubtedly exists on the White Nile'. In reply Stanton suggested the appointment of a Consul at Khartoum who would watch and influence the Governor-General, and who might be able to organize, beyond the boundary of Egyptian authority, a coalition of tribes who would be strong enough to resist the slave traders and with whom legitimate commerce might be promoted. At the same time he suggested that Gifford Palgrave should be appointed to this post. It was agreed, however, that the experiment of a trading Consul should not be repeated and the Foreign Office wondered 'what salary will be sufficient for such a man, and with such pretensions, as Mr. Palgrave?'[5] In any case the small amount of attention that the Foreign Office could spare for north-east Africa was monopolized at that moment by the problem of rescuing the British prisoners

[1] A. M. Chirgwin, *Arthington's Million*, London, Livingstone Press, s.d.

[2] At this date they had a representative at Khartoum as part of a plan to open up an 'Apostel-Strasse' from Egypt to Abyssinia.

[3] See above, p. 51.

[4] F.O. 141/58. Clarendon to Stanton, 28 February 1866, enclosing Arthington to Russell, 31 January. Further correspondence in F.O. 141/61.

[5] F.O. 84/1260 Stanton to Clarendon, 9 May 1866, F.O. 78/2253 Stanton to Clarendon, 10 May 1866, and memo. by Murray, 29 May 1866 and 15 July. Palgrave's *Narrative of a Year's Journey through Central and Eastern Arabia*, one of the greatest travel accounts of the nineteenth century, was published in 1865. The journey revealed the impossibility of undertaking missionary work in the area, so with the consent of his Superiors he severed his connection with the Jesuits. He entered the Diplomatic Service but, although he was a brilliant linguist and a man of considerable ability, his future career was undistinguished. cp. *Dictionary of National Biography*.

held by King Theodore in Abyssinia, the climax of a strange series of events resulting from the small, diverse, and even eccentric factors which constituted British imperial interests in that area.[1]

After Napier's campaign in Abyssinia had achieved the limited objective of effecting a rescue, Palgrave returned to press for a re-establishment of the Khartoum Consulate. 'Parliament and the Nation,' he wrote,

> might readily sanction this . . . in view to the Abolition of the Slave Trade; a popular move, and creditable to ourselves. But the real and ulterior Political importance of such a Post, both as regards the Sudan, a district always ready, troops and all, to separate from Egypt, and in regard to Abyssinia and the Red Sea coast, is self-evident. Also much furtherance to English trade, direct and indirect. . . . When the crisis comes, which must come in some form sooner or later, this Post will be hardly less useful to us, than those which regard Cairo and the Isthmus.[2]

If, however, the Foreign Office had previously been preoccupied with the problem of Abyssinia its costly solution had only under-lined the undesirability of employing adventurous Consuls, and no reply to these somewhat Machiavellian proposals is recorded.

The same caution dictated by economy and apathy, this time personified in Gladstone himself, governed at first the Foreign Office reaction to the Khedive's expedition to the White Nile in 1869. After accepting the command Baker returned to England to order the necessary steamers and equipment, and in an interview with Clarendon he imparted some of his own enthusiasm and confidence in the probable results of the expedition. A favourable report of the interview was prepared for Stanton, but Gladstone, the Prime Minister, remarked 'I *conclude* we undertake no res-ponsiblity with regard to this expedition', and the amended despatch advised Stanton to

> understand distinctly, and make known to all British subjects who may take part in this Expedition, that H.M.G. undertake no responsi-bility whatever for the consequences of it either as regards themselves, or as regards any matter connected with it.[3]

Thus in the plans of the few people who were interested in equatorial Africa, explorers, missionaries, and merchants, the

[1] D. Mathew, *Ethiopia. The study of a Polity, 1540–1935*, 1947.

[2] F.O. 84/1290. Palgrave to Egerton, 5 June 1868.

[3] F.O. 78/2092, Memoranda by Clarendon and Gladstone, 12 and 14 April 1869. F.O. 78/2091, Clarendon to Stanton, 15 April 1869.

southern Sudan came in the 1860's to hold a position of foremost importance. Thwarted by the disturbed state of the area, they attracted the attention of official circles to the situation. The area occupied, however, at that time a minute field in the world-view of the Foreign Office, whose response to appeals for assistance was dominated by the two factors of indifference, and distrust of Egyptian efficiency. The latter was to be a powerful and permanent legacy; the former was quickly broken as the result of the revolutionary change introduced by two events of 1869: the Egyptian expedition to Central Africa and the opening of the Suez Canal.

2. *The impact of Ismāʿīl's intervention*

The expedition of 1869 was one of the events which inaugurated the 'scramble' for Africa. Its significance for Egypt and the Sudan as the major part of Ismāʿīl's grand design has been discussed previously, but it also provoked immediate and important responses in Britain. Far from being an isolated incident standing outside the main stream of African history, it aroused widespread interest and momentarily placed the southern Sudan in the forefront of the developments which led to the European occupation of equatorial Africa. To many people in public life it was a dramatic revelation of the strategic and economic possibilities of alien rule in tropical Africa; and to a small group of people who were beginning to take a close, professional interest in the Lacustrine Kingdoms it came as a spur to action.

Baker's expedition caught the imagination of contemporaries. The scale of its preparation and equipment made it from the start a unique enterprise. Drama surrounded the progress of the expedition, and in letters from Baker to Murchison and other friends published in *The Times* it lost nothing in the telling. The fearful struggle to reach Gondokoro and the subsequent difficulties with the Bari were followed by over a year of suspense, when all that was known for certain was that Baker with his wife and only two hundred followers had plunged into the interior. Disquieting rumours percolated back, Stanton was often asked for news, the Khedive prepared to send a relief expedition to the east coast of Africa, and on 17 April 1873 *The Times* published rumours of his death.[1] Then on 30 June Stanton forwarded a telegram from

[1] F.O. 78/2229. Stanton to Granville, 21 January, 7 and 14 December, 1872. In the last Stanton feared that Baker is in 'a very critical position'.

Baker which was read in both Houses of Parliament: 'The country as far as the Equator annexed to Egyptian dominion; all rebellions, intrigues and slave trade completely put down; country orderly; Government perfectly organized; and road open as far as Zanzibar'. . . .[1] On 13, 14 and 15 August letters from Baker were published in *The Times* which confirmed this news and added his belief that Lakes Albert and Tanganyika were one, thus opening up the prospect of a vast extension of the Egyptian empire. Instead of disaster there was apparently complete success. The leading article of *The Times* on 15 August summed up the achievement:

> The magnificent prospect opened up by Baker Pasha's Expedition may stir even the sluggish Government of Egypt into energy . . . at any rate, unless the aquisitions of Baker be absolutely and shamefully abandoned, the Egyptian rule must so far unseal the trade of Central Africa as to allow a keen solvent of European commerce to penetrate into the heart of that obdurate Continent. . . . The undertaking stands out in the tame history of our times as a bold and romantic episode. . . . He accepted a task hardly less perilous than that of Cortez. . . . Nothing recorded of the Spaniards in Mexico or of the English in India, exceeds in stirring interest the story of the retreat from Bunyoro.

On 8 December the Royal Geographical Society held a reception in his honour: 'the theatre of the London University has seldom, if ever, held a more crowded and brilliant assembly . . . a witness to the intense interest which Sir Samuel Baker's achievements have aroused among his countrymen'. Before 1,500 people, who included the Lord Chancellor, Sir Bartle Frere and several M.P.s, the Prince of Wales welcomed Baker 'as a philanthropist who has carried out a great work for the benefit of human kind'.[2]

This excitement and interest over a dramatic adventure mingled with a realization of its great significance. Consul Hansal, in a letter published in Vienna, was typical in hailing it as bringing a new epoch to central Africa.[3] Unlike Napier's expedition to Abyssinia, which was for contemporaries the only comparable enterprise, Baker's objective was one of permanent conquest and

[1] Hansard, 3rd series, ccxvi. Commons, 30 June 1873.

[2] *The Times* 9 December 1873. Other receptions were held at Brighton, Liverpool (including a speech to the Chamber of Commerce) (*The Times* 23 March 1874), and in the City, where he received the Freedom of the Turner's Company in recognition of his services to the ivory trade (*The Times* 6 March 1874).

[3] *Mit. k-k. geog. Ges.*, Vienna, 1870, p. 279.

colonization, and his contemporaries realized that his methods and plans could be imitated elsewhere. His use of steamers, and even more his plans for their use on the Great Lakes, emphasized the revolution which this could bring to the problem of transport, and his exploits strikingly revealed the power conferred by European weapons. After a lecture to the United Service Institution on 'Experience in Savage Warfare', in which Baker recounted the effects and prestige gained by firearms, rockets, light-artillery and cavalry, the Duke of Cambridge declared that it 'was a wonderful thing that one man should have been able to exercise so much power over those savage hordes. . . . What had been done once could be done again'.[1]

Besides revealing the possibility of establishing some form of administration in central Africa, Baker added to the legend which was growing up about the reputedly great natural riches of the area. In the Bari country the corn tax could be collected from 'an immense area of rich districts' while Fatiko, 'the Paradise of Africa', had 'the perfection of a superb park' with a 'climate as cool as the south of France'.[2] Again this was reflected in a leading article of The Times:

> It is not long since Central Africa was regarded as nothing better than a region of torrid deserts or pestiferous swamps. . . . the veil has since been lifted . . . and there now seems reason to believe that one of the finest parts of the world's surface is lying waste . . . under the barbarous anarchy with which it is cursed.[3]

It is difficult to pin-point changes in the climate of opinion but it seems probable that the impact of Baker's expedition, by focussing attention on equatorial Africa and by demonstrating the possibility of colonization, was one of the most important events which caused a change in Europe's attitude to Africa. The Foreign Secretary, Lord Derby, thanking Baker for a copy of Ismailia which he was reading with interest, wrote:

> Whatever may happen about the slave trade, your expedition cannot fail to have extended British influence in Egypt. . . . I know nothing

[1] The Times 16 December, 1873, cp. also 'the power which modern firearms have given in contending with uncivilized races is even yet, perhaps, imperfectly appreciated.' ibid; 9 December.

[2] F.O. 84/1371. Vivian to Granville, 6 September 1873, enclosing a report by Baker. See also Baker's Ismailia.

[3] The Times leader 9 December on Baker's speech to the Royal Geographical Society.

that is going on in the world just now so remarkable as the steady and rapid progress which we are making in opening-up Africa; and it is evident that the road must lie mainly through Egyptian territory.[1]

Yet even more important than the positive aspects of Baker's example was the fact that the expedition presented a challenge and a warning, which acted as a powerful stimulus to the growth of specific British interests in East Africa. For the British share in the 'scramble' for Africa was not primarily the result of a change in public opinion, of a popular, political demand for imperial expansion. It depended throughout far more on the actions of a few individuals, and, until the end of the 1880's when Rhodes and Salisbury took a controlling interest in the decisive stages of the scramble, the drive for an expansion of British interests in East and Central Africa came in the most part from a small group of private individuals: the humanitarians. Quaker bankers, Scottish and Lancashire business-men, evangelical abolitionists, explorers and Christian missionaries united on a platform of defeating the slave trade by the introduction of a legitimate commerce, and they were able to mobilize support in the country at large. Baker's expedition profoundly alarmed these humanitarians and it started to awaken them to the need for action. The deep-rooted distrust of Egypt as a slave-holding nation, which went back to the early sixties, became linked with an active hostility—tinged with jealousy—on the part of those who were hoping to introduce Christianity and commerce into equatorial Africa, and who were beginning to exercise a paternal, proprietary interest in the area.

From the beginning Baker's expedition met with a mixed response in Britain. As early as May 1870 Wylde, the head of the Slave Trade Department at the Foreign Office, noted in a memorandum 'Unless Sir Samuel Baker's expedition is very sharply looked after, I shall be very much surprised if it does not turn out a slave trade Razzia on a large scale,'[2] and in September of the same year criticism was publicly expressed. In the discussion of a letter from Baker read by Murchison at a meeting of the geographical section of the British Association, a certain Dr. G. Cambell, who was applauded by those present, said that

[1] Baker MSS. Derby to Baker, 1 November 1874. An extract is reprinted in Murray and White, p. 210 without stating the authorship.
[2] F.O. 78/2253. Memo by Wylde, 30 May 1870.

the expedition raised the whole of the enormous question whether Central Africa was to be Christian or Mohomedan, and whether it was to be a free or a slave-holding country ... if this expedition was successful Mohomedanism would be triumphant and Christianity extinguished.[1]

These doubts and criticisms found a rallying point in the Anti-Slavery Society. In the first half of the century, as has been seen, its attention was practically monopolized by the problem of the Atlantic slave trade, but in the 1860's its attention was increasingly turned to the Arab slave trade.[2] In 1866, two years after his return from the Zambezi expedition, Livingstone set out on his long last journey. He was determined to solve the remaining mystery of the Nile-Congo watershed, and he was equipped by the British Government 'with official authority to deal with native chiefs in all the area between the frontier of Portuguese East Africa and those of Abyssinia and Egypt'.[3] The drama of his lone adventures and his persistent revelation of the evils and extent of the slave trade around Lakes Nyasa and Tanganyika aroused great public interest, and missionary and philanthropic circles urged the Government to take sterner measures to restrict this trade. The Committee of the Church Missionary Society presented a memorial to the Secretary of State for India in 1869,[4] and in 1871 a Parliamentary Select Committee was appointed 'to inquire into the whole question of the Slave Trade on the East Coast of Africa.' Previously the British treaties with the Sultan of Zanzibar had provided for the prevention of the export of slaves beyond the coast of Africa, but the evidence presented to the Select Committee revealed that the export of slaves was in fact increasing. The Committee declared that a new treaty providing for the total abolition of the slave trade should be negotiated, and the Sultan should be informed that if this proved insufficient the British Government would take the requisite measures 'to put an end to all slave trade whatever, whether foreign or coasting'.[5] Although primarily concerned with East Africa, the evidence before the Committee incidentally revealed

---

[1] *Liverpool Mercury*, 17 September 1870. Grant was present but at this period made no recorded comment on the challenge of the expedition. Murchison pointed out that there was no Christianity to extinquish.

[2] See above, p. 166.

[3] Coupland, p. 116.

[4] Oliver, pp. 18–19.

[5] Coupland, pp. 165–70.

how considerable was the Red Sea slave trade,[1] and Sir Bartle
Frere, appointed to negotiate the treaty with Zanzibar, visited
Egypt on his outward journey in December 1872.

In two long interviews Ismā'īl discussed with Frere his plans
for Africa. He wanted, he said, to strike at the evil of the slave trade
at its source, for he believed that domestic slavery would soon
wear itself out if the source were stopped. With this object in view,
he had already gone to great expense with Baker's expedition and,
Frere reported, 'he claimed for his Government the position of the
head of civilization on the African continent'. He needed, however,
the 'moral support' of Great Britain to convince his subjects of the
necessity of such a policy. Ismā'īl suggested therefore that perhaps
the Anti-Slavery Society should urge the British Government to
call upon him to take more energetic measures and, as a *quid pro
quo*, the 'moral support' of Great Britain should include a recognition of his claims against Abyssinia and his need for greater
independence from Turkey and France. Frere was impressed by
his ability, convinced of his sincerity, and from personal experience
thought that 'the progress of Egypt had been greater during the
last forty years than that of India'. Her increased wealth had,
however, led to an increased demand for slaves and, as the sources
of the latter were so widespread, Frere believed 'it to be
practically impossible to cut off the supply whilst the demand
continues'. The only solution therefore would be the abolition of
the legal status of slavery by a gradual measure similar to that
introduced in Brazil. Frere was confident that Ismā'īl could be
convinced both of the necessity and of the possibility of such a
measure.[2] In a letter to Sir Thomas Fowell Buxton, the grandson
of Buxton the 'Liberator', Frere put forward his ideas, and showed
how they were linked with the future of equatorial Africa:

> The real thing to do would be to abolish slavery in Egypt and so
> cut off the demand—I do not think it at all impossible he might take
> steps in that direction. It would put him clearly among the civilizing
> powers and in advance of Turkey, and not be so difficult as it will be
> ten years hence. With Egypt free soil no one would object to see

[1] F.O. 84/1341. Granville to Elliott, 10 August 1871. Granville warned the
Ambassador in Turkey that, as a result of the evidence before the Committee,
he would probably have to make 'an earnest representation to The Porte'.

[2] F.O. 84/1389. Frere to Granville, 1 January 1873 enclosing long memoranda
on the slave trade and his conversations with Ismā'īl. See also F.O. 84/1354 and
F.O. 78/2229 for Stanton's account, 20 December, 1872.

His Highness' power extended to the Lake Region: but it would not be so if his new acquisitions were all turned into slave hunting grounds.[1]

The Foreign Office, while not prepared to give the whole-hearted support which Ismāʿīl wanted, arranged a demonstration of anti-slavery sentiment.[2] In the following months memorials from the British and Foreign Anti-Slavery Society and the International Anti-Slavery Society were duly forwarded to the Khedive urging him to abolish slavery.[3]

The news of Baker's apparent success immeasurably increased this concern over Egyptian imperial expansion into equatorial Africa. On 31 October 1873 an important deputation headed by Sir Bartle Frere and the Rev. Horace Waller and including several M.P.s interviewed the Foreign Secretary. They presented a memorial which demanded that the Great Powers of Europe should 'intimate to H.H. the Khedive of Egypt that, while not unwilling to acquiesce in the extension of his rule to the farther regions of the Nile, *the conditions of such extension being the extinction of the slave trade and the abolition of slavery*, they are not prepared to recognise his authority in those countries so long as these may be tolerated within his dominions'. The memorialists were doubtless sincere in their wish that the Khedive should fulfil these conditions; but a reference to the 'beneficial and almost boundless commerce' which could be carried on by European traders 'with those regions of surpassing productiveness' reveals that, under the impulse of Baker's expedition, their thoughts were already turning towards what they hoped would be a surer solution: an active European intervention in the interior to establish legitimate commerce.[4]

[1] A.S.S. MSS. Frere to Buxton, 17 January 1873.

[2] F.O. 84/1354 Minutes on Stanton to Granville, 20 December 1872. Granville considered the proposal for moral support opened too wide an issue, but thought 'we might be stupid, and not understanding apply the pressure he suggests'. It was decided therefore to request Samuel Wilberforce, the Bishop of Winchester, to initiate an agitation.

[3] *Anti-Slavery Reporter*, July 1873.

[4] *Anti-Slavery Reporter*. October 1873, and January 1874. Another deputation in June 1874 urged Lord Derby 'to withhold his sanction to the annexation of the territories of the Upper Nile till slavery had been abolished' (Reporter July 1874). The issue was touched upon in a debate in the Commons on 8 July 1875, the Government defending the Khedive's intentions (Hansard 3rd series, vol. ccv). The Rev. Horace Waller, the editor of Livingstone's 'Last Journal', was a foremost advocate of the idea of legitimate commerce.

It was not a new idea. The early Abolitionists had recognized its importance and Livingstone had done much to convert Christian missions to the alliance between Christianity and Commerce. No active steps had been taken however and, as stated above, Baker was the first to demonstrate the possibilities of introducing such a policy in equatorial Africa. Then following soon after the reports of Baker's apparent successes came the news of Livingstone's death near Lake Bangweulu in May 1873. It was an event which in its effect on British public opinion was comparable to Gordon's death at Khartoum in the following decade. The small group of expert enthusiasts was at last suddenly supported by the general public, while thousands of people lined the streets for his burial in Westminster Abbey. The *Daily Telegraph*, convinced that 'the work of England for Africa must henceforth begin in earnest where Livingstone left it off', commissioned Stanley, who three years previously had successfully 'found' Livingstone at Ujiji on Lake Tanganyika, to undertake a journey across Africa from Zanzibar to the mouth of the Congo, and with widespread support from their congregations the·missionary societies were able to open 'a new chapter in the history of the missionary occupation of East Africa'.[1]

At the time of Livingstone's death there were still no permanent missionary settlements in the interior of East Africa, but within a few years stations were established throughout the length of the Great Lakes. The Scottish Presbyterians sent two missions to the Shire highlands and Lake Nyasa, where they were supported by the Glasgow-financed African Lakes Corporation, which by the use of steamers hoped to undercut the Arabs' use of slave porterage. The U.M.C.A. re-established itself on the mainland and gradually moved in towards Lake Nyasa. The London Missionary Society, aided by Robert Arthington[2] with a grant of £5,000 for a steamer on Lake Tanganyika, established stations based on Ujiji, and on the publication of a letter from Stanley on 15 November 1875 advocating the foundation of a Christian mission in Buganda the C.M.S. were offered £5,000 by an anonymous donor.[3]

The offer was accepted, and at this juncture the alarm and suspicion aroused by Baker's expedition once more became apparent. In a discussion with the C.M.S., Grant, Speke's

---

[1] Oliver, pp. 34-35. [2] See above, p. 168.
[3] Oliver, pp. 35-42. See also above, p. 117.

companion, hastened to stress the vital importance of preserving the independence of Buganda. The letter offering the £5,000 seemed to suggest that the C.M.S. might with Gordon's help approach Buganda by the Nile route, and Gordon's brother suggested to the Committee that, although it might be a year before the way was cleared by the submission of Bunyoro, a small mission should be sent to Khartoum to await the time when an advance might be made to Buganda. Grant, however, 'deprecated very strongly' the approach from the Nile route and urged that 'without loss of time' an attempt should be made to reach Lake Victoria by some route from the Indian Ocean. It was decided to follow this advice.[1]

At this moment another event forced Britain to define more clearly her attitude to Ismā'īl's imperial expansion. On 30 November 1875, the day before this decision of the C.M.S. was taken, a telegram from the Sultan of Zanzibar had been published in the *Pall Mall Gazette*. The Sultan strongly protested against the violation of his territory on the mainland by an Egyptian expedition, under a Scotsman McKillop, who was to open for Gordon a route from the east coast of Africa to the Lakes. Dismayed, even before the discovery of the Fola Rapids, by the long and uncertain lines of communication which the Nile route involved,[2] Gordon had suggested to Ismā'īl at the end of 1874 the desirability of attempting to reach the Lakes from a point near the mouth of the River Juba on the Indian Ocean. Ismā'īl, who had already during Baker's expedition envisaged the need for a supporting penetration from the east coast, accepted Gordon's suggestion and the expedition was despatched. In November 1875 four Egyptian warships landed troops at the mouth of the River Juba and overpowered the Sultan's garrisons.[3]

[1] C.M.S. MSS. Report of the Victoria Nyanza Sub-Committee 1 December 1875. The reason given by Grant (that Mutesa would suspect any party arriving via the Nile) was a valid one and later supported by Gordon. There can however be little doubt of Grant's real motive. As early as January 1875 Gordon had written to Grant asking him for maps of the east coast and telling him to observe secrecy. No maps arrived, and on 12 March 1876 Gordon wrote: 'I think I see a little intrigue going on between Grant and Stanley, Mutesa and Co. I am not sure of it but dear! dear! they have a poor chance. Egypt's base of operations is five days from Mutesa's while their's is at least 900 miles off, a 900 miles which cost Stanley 140 men one way or another . . .'. Gordon MSS. G. to his sister, 12 March 1876.
[2] See above, pp. 109–10.
[3] Coupland, pp. 276–80.

This sudden intrusion into the affairs of Zanzibar came at a moment when British co-operation with the Sultan was reaching a favourable conclusion. Frere's mission to Zanzibar, the threat of a naval blockade, and the skill of the British political agent and Consul, John Kirk, had persuaded the Sultan on 5 June 1875 to sign a treaty solemnly abolishing all slave trading throughout his dominions. British policy was therefore firmly committed to upholding his power at Zanzibar and on the mainland, and it was hoped that his influence in the interior would continue to increase. On the arrival of McKillop's expedition both the Sultan and Kirk lodged strong protests in London, *The Times* stigmatized the invasion as 'a wanton outrage', and in the face of British protests the expedition was recalled.[1] Ismā'īl, realizing the mistake of attempting a *fait accompli*, turned to diplomacy and in January 1876 asked the British Government to support his request for a port on the Indian Ocean. He pointed out that he had spent a great deal of money in suppressing the slave trade in Equatoria and the shorter line of communication was essential if his position was to be maintained.[2] The southern Sudan was losing its initial importance. The Nile was no longer to be the chief highway to the Lakes and the incident forced the Foreign Office to re-consider the future of equatorial Africa.

The Foreign Office was at first inclined to support Ismā'īl's request as it wished to enlist Egyptian co-operation on two important issues. The first reactions to the change brought about by the opening of the Suez Canal, which was to place north-east Africa in the forefront of the Foreign Office world-view, were developing in a haphazard fashion. Faced with the problem of forestalling European rivals in the Red Sea, the Foreign Office, on the advice of the Ambassador in Turkey and Stanton in Egypt, decided to support the extension of Ismā'īl's sovereignty between Suakin and Cape Guardafui, trusting that this would effectively obstruct French and Italian designs. The negotiations were complicated but by November 1875 draft agreements had been despatched to Cairo—they crossed in fact with the news of the expedition to the Indian Ocean.[3]

[1] Coupland, pp. 280–88.
[2] F.O. 78/3189 Stanton to Derby, 9 January 1876.
[3] The memoranda and despatches are in F.O. 78/3185–3189. See also Sabry, pp. 383–409.

At the same time the Foreign Office wished to deal with the slave trade issue in a similar fashion. In July 1873, six months after Frere had left Egypt, Ismā'īl visited Constantinople. The British Ambassador, acting apparently on his own initiative, seized a favourable opportunity to suggest an Anglo-Egyptian agreement on the suppression of the slave trade. Basing his suggestions on those contained in Frere's memorandum he proposed that after an interval of seven years all sale of slaves should be prohibited and that various measures should be taken to make this effective.[1] The Khedive was co-operative and optimistic of the success of the scheme, but several incidents held up the negotiations until the issue became linked with the recognition of Egyptian sovereignty over the Red Sea coast line. Frere's mission had, however, fully awakened the interest of the Anti-Slavery Society in the Egyptian slave trade. By articles in the *Anti-Slavery Reporter*, by deputations to the Foreign Secretary, by letters to *The Times*, and by the vigilance of a group of M.P.s, the Society prevented the Government from treating it as a minor issue. Its activities were in fact an embarrassment, providing welcome material for the Opposition, so that by December 1875, Lord Tenterden, Under Secretary of State, was anxious to get the agreement signed 'as it would have a very good effect on public opinion'.[2]

Thus, since the Foreign Office was anxious to solve both the strategical and the slave trade issues by supporting and influencing Egypt, Ismā'īl's request for an Indian Ocean port was at first favourably received. Wylde thought that, as the Nile route was 'futile in the extreme', his objects 'deserved every encouragement on our part' if they could be carried out 'without violating' the territory of Zanzibar. He suggested that Ismā'īl's request should be forwarded to Kirk stating that Derby was disposed to view the proposal favourably.[3] This evoked, however, a vehement and able reply from Kirk. He challenged the Egyptian claim to the Nile Lakes and the adjacent regions which had been 'explored and hitherto made known by Englishmen alone, where Zanzibar traders had been for years back, but where the Turkish flag is unknown,' and he emphasized that support for Egypt would

---

[1] F.O. 84/1370. Elliot to Granville, 8 July 1873.

[2] F.O. 78/3188 minute by Tenterden, 22 December 1875, also F.O. 84/1450 Tenterden to Rourke, 3 February 1876.

[3] F.O. 78/3188. Wylde on Stanton to Derby, 9 December 1875.

involve the repudiation of Zanzibar at a moment when, after years of patient preparation, the latter had been induced to co-operate loyally. 'The whole scheme is injurious to our commercial and political influence and our policy for the suppression of the slave trade'.[1] This despatch was decisive. In August 1876 when Ismā'īl was again approached on the subject of the slave-trade convention he countered with a repetition of his request for a port, but, wrote Wylde, Kirk 'expressed so decided an opinion against it' that it must be refused.[2]

In December Ismā'īl again objected, pointing out that he saw no advantage in concluding a convention which 'might involve him in responsibilities for suppressing the slave trade without any corresponding advantages to Egypt. What he really wanted was a port near the River Juba'.[3] A few days later however Vivian, who had succeeded Stanton as the British Consul-General, reported that the Red Sea slave trade was estimated at the startling figure of 30,000 per year. 'In no other province than that administered by Colonel Gordon is a negro safe', £8 was being given by the Government for army 'recruits' and Shilluk women and children were being carried off in lieu of taxes. He forwarded this report 'to warn H.M.G. against trusting too much to any anti-slave-trade engagements into which the Viceroy may enter and against encouraging the extension of Egyptian jurisdiction in Africa.[4] Lord Salisbury at the India Office suggested that Ismā'īl's request should be met by an ultimatum: either the convention should be accepted immediately, or the British Government would reserve to themselves perfect freedom of action on the Somali coast. After some hesitation Ismā'īl yielded.[5]

It is difficult to see how the Foreign Office could have supported Ismā'īl's request. One may feel that the 1869 expedition constituted as good a claim to the Lake regions as the activities of British explorers and Zanzibar traders which were put forward by Kirk. But while the Sultan of Zanzibar was proving a sure ally

---

[1] Sir J. M. Gray, 'Sir John Kirk and Mutesa', *Uganda Journal*, 1950, p. 5.
[2] F.O. 78/3189. Wylde on Cookson to Derby, 8 August 1876.
[3] F.O. 78/3189. Vivian to Derby, 2 December 1876.
[4] F.O. 84/1450 Vivian to Derby, 8 December 1876.
[5] F.O. 78/3189. Mallet to F.O., 27 January 1877. Vivian to Derby, 21 February 1877. This is an interesting confirmation of Salisbury's early interest in the problem. Throughout the negotiations the India Office had pressed the Foreign Office to pursue a firm policy towards Egypt.

against the slave trade, reports continued to reveal the untrust-
worthiness of Egypt on this matter and, as in the 1860's, this was
united with fears of a monopoly which would exclude British trade.
It is also of course doubtful whether Ismā'īl would have been able
to exploit the route from the Indian Ocean as the financial weakness
of Egypt was already becoming apparent.[1] The request nevertheless presented a genuine dilemma, and the decision to support
Kirk's defence of the Sultan and Mutesa necessarily involved the
repudiation of a man whose character and aims had won the respect
and sympathy of men so varied as Baker, Frere, Gordon and Stanton.

Besides forcing the Foreign Office to define its attitude to the
future expansion of Egypt in Africa, McKillop's expedition gave
the final impulse for the first attempt to establish a British trading
company on the mainland of the Sultan's dominions. The response
generated by Baker's expedition in the thoughts of those interested
in introducing legitimate commerce into equatorial Africa and the
sense of urgency and caution imparted by Grant to the C.M.S.,
were joined, after McKillop's expedition, with the resolve to take
active steps without further delay.[2] The economic potential of the
Lacustrine Kingdoms and the strategic importance of a new route
to them and to the sources of the Nile were now apparent, and it
was also realized that the slave trade could be brought to a close
only by the firm penetration of European commerce. Commercial
and humanitarian interests in Britain were anxious therefore to
appropriate Gordon's idea of a new route based on a port on the
Indian Ocean.[3] By May 1876 it was publicly announced that there
was 'a movement on foot to organise an East African Company'.[4]
The most powerful supporter of this movement was William
Mackinnon, creator and controller of the 'British India Steam
Navigation Co.' which served every important port on the Indian
Ocean. In 1876 with Buxton's collaboration he started to finance
the construction of a road from the coast to Lake Nyasa, and at the
same time he hoped to take over a large concession on the mainland from the Sultan of Zanzibar.[5] In January 1877 Gordon
returned to England from Equatoria thoroughly disheartened by

[1] See above, p. 120.
[2] Coupland (p. 301) tends to overestimate the effect of McKillop's intrusion
for he seems to have been unaware of the earlier response to Baker's expedition,
cp. above, p. 177.   [3] Coupland, pp. 300–1.
[4] *Anti-Slavery Reporter* July 1876. Report of annual meeting on 26 May.
[5] Coupland, pp. 302–6.

the evidence of the slave trade he had seen on his return journey. He felt acutely 'the inutility of opening new countries to the Khedive,' for he was convinced that 'the same lot would fall on the people I had conciliated, the moment I left'.[1] Through Waller he was brought into contact with Mackinnon, and Gordon was on the point of accepting service with him when he received a telegram from the Khedive entreating him to return. Gordon therefore left Mackinnon, whose plans for an East African Company came to fruition several years later, after receiving a further impulse from German activity.[2]

Gordon returned as' Governor-General of the whole Sudan,[3] and his appointment evoked further uneasiness amongst the humanitarians who feared an extension of Egyptian activity. In February 1877 an influential group, including the Archbishop of Canterbury, Buxton, and several other M.P.s, met at the house of the Baroness Burdett-Coutts. They decided to present a memorial to Lord Derby, the Foreign Secretary, urging him to prevent the annexation of Buganda by Egypt, and to keep it 'free and open to English commerce, industry, and civilization'.[4] The following November Kirk forwarded a letter from a C.M.S. missionary reporting that Mutesa had been ordered to pull down a 'Christian flag' by the Egyptians. 'I am very much afraid,' Grant commented to Baker,

> the poor fellow will get himself into trouble with Egypt and I wish we could do something to aid him. . . . The Mission will no doubt support him but unless we keep up an agitation in his favour at home, the Egyptians with Gordon and the American officers at their head will try to crush him.[5]

[1] Waller MSS. Gordon to Waller, 4 January 1877.
[2] Coupland, pp. 294–5; and see below, pp. 194–5.
[3] Ismā'īl's decision to appoint Gordon to this post is an interesting example of the indirect way in which British pressure was gradually being brought to bear. Graham (later General Sir Gerald Graham, an intimate friend of Gordon) had an interview with Derby on 1 February in an attempt to persuade him to support Gordon's claim to complete power. Although Graham thought that he had made no impression on Derby, the following day Vivian was instructed to give his support. On 16 February Gordon wrote to thank Vivian for his 'straightforward representations' (Gordon MSS. Graham to G., 1 February; F.O. 84/1472, Derby to Vivian, 2 February; Vivian to Derby, 18 February).
[4] F.O. 141/108. Derby to Vivian. 29 March 1877, transmitting two memorials. The arguments are clearly only a development of those put forward in 1873. See p. 177 above.
[5] Baker, MSS. Grant to Baker, 9 January 1878. In the same letter Grant wrote: 'while in Scotland I set three associations a-going in aid of African exploration'. *The Times* of 31 January 1877 published a letter from Grant

These fears of an Egyptian advance were not groundless. At the time of Gordon's return from Equatoria, Stone, the American Chief of the Egyptian General Staff, strongly advised Ismā'īl to occupy Buganda and Karagwe without loss of time. The activities of the English missionaries, of the Sultan of Zanzibar, and of Leopold II, King of the Belgians, were, he thought, sufficient warning that the Egyptian claims would soon be challenged, and at this early date he emphasized the need to safeguard the Nile Waters: 'I tremble for the future of Egypt if she loses these Equatorial provinces. . . . The Great Power which possesses the sources of the Nile will also possess for ever domination over lower Egypt'.[1] Gordon therefore in 1877 fully intended his subordinates to advance and launch a steamer on Lake Victoria; but, it will be remembered, he informed the British Consul-General that he was willing to respect the independence of Mutesa as long as the latter maintained a friendly neutrality.[2] By his acceptance of the C.M.S. missionaries Mutesa had thus gained diplomatic support, yet the Egyptian advance was halted this time, not by the protests of Kirk and the humanitarians, but by internal weaknesses. As related in previous chapters, the problems confronting the rest of Ismā'īl's empire cast those of Equatoria into insignificance.[3] Gordon, as Governor-General, was far too occupied with the struggle against Sulaimān and with the intrigues of Abyssinia to spare any real attention for the south, and with the ever-worsening state of Egyptian finances there was no possibility of despatching the men and materials needed for an advance. Instead retrenchment was ordered. 'I see Grant is still harping on Egypt attacking Mutesa,' Gordon wrote to Watson, who had served under him in Equatoria, 'go and see him, if you have time to waste, and tell him that in six months the whole of our posts will be withdrawn from his vicinity because they do not pay their cost and Mutesa will be left to his fate.'[4]

Thus by 1880 the initiative in the process of penetration inaugurated by Ismā'īl was passing into other hands. The knowledge that there was no navigable connection between Lakes Albert and

warning that the 'chief object of Gordon's return is the annexation of Lake Victoria'.

[1] Douin, vol. III (iiib), pp. 340–42.
[2] See above, p. 135.
[3] See above, pp. 120, 137.
[4] B.M. Add. MSS. 41340. Gordon to Watson, 14 November 1878.

Tanganyika had shattered the dream of the vast empire envisaged by Baker, and Gordon's survey of the Fola Rapids had made it increasingly obvious that the Nile could no longer be regarded as the natural highway to the Equatorial Kingdoms. Livingstone's death had stimulated the missionary occupation of Lakes Nyasa and Tanganyika, while Stanley's exploration of the Congo focussed attention upon an alternative and greater route into the centre of Africa. In 1876 while Stanley was still in Africa King Leopold founded the African International Association, and, although the numerous individuals sent under its auspices to East Africa achieved relatively little, the instrument was at hand for the future development of the Congo Free State.[1] The White Nile was no longer the focal point of interest, and Khartoum had become merely one of several gateways into the interior. But the southern Sudan was still uniquely important in one respect: the sole patch of civilized government planted in the heart of Africa continued until 1889 to exert a powerful influence on those who hoped to introduce legitimate commerce and to establish a claim to equatorial Africa.

3. The response of private enterprise

Although in the 1870's events in the southern Sudan had stimulated those who hoped to open up equatorial Africa, the humanitarian attitude to the area itself had remained essentially negative.[2] Just as the Foreign Office hoped to achieve its strategical ends by working through Egypt, so the Anti-Slavery Society was content with a policy which aimed at compelling Egypt to suppress the slave trade, and the conventions of 1877 dealing with slavery and sovereignty in the Red Sea marked the climax of both these policies. When Gordon returned to England in 1880 after retiring from his post as Governor-General, it was not immediately evident, despite Ismā'īl's fall in 1879, that this policy was bankrupt. While

---

[1] Coupland, pp. 328–34.

[2] This work of vigilant criticism exhibited many of the evils of long-range humanitarianism. The Anti-Slavery Society was only too ready to give publicity to exaggerated and inaccurate accounts, and, not having to face the responsibilities of action (particularly when Egypt was involved), it was tempted to ignore the complexity of the problem. A letter to the Society, written by Gordon in 1874, contains some scathing comments on the evils of long-range criticism and he was continually urging them to send out an observer to gain a first-hand impression of the situation (B.M. Add. MSS. 47609. Gordon to Sturge and Cooper, 18 May 1874; also Waller MSS. Gordon to Waller, 18 May 1874).

entering into negotiations with Mackinnon and Leopold about
positive plans for an expedition from the east coast inland, Gordon's
concern for the Sudan was restricted to a powerful agitation to
re-establish the Khartoum Consulate. To him it still seemed
possible that in the Sudan the slave trade could be suppressed by
force and that a Consul with a roving commission might compel
the local authorities to continue the struggle. Gordon therefore
urged the C.M.S. and kindred societies to contribute £1,500 per
annum for this purpose,[1] and, abandoning the reserve which had
previously marked his relations with the Anti-Slavery Society,
he gave his full support to its energetic secretary Charles Allen.
At a time when he had very little money he subscribed £100 and
urged Allen 'to go round the counties and make one *good supreme
effort*, which will restore the power of the Anti-Slavery Society
over the lukewarm Consuls and the Foreign Office', adding 'I am
thinking of going into Parliament'.[2] Finally, in March 1881, in
company with Shaftesbury, Brougham, Cardinal Manning, three
Anglican Bishops, the Lord Mayor, and several M.P.s, he presented a long memorial to Gladstone urging the Government to
appoint a Consul. The pressure could no longer be resisted, but a
series of setbacks prevented a succession of intended Consuls from
reaching Khartoum, and, although a Consul, by the supply of
accurate information to Cairo, might have exerted a powerful
influence in the crucial years which followed, no tangible results
were achieved.[3]

The British occupation of Egypt in 1882,[4] although it was
eventually to have far-reaching results for the southern Sudan,
did not immediately affect the situation. For the moment the main
preoccupation of the Foreign Office was to avoid all further
commitments and to escape as soon as possible from this unfortunate entanglement. The initiative remained therefore with private
enterprise, and the collapse of Egypt, together with the success of
the Mahdi's movement, revealed to the humanitarians the bankruptcy of their previous attitude to the Sudan. It became increasingly obvious that, as in other areas, the problem was essentially one

[1] C.M.S. Committee Minutes, vol. 45, 9 February 1880, report of interview
with Gordon.
[2] B.M. Add. MSS. 47609. Gordon to Allen, 5 November 1880.
[3] *Anti-Slavery Reporter,* April 1881. F.O. 78/3467 and 3586 for abortive
attempts to install a Consul at Khartoum. It was regarded as a very minor issue.
[4] See above, p. 152.

of introducing legitimate commerce. In humanitarian activities the mobilization of protest was therefore replaced by the plans of a small yet influential circle of philanthropists.[1] These plans crystallized round two projects: the Suakin-Berber railway, and an approach from the Congo; the future of the southern Sudan was intimately linked with both, and the province of Equatoria provided the chief hope that profits would follow philanthropy.

In 1876 Augustus Wylde, the son of the head of the slave trade department of the Foreign Office, was appointed Vice-consul at Jeddah, where he combined these duties with the Red Sea agency for Mackinnon's steamship company. In both capacities he travelled extensively in Abyssinia and the Sudan and in both activities he was frustrated by the Jeddah merchants. He found that their agents at the principal markets in the Sudan and Abyssinia were able to underbid all attempts to establish a trade in Manchester piece goods, as the export of slaves solved their transport problems and yielded high profits. In 1878 he had several long conversations with Gordon when both agreed that 'the present state of things' would continue until 'European merchants or natives' could be found to do a legitimate commerce, and in 1880, realizing that a railway was indispensable, he told Gordon that 'the Sudan slave trade must be put a stop to through Suakin as the great outlet of the Sudan is through there. The Korosko and Nile route is impracticable compared to the Berber-Suakin route which is more speedy and where tonnage and freights can always be procured cheaply'.[2]

[1] Under Wilberforce and Buxton the humanitarian front reached the status of a nation-wide crusade and the Society was a pioneer in the mobilization of public opinion. The radius of its influence, however, considerably contracted in the second half of the century. Allen told Waller in January 1881 that the subscription list 'would have been a miserable affair but for Colonel Gordon's donation', and in November 1882, at an important public meeting on the slave trade in Egypt at which Shaftesbury, Buxton, and Forster were present, Manning contrasted the scanty attendance with the multitudes that used to throng Exeter Hall. The Society remained however an important centre of humanitarian interests, its secretary was the friend and adviser of the leading philanthropists, and it was one of the chief channels by which they hoped to arouse public interest in their plans (Waller MSS. Allen to Waller, 29 January 1881. *Anti-Slavery Reporter* December 1882).

[2] Two valuable reports by Wylde on the Red Sea slave trade are in F.O. 84/1450 dated Cairo 25 November 1876 and F.O. 141/117 enclosed in Salisbury to Lascelles, 23 October 1878. The letter to Gordon, 7 October 1880, is in B.M. Add. MSS. 47609; it contained a suggestion that with Mackinnon's help Gordon should start a company in the highlands of Abyssinia: it would 'be the death of the slave trade as far as Abyssinian and Galla slaves are concerned'.

By the summer of 1882 Wylde had returned to England and a private committee under the Duke of Sutherland was formed to consider the project of a railway from Suakin to Berber. At a meeting of the 'Suakin-Berber syndicate' in November, Wylde, with the assistance of Lee Smith, late engineer-in-chief of the Egyptian railways, put forward definite estimates: the three hundred miles of line would cost about one and a half million pounds to construct, and the annual profit, after working expenses had been deducted would be about £180,000. 'An enormous extent of country will be brought within easy reach of civilization.' Already there were two small steamers on Lake Albert, and Wylde thought that once the railway was built the equatorial Lakes would be reached in a month from London. In December a letter from Gordon was printed describing the railway as 'a sine qua non for the well-being of the Soudan,'[1] and in February 1883 R. W. Felkin, in a lecture to the Royal Society of Arts, drew attention to 'the most important part of the Egyptian dominion: . . . the vast equatorial possessions, the extent and significance of which do not seem to be fully realized, either by governments or business men'. Estimating the population of the equatorial regions ruled over by Egypt at over ten million and the populations of the areas which would trade with Egypt—Wadai, Bornu, Bunyoro, and Buganda—at over thirty-eight million, he sketched a picture of Emin's province of Equatoria where 'crime is unknown, slavery does not exist, the people live at peace with each other, and on the most friendly terms with the Government'. He ended by declaring that the Suakin-Berber railway was 'the most feasible way of opening up Central Africa. It puts Zanzibar out of the question, and would probably be a great rival to the Congo, though both Red Sea and Congo routes would pay, there being room and capabilities for both'.[2]

---

[1] *Anti-Slavery Reporter*, May 1885, reprinted the minutes of the syndicate together with Gordon's letter.

[2] *J. Soc. of Arts*, March, 1883. Felkin (1853–1926) played an important part in forming and publicizing the philanthropic interest in Equatoria. In 1878 he had accompanied the first party of C.M.S. missionaries to reach Buganda by the Nile route, and returned the following year due to ill-health. He spent several weeks with Emin and a firm friendship developed. They corresponded regularly and in October 1882 Felkin wrote to the *Scotsman* urging the retention of Equatoria. He was also a close friend of Charles Allen, and early in 1883 Emin wanted them to approach the British Government to whom he would then send a full report (Hill, *Biographical Dictionary*; A.S.S. MSS. Felkin to Allen, 1 July 1883).

Other authorities contributed to the mythical picture of Equatoria which these high hopes encouraged. In June, the German explorer, Schweinfurth, described the route through Equatoria as 'the best, safest and most direct way of reaching the central part of the middle Congo—that centre of development towards which all the civilizing and philanthropic hopes are rightly directed,' and in September Allen, quoting the brightly optimistic reports of Gessi, Lupton, and Emin, re-emphasized the potentialities of this 'remarkably fertile area'. In the absence of accurate information the scramble for Africa was in many cases conducted on the basis of reports such as these and for a brief period the project of a railway restored to the southern Sudan its strategic importance as a highway into central Africa.[1]

Meanwhile the Suakin-Berber syndicate sent a deputation to the Foreign Office, but finding no response it was decided to investigate the possibilities at Cairo. An Egyptian Commission, consisting of two previous Governors-General, two French engineering experts, and Watson and Mason, both of whom had served in Equatoria, reported in favour of the railway in June 1883. But the requisite concession was not granted by the Egyptian Government, and the proposal was temporarily shelved.[2]

At this juncture Gordon introduced a fresh approach to the problem. In 1880 he had nearly accepted service under Leopold who wished him to command an expedition in East Africa, and in 1882 Mackinnon, at Leopold's request and with Kirk's support, urged him to 'control and work out the great problem of African civilization' on the Congo, taking over from Stanley who was expected to retire shortly after opening-up the lower reaches of the Congo. Gordon, intending 'to mix no more in affairs,' declined the offer and escaped to Palestine in an attempt to find peace. While there, however, he received another letter from Mackinnon, written after an interview with Harry Johnston, 'who recently visited all the stations and gives a very satisfactory account', urging him to reconsider his decision. Gordon, believing that the War Office raised no objection, decided to go.[3]

---

[1] *Anti-Slavery Reporter*, July and September 1883. Schweinfurth was a regular correspondent with Allen. Gessi had been anxious to arouse Italian interest in the area; Zaghi, *Vita di Gessi*, pp. 134, 135.

[2] A. B. Wylde, *1883–87 in the Soudan*, vol. ii, p. 135.

[3] Mackinnon's letters dated 22 July 1882 and 12 October, 1883 are in Gordon

After long conversations with Leopold in Brussels, Gordon sent Allen, secretary of the Anti-Slavery Society, a resumé of his plans written for publication in *The Times*. The defeat of Hicks Pasha's expedition by the Mahdi in November 1883 had made it clear that the Sudan, south and west of Khartoum, would have to be abandoned, and it seemed certain that this would lead to an increase in the already considerable slave trade of Kordofan and the Bahr el Ghazal. Gordon intended to suppress this trade by stopping it at its source. He hoped to lead an expedition up the Aruwimi tributary of the Congo, and, striking overland, to reach Emin's posts on the River Wele and the headwaters of the Bahr el Ghazal. He thought he would be firmly established on the Bahr el Ghazal by 1886, and he hoped by then to be able 'to take every province back' while the Egyptian forces in the north kept the Mahdi fully occupied.[1]

An approach from the south was a revolutionary conception. At that period it would have imposed a severe strain on Leopold's resources and Stanley did not favour it for this reason, but, even when the War Office claimed Gordon's services and decided to send him to Khartoum, Gordon persevered with his plans. From Korosko on his way to Khartoum he wrote a long letter to Leopold offering to take over the southern provinces, after accomplishing his mission in the north, and to administer them for the Congo. He thought they might cost £50,000 p.a. at first, but suggested that Leopold might economize elsewhere and added 'Your Majesty may also hope to see the object of your vast expenditure fulfilled within a few years, and with it the cutting off of the slave trade in a way nothing else can do'.[2] Ten years later, when Belgian forces pressing towards the Nile were causing much anxiety to the

MSS. Gordon's correspondence with Waller (Waller MSS.) and Allen (B.M. Add. MSS. 47609) throws light on his relations with Leopold. B. M. Allen (Charles Allen's son), *Gordon and the Sudan* contains details of Gordon's movements. One of the reasons Gordon gave for his earlier refusal was that he had told Leopold 'three years ago that till he got a Charter he could never hold any jurisdiction over Foreigners out in Africa, and the Stanley-Brazza affair shows this clearly. One would only court failure in going and the more successful one was, the more certain would be the difficulties. . . .' A further illustration of the way private enterprise was hampered by lack of public sanction (Waller MSS. Gordon to Waller, 9 November 1882).

[1] B.M. Add. MSS. 47609. Gordon to Allen, 5 January 1884.
[2] Gordon to Leopold, 1 February 1884, printed in B. M. Allen, pp. 448–9.

Foreign Office, Leopold pointed out that it was Gordon who first drew his attention to the value of the area.[1]

Gordon's death at Khartoum in January 1885 led to the fall of Gladstone's Government and focussed the attention of Britain upon the Sudan. The humanitarians intensified their activities as it seemed possible that various projects might be floated on the wave of concern and emotion. The Suakin-Berber railway and the approach from the south were again canvassed with renewed vigour.

During the Khartoum relief expedition of 1884 the War Office had turned its attention to the possible strategical value of a railway from Suakin to Berber, and immediately after Gordon's death, when it seemed that the campaign against the Mahdi would be greatly extended, it was agreed by all authorities that the railway would be of considerable value. On 14 February 1885 the Liberal Government, in an attempt to restore its waning prestige, ordered its constuction.[2] The news was received with delight by *The Times*, and on 7 March Stanley, recently returned from the Congo, proposed a Gordon Association for the Nile on the model of the Congo International Association. 'The first and indispensable requisite' was the construction of the railway; the Association would then make treaties with the chiefs (including presumably the Khalifā 'Abd Allāhī) and 'merely act as an impartial riverain authority for the prevention of disputes, the settlement of differences, and the maintenance of a free river road to the heart of Africa'.[3]

The scheme was fully supported by the humanitarians. Wylde reiterated that if the railway was built Suakin would rival Alexandria, and when at the beginning of May the Government, having squandered nearly a million pounds, decided to abandon the mismanaged fiasco, the humanitarians organized a protest and attempted to arouse the interest of private enterprise. The Anti-Slavery Society memorialized the Government demanding that the plant should remain at Suakin in order to permit an early resumption; Bennet Burleigh, the *Daily Telegraph* correspondent, wrote a

[1] F.O. 10/614 Plucknett to Kimberley, 29 April 1894, and F.O. 10/616, Plucknett to Kimberley, 23 June 1894.

[2] Hill, 'The Suakin-Berber railway, 1885' *S.N.R.* 1937.

[3] *Anti-Slavery Reporter*, March 1885. Reprint of the *Pall Mall Gazette*'s report of an interview with Stanley. See also his introduction to *The Congo Free State*.

strong article in favour of the railway, asking the City to support
an attempt 'to open up the whole of vast equatorial Africa . . . compared to which the Congo State is a small affair'; and the Baroness
Burdett-Coutts wrote an eloquent letter stating that conferences
on the Sudan had been held at her house, that the 'opening out of
Sudan markets to English enterprise and the suppression of the
slave trade, although not absolutely identical, are like parallel
lines . . . thus all interested in the one feel an equal interest in the
other,' and that 'ready assistance from influential quarters' would
be forthcoming to form a Company on the lines of the British
North Borneo Company should a railway be built. In June
Cardinal Manning, possibly attempting to influence the Mansion
House Committee who were deciding how to distribute the funds
for a Gordon memorial, wrote in the *Tablet* that 'a Nile Association
analogous to the Association of the Congo' would be a true mem-
orial for Gordon: 'the heart of Africa would be opened to the
Christian world'. And the C.M.S., who had founded a Gordon
Memorial Mission, also regarded a highway into the Sudan as
Gordon's best memorial.[1]

They did not, however, arouse public enthusiasm to a degree
sufficient to force the Government either to retract its decision or
to support and sanction a private company. The alternative
project was therefore revived. On 22 July 1885 at a meeting in the
Mansion House presided over by the Lord Mayor, Sir Robert
Fowler, M.P., the humanitarians made what was perhaps their
greatest public effort to mobilize private enterprise in the support
of a venture in tropical Africa. After the Bishop of Gloucester had
denounced slavery in Egypt and Waller had evoked the memory of
Gordon, Stanley made a long and passionate speech. Emphasizing
that the Nile route was temporarily blocked and impassable, he
read from Gordon's journals extracts of a letter from the Emir
Karam Allāh to the Mahdi describing the chaos and the suffering
which existed in the Bahr el Ghazal. He then recalled Gordon's
plan to save these areas, which he described as 150,000 square

---

[1] *Anti-Slavery Reporter*, May and June 1885. Reprints from the *Daily
Telegraph*, the *Church Missionary Gleaner*, and the *Tablet*. In a pamphlet on
African Development: the Sudan, written probably in 1887 or 1888, Baker stated
that if the Khedive would guarantee 4½ per cent. 'a railway would be constructed
by public money without delay' and added 'should he grant a concession to a
public company similar in independent action to the original East India Company,
no British troops would be required'.

miles of rich and fertile country, and urged 'all who lament the death of Gordon' to unite their influence and to raise sufficient funds to send forward an expedition via the Aruwimi, a tributary of the Congo, which would contact the remnants of Egyptian administration and weld the tribes into 'a confederacy for their own self-preservation'. The appeal was warmly seconded by J. H. Hutton, President of the Manchester Chamber of Commerce, and by Manning who, stating that Stanley needed only £5000 p.a. to support the proposed staff of pioneers, 'looked to the merchants of this country to provide the tribes . . . with the first elements of civilisation and also of self-defence'.[1]

After this meeting the Baroness Burdett-Coutts and Cardinal Manning formed a committee which asked Schweinfurth to lead the expedition. While welcoming the 'great conception of re-conquering the area of the Upper Nile . . . approaching from the south', he declined the task on grounds of health and suggested that Joseph Thomson would alone be equal to it. Thomson however was temporarily engaged in Nigeria, and, as apparently the public response was slight, the plans remained in abeyance until news of Emin revived interest in the whole question.[2]

Meanwhile in East Africa events had been moving rapidly. In November and December 1884 Carl Peters, the young founder of the *Gesellschaft für Deutsche Kolonisation*, surreptitiously signed treaties with twelve African chiefs giving his Company sovereignty over a large area on the mainland. He returned with the treaties to Germany, and on 3 March 1885 Bismarck, secure in the knowledge that Britain was thoroughly occupied with the crisis following the fall of Khartoum, published a *Schutzbrief* taking the territories obtained by Peters under Imperial protection. Their boundaries were extended to meet the recently recognized Congo Free State, and a German squadron was sent to Zanzibar. The basis of British policy at Zanzibar—the co-operation between Kirk and the Sultan and the maintenance of the latter's authority—was irreparably damaged. Bismarck recognized British interest in the northern part of the interior and a Delimination Commission was established which finished its work by 9 June 1886. In July Kirk left Zanzibar, and in October the British and German Governments agreed on

[1] *Anti-Slavery Reporter*, August 1885.
[2] A.S.S. MSS. Schweinfurth to Allen, 17 August 1885. *Anti-Slavery Reporter*, August 1890 re committee.

respective spheres of influence.[1] Earlier in 1886 the British East African Association had been formed, with Mackinnon as Chairman, and Buxton and Hutton among the Directors. The Association's immediate sphere of operations was Mombasa but its hopes were centred on the Equatorial Kingdoms and Buganda in particular, where the C.M.S. and Roman Catholic missionaries were in a precarious position. Mutesa, who died in October 1884, was succeeded by Mwanga, a youth strongly influenced by Arab traders who were increasingly hostile to all European intruders. In October 1885 the Anglican Bishop, James Hannington, was murdered and in the following May more than thirty young Baganda converts were burned alive. At Zanzibar little could be done to aid the missionaries, until news of Emin, with the remnant of Egyptian power in Equatoria, suddenly seemed to offer the nearest means of succour.[2]

After the fall of Khartoum there were vague hopes in Europe that Emin, together with the explorers Junker and Casati, might succeed in reaching a station on the Upper Congo. When they did not appear, Junker's brother commissioned a German, Dr. Fischer, to lead an expedition to Equatoria. Setting out from Zanzibar, Fischer failed in his attempt to reach Emin, and no news was received until letters, brought out by Junker, reached the coast at the end of September 1886. From these it was learnt that Emin had succeeded in withdrawing to Wadelai, that he had lost 'a good many gallant men', that there remained only 'a little flock of men in the midst of thousands of negroes', and that, if he was to evacuate those who wished to leave, he would need assistance.[3]

The situation presented an opportunity for imperial intervention. Holmwood, Vice-Consul at Zanzibar, reported that 'both Dr. Junker and Mr. Mackay (the foremost C.M.S. missionary in Buganda) strongly urge the necessity of the immediate relief of Wadelai if it is not to be abandoned to the same fate as that which overtook Khartoum'. As Mwanga's hostility was 'the direct cause of Emin's isolation', he thought it 'would be a good opportunity for dealing at the same time with Uganda'. It also opened up prospects of future expansion: 'a safe "depot" on the Albert Nyanza would provide a base from which any further operations

---

[1] Coupland, pp. 400-75.   [2] Oliver, pp. 103-6.
[3] F.O. 84/1775. Emin to Kirk, 1 January 1886, enclosed in Holmwood to F.O. 23 September 1886. See also Schweitzer, pp. 255-358.

that might be decided upon for the retention of the Upper Nile could be undertaken effectively and without anxiety'. Holmwood went on to suggest an expedition of 1200 porters carrying ammunition and supplies, an armed guard of at least 500 Africans and if possible a body of seasoned Nubian or Egyptian troops; these, when united with Emin's people would provide 'an overwhelming force' capable 'of dealing with Uganda'.[1] Kitchener, then in command at Suakin and previously the British representative on the Zanzibar boundary commission of 1885, recommended that an expedition costing £10,000 should be sent via the Masai route. 'When they arrived they should obtain blacks and push north, sending down ivory for more rifles.'[2]

Emin's position seemed thus to offer a chance for a decisive imperial advance, and these plans received further support with the arrival of later letters from Emin and Mackay. At the end of 1884 Mackay had already been urging Kirk to frustrate German designs on the Lakes, and Emin's letters reveal that it was Mackay's influence which fortified his hope that England would come to his relief. 'Surely,' Mackay wrote to Kirk, 'the only vestige left of peace and civilized order in the whole of the Upper Nile Basin will not be removed by England's orders.'[3] In a long letter to Felkin, Emin explained his determination to

hold out here with my people. This resolution has been greatly strengthened by the letters which I have received from Mr. Mackay a few days ago. . . . I have certainly some glimmerings of hope that as Egypt appears to be unable to lend us aid England may at some future day take advantage of the position in which we find ourselves to remain true to her former traditions of a humanitarian and civilising mission. At the present time when the European Powers are racing neck and neck to gain possession of districts in Africa, is it really possible that no one in England should have been enlightened enough to see how easy it would be to occupy the whole of our province, as also the Mombuttu and Makraka country, and this too without any cost.[4]

[1] F.O. 78/3930. Holmwood to Baring, 25 and 27 September 1886, enclosed in Portal to Iddesleigh, 19 October 1886.

[2] F.O. 78/3939. Kitchener to Portal (telegram), 24 September 1886, enclosed Portal to Iddesleigh, 25 September 1886.

[3] F.O. 84/1775 Mackay to Kirk, 24 August 1886, enclosed in Holmwood to F.O. 18 October 1886.

[4] F.O. 84/1794 Emin to Felkin, 7 July 1886, in Felkin to Iddesleigh, 23 November 1886.

Anxious to assist in this annexation of the area by England, Emin continued to discuss with Mackay 'the prospects of realizing your dreams: from the Zambezi to the Bahr el Ghazal'.[1]

Yet if Consuls, strategists, missionaries and foreigners clearly realized that the Upper Nile Valley was becoming a key-point of Britain's strategic interests, the Cabinet in England were by no means prepared to take any hasty action. The Intelligence branch of the War Office was quite unready to offer any advice on the proposals to launch a military expedition some eight hundred miles into the interior to Africa: 'our interests there are not so great that we have ever made this a special subject of study'. Through the Royal Geographical Society they were placed in touch with Joseph Thomson and from him they learnt that lack of food and water made it impossible to send a large military force through Masai country. A small relief caravan it was thought might get through by that route but only with 'very considerable risk', and an attempt on the part of five hundred soldiers to fight their way through to Uganda would be 'far too full of risks', while lack of provisions· precluded a larger expedition via Lake Victoria. Wolseley, the Adjutant-General, concluded therefore that 'the question should be regarded as one for diplomacy and not as a military one,' suggesting that a small scale mission might be sent to bribe Mwanga. Salisbury, the Prime Minister, fully agreed that an armed expedition was 'quite out of the question'. He thought Wolseley's suggestion was worth considering but only if it was within 'the narrow surplus of the Egyptian Treasury,' and his lack of interest in the Upper Nile Valley at this date is clearly revealed by his opinion that 'the Germans should be placed in possession of our information. It is really their business if Emin is a German'.[2]

It became apparent that the Government would of its own initiative take no decisive action. To those, however, who for various reasons were interested in Equatoria it seemed that Emin's message offered a most favourable opportunity for launching their schemes with some degree of Government recognition and support. Now at last it seemed that sufficient official encouragement might be obtained to enable private individuals to succeed in attracting

[1] Oliver, pp. 129-32.
[2] F.O. 84/1790 Brackenbury to Wolseley, 29 September 1886. F.O. 84/1775 Minutes by Wolseley and Salisbury on Holmwood to Iddesleigh, 23 September 1886.

capital and in establishing a solvent enterprise in the centre of Africa; an Emin relief expedition might accomplish for the southern Sudan what it was hoped a Charter would secure elsewhere. From being an individual known only to a few savants, Emin, as 'Gordon's heir,' became a public figure. To the semi-mythical account of the wealth and value of Equatoria was added the picture of the gallant defender of civilization threatened and surrounded by the forces of fanaticism.

As usual the Anti-Slavery Society opened the campaign. On 8 November Allen forwarded a resolution to Iddesleigh at the Foreign Office which stated that 'the position of Emin Bey presents a very strong claim upon Her Majesty's Government'. Both the British and Egyptian Governments 'are bound to be sparing of neither exertion nor expense in order to rescue him . . . or to enable him to hold a friendly position amongst the natives of his province'.[1] Felkin was still practising medicine in Edinburgh and he discussed with Allen some of the plans for the campaign. 'We too are going to try and get up a petition to the Government. . . . In order to get the Scotch to stir I must have a good humanitarian, utilitarian, and several other "arian" objects in my paper. Can you help me? Do try—think of all poor Emin has tried to do and really has done, of his "long weary holding out".' Later he reported that he had asked Joseph Thomson to write to *The Times* as he had private information that unless the papers and the public took up the matter it would fall through. 'I understand the Royal Geographical Society petitioned last week. Could you not get Wylde or Horace Waller to write to the *Standard* or *Daily Telegraph*. . . . Burleigh of the D.T. said he would write a Leader on the subject if he had one or two strong letters to go on. . . . I should not be at all surprised if the German Government do not act before ours, their fingers are itching to extend their territory and this gives them a splendid opportunity.'[2]

At Felkin's instigation the Scottish Geographical Society forwarded a resolution to Iddesleigh suggesting that Joseph Thomson should lead 'a *pacific* relief expedition' to Lake Albert from the south of Lake Victoria.[3] Felkin turned also to another

[1] F.O. 84/1793 Allen to Iddesleigh, 8 November 1886.
[2] A.S.S. MSS. Felkin to Allen, 17 and 20 November 1886.
[3] F.O. 84/1794 White (Secretary of the Scottish Geographical Society) to Iddesleigh, 23 November 1886.

group of Scotsmen interested in Africa, and as a result the African Lakes Company[1] decided to send an expedition via Lakes Nyasa and Tanganyika to Emin. When the preparations for Stanley's expedition later became known, they offered to continue with their plans, for 'it is manifest that Emin will require for the maintenance of his position, not an expedition only, but repeated communications at regular intervals, and there seems to be little doubt that our route is the most accessible and reliable for such a service'.[2] This problem of communications was crucial, Felkin thought, for Emin had asked him to obtain 'a definite arrangement with a syndicate of English commercial men' which would enable him to continue to administer the area either under the protection of England or as an independent state on the model of Sarawak. Felkin was concerned, therefore, not to rescue Emin but, by supplying him with ammunition and barter goods, to enable him to maintain his position until such an arrangement could be made. Two years later Felkin eventually signed such an agreement with Mackinnon, stipulating however that Emin remained quite free to reject it.[3]

Meanwhile others, whose concern for Emin was by no means so personal or paramount as Felkin's, hastened to bring forward their schemes. In May 1884 Francis Fox, an active, influential Quaker and owner of the Atlas Engineering Works at Bristol, visited Egypt to consider some irrigation schemes for the Egyptian Government. Conversations with Baring, Zubair and others awakened in him a deep interest in the Sudan, and after Gordon's death he was in close contact with Manning and the explorer Cameron. He also paid a visit to Edinburgh to discuss plans for the Sudan with Felkin.[4] With Wylde he was principally interested in opening up the Sudan from the Red Sea coast,[5] but he extended his interest

[1] See above, p. 178.

[2] F.O. 84/1796 Ewing (Secretary of the African Lakes Co.) to Stanley enclosed in Ewing to Anderson, 30 December 1886. F.O. 84/1857 Memorandum by James Stevenson, 31 January 1887, mentions Felkin's part in the negotiations.

[3] In 1898 Felkin wrote an introduction to the English edition of G. Schweitzer's *Emin Pasha: his life and work* to defend himself from the German accusation that he had acted in bad faith towards Emin. The details of the negotiations are printed there: see especially Emin's letter on p. xxxii.

[4] J. E. C. Montmorency, *Life of F. W. Fox*. From 1888–1918 Fox was a leading member of the Aborigines Protection Society.

[5] *The Times* of 3 June 1887 printed a long report by Fox on a new Suakin-Berber syndicate scheme. It was however turned down by the Egyptian Government (Shibeika, p. 311.) In 1889 Wylde started a 'pilot' scheme near Tokar.

to the other alternative of an approach from the Congo, and the news from Emin offered a favourable opportunity. On his visit to Felkin he disclosed that he and J. T. Wills, the son of Justice Wills and almost certainly another Quaker, were hoping that an expedition would be sent via the Ubanghi and Wele rivers, and that 'their main object was to get a station in the Nyam-nyam (Zande) country which they would take care not to give up'.[1]

A few days later Wills embodied the proposals in a long letter to Iddesleigh suggesting that the services of Dr. Junker, the authority on the Upper Ubanghi, should be secured immediately. Then 'with Government assistance of a certain definite amount' a private company could be formed for the 'permanent maintenance of Emin Bey's province'. This would 'secure the back entrance of the Egyptian Sudan, and a most valuable ivory trade, to English enterprise'.[2] Assistance from the Government was not, of course, forthcoming for so vague a scheme, and in a lecture to the Royal Geographical Society in March 1887 Wills appealed to a wider audience: 'turn away the ivory from Khartoum to the Congo and the great incentive to the slave trade is gone; philanthropy is cheap, for the profits will be enormous. Ivory is now worth 20–25 times the cost of transport from Stanley Pool and the remaining £900 a ton will pay for steamers, stations, and the rest'.[3]

While Allen and Felkin were mobilizing public opinion in an attempt to force the Government to act, a private approach was made to the Foreign Office. Towards the end of October Mackinnon and Hutton contacted Sir Percy Anderson, head of the African Department of the Foreign Office, and Sir James Ferguson the Under-Secretary. They suggested that Stanley might be employed to lead a relief expedition and on 15 November they put their proposals in writing. 'There is a general feeling in the country,' wrote Mackinnon, 'that the Government should in some way or other take immediate action in the matter.' Stanley offered his

---

[1] A.S.S. MSS. Felkin to Allen, 20 November 1886. Felkin was unsympathetic to the project as he felt they would not succeed in giving Emin any effective help.

[2] F.O. 84/1794 Wills to Iddesleigh, 25 November 1886. Wills added that his information had been collected 'some time ago in reference to a Soudan Company'.

[3] *Proc. Roy. Geog. Soc.* 1887. This is a striking example of the way in which it was hoped that the ivory trade would finance European penetration into central Africa. In the discussion which followed the lecture Sir Francis de Winton, an intimate adviser to Leopold, confessed his great interest in the question.

services gratuitously and estimated that the expedition would need £20,000. 'No responsibility for his personal safety' would rest on the Government but their help in the way of transport and recommendatory letters was needed. In further interviews Mackinnon offered to find £10,000 for 'the establishment of trading posts en route' and Hutton said that others, including himself, would subscribe 'their object being to form a large trading colony from the Mombasa base'. Ferguson felt that had any of the Sudan loan remained funds might have been available, but this was not the case and the matter was referred to the Cabinet. Salisbury remained cautious and hostile to the scheme. He informed Ferguson that 'the Cabinet had decided not to entertain the proposal as it would involve the Government in responsibilities similar to those in General Gordon's case'.[1]

Immediately after this Cabinet decision had been taken an important telegram arrived from Baring, the British Agent and Consul-General in Cairo, who was still waiting to hear what instructions he should give to the Egyptian Government. Schweinfurth had approached him with the suggestion that Junker should lead an expedition of 300 Zanzibari troops and 1000 porters, dethrone Mwanga by aiding the party opposed to him, and bring relief to Emin. Schweinfurth anticipated contributions from English missionary societies, and suggested that the Egyptian Government should contribute £10,000, a sum which Baring considered quite reasonable.[2] While feeling that this project, like Holmwood's earlier ones, would involve far too many risks, Anderson and Ferguson seized on the fact that here was a definite offer of £10,000. Mackinnon was informed the same day, and was 'not indisposed' to provide the remaining expenses, stipulating however that 'the employment of an Anglo-Saxon . . . was a sine qua non'. On 27 November he submitted his fresh proposals, and they were approved after it was made quite clear that the Government had no responsibilities in the matter. Stanley was to accept full responsibility for all the arrangements, and Mackinnon, convinced that 'the risk could not be compared to that of a Soudan

[1] F.O. 84/1793 Mackinnon to Ferguson, 15 November 1886, enclosing Stanley to Mackinnon, 15 November 1886. F.O. 84/1794 Minutes by Ferguson, 20 and 23 November.

[2] F.O. 78/3932 Baring to Iddesleigh, 23 November 1886, enclosing memorandum by Schweinfurth, 21 November. Schweinfurth was later one of the chief promoters of the German Emin Relief Expedition.

expedition,' merely demanded that he should receive 'a just proportion' of the ivory which Emin was reputed to possess. As this was estimated at £60,000 there was good reason to believe that philanthrophy might be profitable, particularly if it was found possible to utilise Emin's experience and troops to form the basis for a future trading colony.[1]

Preparations were rapidly made. Stanley was recalled from the middle of a successful lecture-tour in the United States. An Emin Relief Committee was formed with Sir Francis de Winton as secretary, and Grant and Waller among the members. The Baroness Burdett-Coutts and Buxton were among the subscribers. Stanley arrived in England on 24 December and immediately informed Anderson that he had come to the conclusion that the Congo would be 'the quickest, easiest and safest route' by which to reach Emin. A few days later the French Ambassador, anxious for the safety of the French missionaries in Buganda, intimated that he hoped the expedition would avoid the East African route. The Relief Committee however were converted to Stanley's choice only after Leopold had let it be known that he could not dispense with Stanley's services unless the Congo route was taken. He also had realized that this was an opportunity not to be missed, and Stanley was instructed to inform Emin that Leopold was prepared to maintain him in his province provided it did not cost more than £15,000 p.a. The British Treasury were persuaded to supply the necessary coal for a steamer to transport the expedition from Zanzibar to the Congo (a matter of over a thousand tons) and on 20 January 1887 Stanley left England.[2]

At last the plans of the humanitarians were translated into action, although the measures envisaged were on a more modest scale than some of the earlier proposals. The sums involved seem, and were, puny in comparison to the results which it was hoped to achieve. Philanthrophy showed a marked reluctance to face risks although there seemed a good chance of a profitable return, and this modest venture was launched only when an official contribution was received. Equatorial Africa was still largely an unknown quantity, and although this fact fostered extravagant accounts of

[1] F.O. 84/1794. Minutes by Anderson, 24 and 30 November 1886; Mackinnon to Iddesleigh, 27 November.

[2] F.O. 84/1795 Anderson to Pauncefote, 24 December 1886. F.O. 84/1796 Anderson to Mackinnon, 29 December 1886. F.O. 84/1857 F.O. to Admiralty, 22 January 1887.

the territory it also accounted for the lack of business interest. Throughout the decade the humanitarians had encountered the firm and understandable resolve of the British Government to avoid commitments. In Uganda their actions eventually succeeded in overcoming official reluctance, but in the southern Sudan they failed. When Stanley eventually arrived in Equatoria the situation had so deteriorated that there was no chance of building on the slender foundations which had existed,[1] and there remained only the weary evacuation to Zanzibar.

With the departure of Emin the immediate interest of the southern Sudan to the outside world disappeared. European businessmen were no longer presented with a unique opportunity of taking over what had seemed from a distance to be a flourishing concern. Confronted with reality they saw that private individuals, without an imperial intervention, had no hope of establishing a legitimate commerce in Equatoria. Private enterprise proved inadequate in other areas in tropical Africa and the imperial factor was brought in elsewhere eventually, but its early failure in the southern Sudan proved to be of peculiar importance. The Government was from the first the supreme and dominant factor in the next period of the country's history. Traders and missionaries henceforth occupied a minor role, and the British presence in the southern Sudan was almost exclusively a matter of imperial strategy. The reconquest in 1898 depended not on a desire to develop the resources or to meet the needs of the area itself, but on the decision to safeguard the Nile's waters as an inevitable extension of the British occupation of Egypt. Britain merely wished to prevent a rival Power from securing a stronghold in the Upper Nile valley, and government policy was mainly concerned with the bare establishment and maintenance of law and order. With the evacuation of Equatoria and the development of alternative routes into tropical Africa, the fascination of the southern Sudan, as a gateway into the interior and as a foundation for the future, had vanished. The Nile was no longer an important route to the Equator, but its waters linked the area to the north, and the southern Sudan, remote and savage while its neighbours advanced, became a problem-child of the twentieth century.

[1] See above, pp. 162–3.

SOURCES

Manuscript

A.E.

Archives de Ministère des Affaires Etrangères, Quai d'Orsay, Paris.

Correspondance consulaire, Alexandre et Caire.

Correspondance commerciale, Alexandre et Caire.

In this consular and diplomatic correspondence there is a considerable amount of information about Egyptian policy on the White Nile. Several letters from Thibaut, French consular agent at Khartoum from *c.* 1829–1869 and a trader on the White Nile, are forwarded, and there is an important series of reports on the slave trade and general conditions in the Sudan by Garnier, the principal interpreter at Alexandria who visited the Sudan in 1864–5.

Mémoires et Documents. Egypte/1.

Mémoires et Documents. Afrique/74.

These contain long reports by Brun Rollet, Vaudey and Lejean on the ivory trade and general conditions in the Sudan.

A.S.S. MSS.

Papers of the Anti-Slavery Society, at Rhodes House, Oxford.

A valuable source for the plans and interests of the British humanitarian circles.

A.S.T.

Archivio di Stato, Turin.

Consolati Nazionali Alessandria e Cairo.

The consular correspondence contains letters from Brun Rollet and Vaudey, when they were acting as Consular agents for Sardinia in Khartoum.

B. MSS.

Papers of Sir Samuel and Lady Baker, in the possession of his descendants.

This includes correspondence with a wide circle of friends and also a few letters written during the expedition of 1869–73.

B.M. Add. MSS.

British Museum, Additional Manuscripts.

41340. Letters from Gordon to Sir Charles Watson Pasha, who as a young officer served under Gordon in Equatoria.

47609. Letters from Gordon to C. S. Allen, the secretary of the Anti-Slavery Society.

C.M.S. MSS.

Archives of the Church Missionary Society, London. The early papers and minute books of the C.M.S. mission to Uganda contain accounts of Egyptian activities on the upper Nile. There is also a long and important letter from Emin to Gordon, dated 27/X/78.

Emin MSS. The diaries and letters of Emin Pasha at the Hamburgishes Staatsarchiv.

The diaries, except for the final volume, have been published, and the greater part of his correspondence with Junker was published by R. Buchta, *Der Sudan unter ägy. Herrschaft*, Leipzig, 1888.

F.O. Foreign Office files at the Public Record Office, London.

F.O. 84 Slave Trade. Turkey (Egypt).

An indispensable source for British policy towards the southern Sudan. Also contains much information about conditions in the interior.

F.O. 78. Turkey (Egypt). Consular and Diplomatic correspondence.

Contains correspondence from Petherick, while he was Consul at Khartoum (1859–63). Also valuable for British policy.

F.O.141. Miscellaneous correspondence with the British Consul-General, Cairo. Several boxes contain important letters from Petherick and other European traders in the Sudan.

G. MSS. Papers of General Gordon, in the possession of his descendants.

Gordon wrote voluminous letters to his sister Augusta. Many of them were published by G. B. Hill *Colonel Gordon in Central Africa*, 1881, but much of great interest remained unpublished. There is also some correspondence between Gordon and Baker.

J.B. MS. The diary of Admiral Julian Baker, in the possession of his descendants.

An important corrective to Baker's published account of the 1869–1873 expedition.

Kir. MS. The diary of Father Kirchner, Missioni africane, Verona.

In 1858 Kirchner visited the mission stations on the White Nile and Bahr el Jebel; from 1859–61 he was pro-vicar apostolic in succession to Knoblecher. His diary contains much information about conditions in the southern Sudan.

Knobl. MS. The diary of Father Knoblecher, Biblioteca Palatina Vindobonensis, Codex 14152, Vienna. This is the journal of Knoblecher's first visit to Gondokoro in 1849. Most valuable for its careful account of conditions before the removal of the Government monopoly.

M.A. MSS.	The archives of the Missioni africane, Verona. Correspondence of Comboni, Uberbacher, and other missionaries.
Meyer MSS.	*Notizien über die Bezugsquellen von Elfenbein*, Carl Westendarp, 1859–1865, in the possession of the firm of H. A. Meyer, Hamburg. Notes written during a visit to Egypt by one of the directors of the leading firm of ivory importers.
Mi. MS.	A copy of the diary of Giovanni Miani, in the possession of Prof. Carlo Zaghi, Naples. Covers the period of Miani's journeys to the Yei and Galuffi beyond Gondokoro, 1859–1861.
Mor. MS.	The diary of Father Morlang, Missioni africane, Verona. From 1856 to 1860 Morlang was stationed at Gondokoro, and he revisited the area 1861–3. His diary is a very important source for the history of these years.
Mus. Af. It. MSS.	Documents from the Museo d'Africa Italiana, Rome. A very full collection of the correspondence of Gessi, Casati, and other Italian explorers. Much of it has been published by Carlo Zaghi.
O.S.	Österreichisches Staatsarchiv, Vienna. Politisch Archiv General-Konsulat Ägypten. Consular and diplomatic correspondence from Cairo. The most important reports of the Austrian Consul at Khartoum were often forwarded to Vienna, but many seem to have been retained in Cairo or Alexandria. Administrativ Registratur. F 27. Fasc. 9. Fasc. 6. Correspondence dealing with the work of the Vicariate of Central Africa. Administrativ Registratur F 8. Consular returns from Khartoum. Allgemeines Verwaltungsarchiv, Handelsministerium. Contains the provisional instructions for the Consulate at Khartoum.
Vay. MS.	The journal of A. Vayssière, kept at the Société de Géographie, Paris. There is now a microfilm copy at the Royal Commonwealth Society, London. A very interesting account of a journey made by two French ivory-traders, the other trader being the notorious de Malzac. Vayssière's authorship is attested by internal evidence, and by the fact that *Petermann's Mitteilungen*, *Ergänzungsband* 1860–1, Blatt 6, contains an itinerary from the journal supplied by Vayssière and de Malzac.

W. MSS.   Papers of the Rev. Horace Waller, at Rhodes House,
                     Oxford.
                     Contains important correspondence with Gordon.

Typescripts

Carlo Tappi.   'L'Istituto Neri'.
                     'Due Parole d'introduzione'.
                     Missioni africane, Verona.
                     Two short accounts of the work of the Verona Fathers.
                     The author quotes extensively from their archival
                     material.

Printed

This is a list of works referred to in the footnotes; for a bibliography see
R. L. Hill, *A Bibliography of the Anglo- Egyptian Sudan, from the earliest
times to* 1937, Oxford, 1939.

Unless otherwise indicated works in English have been published in
London, those in French in Paris.

ALLEN, B. M., *Gordon and the Sudan,* 1931.

ALMAGIÀ, R., 'Angelo Vinco; relazione delle sue esplorazione sull' alto Nilo
(1849–1853)', *Annali Lateranensi,* vol. iv, Rome, 1940.

AUMONT ET DE VILLEQUIER, DUC D', 'Du Caire à Gondokoro et au mont
Redjaif, 1855', *Bull. Soc. Khéd. Géog.,* vol. ii, Cairo, 1883.

BAKER, S. W. *The Albert N'yanza, Great Basin of the Nile, and explorations
of the Nile Sources,* 1867 ed., 2 vols. *Ismailia. A narrative of the
expedition to Central Africa for the suppression of the Slave Trade
organised by Ismail, Khedive of Egypt,* 1874, 2 vols.

BEATON, A. C., 'A chapter in Bari history', *Sudan Notes and Records,*
vol. xvii, Khartoum, 1934.
—— 'The Bari: clan and age-class systems', *Sudan Notes and Records,*
vol. xix, Khartoum, 1936.

BELTRAME, G. *Di un viaggio sul fiume bianco nell' Africa Centrale,* Verona,
1861.
—— *Il fiume bianco e i Dénka,* Verona, 1881.

BINDER, E. KURT, *Reisen und Erlebnisse eines Siebenbürger Sachsen um die
Mitte des vorigen Jahrhunderts im Orient und in Afrika,* Hermann-
stadt, 1930. (A microfilm copy is now in the library of the Royal
Commonwealth Society.)

BOHNDORFF, F., 'Reise nach Dor Abu Dinga', *Das Ausland,* Munich,
1884.

BONO, A. DE, *Recenti scoperte sul fiume Bianco,* Alexandria, 1862.

BRUN-ROLLET, A., *Le Nil Blanc et le Soudan,* 1855.

BUCHTA, R., *Der Sudan unter ägyptischey Herrschaft* .. , *nebst einem Anhange Briefe Dr. Amin Paschas und Lupton Beys an Dr. Wilhelm Junker*, 1883–5, Leipzig, 1888.

BUET, C., *Les premiers explorateurs français du Soudan équatorial*, 1883.

BURCKHARDT, J. L., *Travels in Nubia*, 1822 ed.

CALONNE-BEAUFAICT, A. DE, *Azande*, Brussels, 1921.

CASATI, G., *Ten years in Equatoria and the return with Emin Pasha*, 1891, 2 vols.

CASTLEBOLOGNESI, A., 'Voyage au fleuve des gazelles', *Tour du Monde*, vol. v, 1862.

CHAILLÉ-LONG, C., *Central Africa* ... *expeditions to the Lake Victoria Nyanza and the Makraka Niam-Niam*, 1876.

CHIRGWIN, A. M., *Arthington's Million. The romance of the Arthington Trust*, Livingstone Press, London, s.d.

COUPLAND, R., *The Exploitation of East Africa, 1856–1890: the slave trade and the scramble*, 1939.

CRAZZOLARA, J. P., *The Lwoo. Part I Lwoo Migrations*, Verona, 1950.

—— *The Lwoo. Part II Lwoo Traditions*, Verona, 1951.

CRESTANI, E. *Don Angelo Vinco. Missionario-Esploratore*, Verona, 1941.

CROMER, THE EARL OF, *Modern Egypt*, 1908, 2 vols.

DANDOLO, E., *Viaggio in Egitto, nel Sudan, in Siria ed in Palestina*, Milan, 1854.

DEHÉRAIN, H., *Le Soudan égyptien sous Mehemet Ali*, 1898.

DOUIN, G., *Histoire du règne du Khédive Ismail*, Cairo, 1936–1941, 3 vols.

—— *Histoire du Soudan égyptien. Vol. I; La pénétration, 1820–1822*, Cairo, 1944.

DUNNE, J. HEYWORTH, *An introduction to the history of education in modern Egypt*, 1939.

EMILY, J., *Mission Marchand. Journal de route*, 1913.

EMIN PASHA (E. SCHNITZER), *Die Tagebücher von Dr. Emin Pascha herausgegeben* ... *von Dr. Franz Stuhlmann*, Braunschweig, Berlin, Hamburg, 1917–1927, 5 vols.

—— *Emin Pasha in Central Africa: being a collection of his letters and journals*, ed. G. Schweinfurth, etc., 1888.

EVANS-PRITCHARD, E. E., 'A History of the Kingdom of Gbudwe (Azande of the Sudan)' *Zaïre*, vol. x, Brussels, 1956.

—— *The Divine Kingship among the Shilluk*, 1948.

—— *The Nuer. A description of the modes of livelihood and political institutions of a Nilotic people*, 1940.

—— 'The Nuer, tribe and clan', *Sudan Notes and Records*, vol. 16–18, Khartoum, 1933–5.

GRANCELLI, D. C., *Mons. Daniele Comboni e la missione nell' Africa Centrale*, Verona, 1923.

GRANT, J. A., *A walk across Africa*, 1864.

GRAY, SIR J. M., 'Mutesa of Buganda', *Uganda Journal*, 1934
—— 'Sir John Kirk and Mutesa', *Uganda Journal*, 1950.
—— 'Speke and Grant', *Uganda Journal*, 1953.

HANSAL, M. *Neuste Briefe aus Chartum in Central Africa*, Vienna, 1855.

HASSAN, VITA, *Die Wahrheit über Emin Pasha, die ägyptische Äquatorial-provinz* (etc.), Berlin, 1893, 2 vols.

HEUGLIN, M. T. VON, *Reise in das Gebiet des Weissen Nil und seiner westlichen Zuflüsse*, 1862–1864, Leipzig, 1869.

HILL, G. B. (ed.), *Colonel Gordon in Central Africa*, 1881.

HILL, R. L., *A Biographical Dictionary of the Anglo-Egyptian Sudan*, Oxford, 1951.
—— *Egypt in the Sudan*, 1820–1881, 1959.
—— 'The Suakin-Berber railway', *Sudan Notes and Records*, vol. xx, Khartoum, 1937.

HOFMAYR, W., *Die Schilluk. Geschichte, Religion und Leben eines Niloten Stammes*, Mödling, 1925.

HOLT, P. M., *The Mahdist State in the Sudan*, 1881–1898, Oxford, 1958.

HUNTINGFORD, G. W. B., *The Northern Nilo-Hamites*, 1953.

HUTEREAU, A., *Histoire des Peuples de l'Uele et l'Ubanghi*, Brussels, 1913.

JACKSON, H. C., *Black ivory and white; or the story of El Zubeir Pasha, slaver and Sultan, as told by himself*, Oxford, 1913.

JEPHSON, A. J. M., *Emin Pasha, and the rebellion at the Equator*, 1890.

JOHNSTON, SIR HARRY, *The Nile Quest*, 1903.

JUNKER, W. J., *Travels in Africa during the years* 1875–1886, 1890–1892, 3 vols.

KAUFMANN, A., *Das Gebiet des Weissen Flusses und dessen Bewohner*, Brixen, 1861.

LEJEAN, G. M., *Voyage aux deux Nils*, 1865.

MACMICHAEL, H. A., *A History of the Arabs in the Sudan*, Cambridge, 1922, 2 vols.

MARNO, E., *Reise in der aegyptischen Aequatorial-Provinz und in Kordofan*, 1874–1876, Vienna, 1878.
—— *Reisen in Gebiete des Blauen und Weissen Nils*, Vienna, 1874.

MATHEW, D., *Ethiopia. The study of a polity*, 1540–1935, 1947.

MAZUEL, J., *L'Oeuvre géographique de Linant de Bellefonds*, Cairo, 1937.

MELLY, G., *Khartoum, and the Blue and White Niles*, 1851, 2 vols.

MURRAY, T. D., and A. S. WHITE, *Sir Samuel Baker. A memoir*, 1895.

NACHTIGAL, G., *Sahara und Sudan*, Leipzig, 1889, 3 vols.

OLIVER, R., *The Missionary Factor in East Africa*, 1952.

PETHERICK, J., *Egypt, the Soudan, and Central Africa*, 1861.
—— *Travels in Central Africa, and explorations of the White Nile tributaries*, 1869, 2 vols.

PIAGGIA, C., *Le memorie di Carlo Piaggia*; ed. G. A. Pellegrinetti, Florence, 1941.

PENEY, A., 'Les dernières explorations', ed. E. F. Jomard, *Bull Soc. Géog. de Paris*, 1863.

PONCET, J., 'Excursions et chasses à l'éléphant au fleuve blanc', *Nouvelles Ann. des Voyages*, 1863–4.

Provinces of the Equator. Summary of letters and reports of the Governor-General, Pt. I, Year 1874, Cairo, 1877.

Pruyssenaere, E. de, 'Vingt-six lettres', ed. H. Wauwermans, *Bull. Soc. Royale Géog. d'Anvers*, 1930.

RUSSEGGER, J., *Reisen in Europa, Asien und Afrika*, Stuttgart, 1843.

SABRY, M., *L'Empire égyptien sous Ismail et l'ingérence Anglo-Française (1863–1879)*, 1933.

SAMMARCO, A., *Il viaggio di Mohammed Ali al Sudan*, Cairo, 1929.

SCHWEINFURTH, G., *The heart of Africa. Three years' travels and adventures in the unexplored regions of central Africa, 1868–1871, 1873*, 2 vols.

SCHWEITZER, G., *Emin Pasha his life and work*, 1898, 2 vols.

SELIGMAN, C. G., and B. Z., *Pagan tribes of the Nilotic Sudan*, 1932.

SELIM, 'Voyage aux sources du Nil Blanc', ed. E. F. Jomard, *Mémoires Soc. Géog. de Paris*, vol. xviii, 1842.

SHIBEIKA, M., *British policy in the Sudan, 1882–1902*, 1952.

SHUKRY, M. F., *Equatoria under Egyptian Rule. The unpublished correspondence of Col. C. G. Gordon with Ismail, Khedive of Egypt and the Sudan, during the years 1874–1876*, Cairo, 1953.
—— *The Khedive Ismail and slavery in the Sudan*, Cairo, 1938.

SLATIN, R. C. VON, *Fire and Sword in the Sudan*, 1896.

SOMBORN, A., *Die Elfenbein und Beinschnitzerei*, Heidelberg, 1899.

SPEKE, J. H., *Journal of the Discovery of the Nile*, 1906 ed.

STANLEY, H. M., *In Darkest Africa, or the quest, rescue, and retreat of Emin, Governor of Equatoria*, 1890, 2 vols.

TAPPI, C., *Cenno storico della missione dell' Africa centrale*, Turin, 1894.

TAYLOR, B., *Life and landscapes from Egypt to the Negro kingdoms of the White Nile*, 1854.

THEOBALD, A. B., *The Mahdiya; a history of the Anglo-Egyptian Sudan, 1881–1899*, 1951.

THIBAUT, G., 'Voyage au Fleuve Blanc', ed. D'Escayrac de Lauture, *Nouvelles Ann. des Voyages*, 1857.

TONIOLO, E., 'The first centenary of the Roman Catholic Mission to Central Africa', *Sudan Notes and Records*, vol. xxvii, 1946.

TRIMINGHAM, J. S., *Islam in Ethiopia*, 1952.

—— *Islam in the Sudan*, 1949.

TUCKER, A. N., *The Eastern Sudanic Languages*, vol. I, 1940.

VOSSION, L., *Le commerce de l'ivoire*; *à Khartoum et au Soudan égyptien*, 1892.

WERNE, F., *Expedition to discover the sources of the White Nile*, 1849, 2 vols.

WESTENDARP, W., 'Das Gebiet der Elephanten und der Elfenbein-Reichtum Indiens und Afrikas', *Mitt. der Geog. Gesell. Hamburg*, 1878–9.

WILSON, C. T. and R. W. FELKIN, *Uganda and the Egyptian Sudan*, 1882, 2 vols.

WINGATE, F. R., *Mahdism and the Egyptian Sudan*, 1891.

WYLDE, A. B., *1883 to 1887 in the Soudan*, 1888.

ZAGHI, C., *Gordon, Gessi, e la riconquista del Sudan*, Florence, 1947.

—— *Vita di Romolo Gessi*, Milan, 1939.

Periodicals

Annali Lateranensi, Roma.

Anti-Slavery Reporter, London.

Bulletin de la Société de Géographie de Paris, Paris.

Bulletin de la Société Khédiviale de Géographie, Cairo.

Das Ausland, Stuttgart.

Journal of the Royal Society of Arts, London.

Mitteilungen der Geographischen Gesellschaft, Hamburg.

Mitteilungen der kaiserlich-königlichen Geographischen Gesellschaft, Wien.

Nouvelles Annales des Voyages, Paris.

Petermann's Mitteilungen, Gotha.

Proceedings of the Royal Geographical Society, London.

Sudan Notes and Records, Khartoum.

Uganda Journal, Kampala.

Zaïre, Bruxelles.

INDEX